BRITISH LITERATURE UNLOCKED VOLUME VI

MODERN TO POSTMODERN: BRITISH LITERATURE FROM 1901 TO THE PRESENT

ANKIT SHARMA

A Complete Guide for UGC NET

TO THE POINT NOTES BASED ON PREVIOUS YEARS QUESTION PAPERS

Foreword

The journey through British Literature is one marked by profound ideas, artistic transformations, and socio-political upheavals, all of which have shaped the literary canon as we know it. In "British Literature Unlocked: A Complete Guide for UGC NET," this literary heritage is meticulously unpacked, volume by volume, to serve as an essential resource for UGC NET English aspirants. Spanning six volumes, this series guides readers from the ancient foundations of the Greco-Roman period all the way to the nuanced expressions of the Modern and Postmodern ages. With each era, readers will find to-the-point notes, questions from the last decade of UGC NET exams, mnemonic codes, and strategic insights designed to simplify and streamline the study process, making preparation not only thorough but also deeply engaging.

Volume by Volume Breakdown
Volume I: Greco-Roman to Chaucer: Dive into the roots of Western literary thought, tracing the influences of classical antiquity up through the Middle Ages and Chaucer's groundbreaking contributions. This volume introduces foundational concepts and sets stage for the evolution of British literature.

Volume II: Elizabethan to Jacobean: Enter the vibrant Renaissance period, where the works of Shakespeare, Marlowe, and their contemporaries reflect the artistic flourishing and complex socio-political shifts of the time. Each page delves into the drama, poetry, and prose that defined these eras.

Volume III: The Age of Milton, Restoration, and The Augustan Age: Explore an age marked by poetic grandeur, the restoration of the monarchy, and the Augustan pursuit of clarity and wit. This volume captures the transformations in language, form, and ideology as literature moved into a reflective phase of transition.

Volume IV: The Age of Transition and The Age of Romanticism: Witness the emotional and imaginative power of the Romantic movement, a response to the rigid rationality of the previous era. This volume celebrates the Romantic poets and novelists who embraced nature, individualism, and emotion in revolutionary ways.

Volume V: The Victorian Age: This volume covers the prolific Victorian era, an age of dramatic change and conflict that grappled with industrialization, social reform, and expanding empire. Here, readers can explore the complex morality, realism, and unique characters of Victorian prose and poetry.

Volume VI: Modern and Postmodern Literature: The journey concludes with an in-depth look at Modern and Postmodern literature, where literary form, narrative structure, and thematic depth are pushed to their limits. From the experimental techniques of Modernism to the playful and questioning nature of Postmodernism, this volume brings British literature into the contemporary era.

Why This Book is Essential?

Designed for aspiring NET scholars, "British Literature Unlocked" offers a unique blend of academic precision and strategic insight. With mnemonics that transform complex historical timelines and literary movements into memorable codes, this guide ensures that vital information is readily accessible. Each volume is filled with analysed questions from the last ten years of UGC NET exams, helping you understand not only what to study but also how to approach the exam strategically. This guide offers a structured pathway through the vast landscape of British literature, reducing overwhelm and empowering students to confidently tackle their preparation.

An effective study companion, "British Literature Unlocked" is the result of years of dedicated analysis, scholarly research, and an in-depth understanding of the UGC NET requirements. The goal is to provide readers with more than just a study guide—it is to offer them a roadmap that navigates through the richness of British literary history with ease and engagement. As you turn these pages, may you not only prepare but also find joy in the timeless world of British literature, its stories, and its legacy.

This series invites you on an enlightening journey, guiding you through the ages and unlocking the potential for both academic success and a deeper appreciation of the literary arts. Welcome to "British Literature Unlocked: A Complete Guide for UGC NET."

CHAPTER 1

Introduction

- ➢ Transition from **Victorian to Modernist** literature period.
- ➢ Industrial growth sparked social and economic changes.
- ➢ **Rise of urbanization** influencing literary themes.
- ➢ Questioning of traditional values and norms began.
- ➢ Impact of **psychological theories**, especially **Freud.**
- ➢ Influence of **Darwinism** on literary worldviews.
- ➢ Expansion of **British Empire** and colonial themes.
- ➢ Emergence of **existential and absurdist** ideas.
- ➢ Rise of **symbolism and impressionism** in literature.
- ➢ Increased focus on individual's internal struggles.
- ➢ **Stream-of-consciousness** technique gains popularity.
- ➢ Questioning of religious beliefs and traditions.
- ➢ Themes of **alienation and disillusionment** emerge.
- ➢ Influence of Nietzsche's philosophy on literature
- ➢ Impact of **wars on writers' perspectives.**
- ➢ Rise of **English War Poets** during conflicts.
- ➢ Exploration of class divisions and inequality.
- ➢ Prose styles moving towards simplicity, **realism.**
- ➢ Importance of the **Irish Literary Revival.**
- ➢ **George Bernard Shaw's** role in social criticism.
- ➢ Emergence of nationalist themes in **Irish drama.**
- ➢ **H.G. Wells' sci-fi themes** in early 20th century.
- ➢ **Joseph Conrad** explores imperialism and alienation.
- ➢ Role of **literary magazines** in shaping thought.
- ➢ Early 20th century paved way for Modernism.

Joseph Conrad (1857-1924)

Life:

- ➢ **Joseph Conrad** born on **December 3, 1857** in Ukraine.
- ➢ Only child of **patriotic Polish parents.**

- **Father**: Translator, **poet**, and man of **letters**.
- **Mother**: Gentle, wellborn, keen mind, **frail health**.
- **Father arrested** for revolutionary plots against **Russians**.
- **Exiled to northern Russia** with family.
- **Mother died** from hardships, aged **thirty-four**.
- **Sent to uncle** for education after **mother's death**.
- Never saw **father again**, who died soon after.
- **Strong bond** with father caused **melancholy**.
- **Melancholy** influenced Conrad's **adult writing**.
- Received **education** in **Cracow**, Poland.
- Chose **not to return** to father's homeland.
- **Suffered** under Russia's rule over **Poland**.
- Decided to **pursue the sea** as vocation.
- Reached **Marseilles** at **seventeen** to sail.
- Sailed almost **continuously** for **twenty years**.
- **Sea** became primary theme in **Conrad's work**.
- Little **"romance"** in Conrad's novels.
- **First love affair** in Marseilles **ended poorly**.
- Claimed to be **wounded in duel**.
- Likely **attempted suicide** instead.
- **Sea background** parallels heroes' **inner turmoil**.
- **<u>Said's academic journey began with the publication of "Joseph Conrad and the Fiction of Autobiography" (1966)</u>**.
- **Conrad left Marseilles** in April of **1878**.
- Saw **England** for the first time, age **twenty-one**.
- **Knew no English** but joined an English ship.
- Learned **English** while sailing **Lowestoft to Newcastle**.
- **Made first mate** at age **twenty-four**.
- Incident in **Singapore** inspired plot for **Lord Jim**.
- Met **Jim Lingard**, basis for **Lord Jim** character.
- Crew nicknamed **Jim as "Lord Jim"** aboard **Vidar**.
- Became a **British subject** in **1886**.
- Wrote **first short story**: "The Black Mate."
- **First story failed** in literary competition.
- Began **Almayer's Folly** while at **sea**.
- Transferred to a **Congo River steamer**.
- Took **notes** that inspired **Heart of Darkness**.
- Completed **Almayer's Folly** at age **thirty-seven**.
- Married **Jessie George, seventeen years younger**.
- **Heart of Darkness** serialized in **Blackwood's Magazine**.

- ➤ **Lord Jim** became his **twelfth work of fiction.**
- ➤ Novel's structure has **inventive narrative techniques.**
- ➤ **Multiple narratives**, symbolism, and **time shifts.**
- ➤ **Financial straits** marked **Lord Jim's creation.**
- ➤ Produced **major novels** like **Nostromo, Typhoon.**
- ➤ Later works include **The Secret Agent, Victory.**
- ➤ Recognized widely for his **literary genius.**
- ➤ Short man with **sharp Slavic features.**
- ➤ Went to **Poland** with family during **WWI.**
- ➤ Barely escaped **imprisonment** in wartime **Poland.**
- ➤ Declined a **British knighthood** yet earned **literary honor.**
- ➤ He suffered a **heart attack in August 1924** and was buried at Canterbury.

Notable Works

- ➤ *Almayer's Folly (1895)*
  - o Conrad's first novel, published 1895.
  - o **Set in late 19th century** Borneo **jungle.**
  - o Focuses on **Dutch trader Kaspar Almayer's** life.
  - o Explores his bond with **mixed-heritage daughter Nina.**
- ➤ *An Outcast of the Islands (1896)*
- ➤ *The Nigger of the 'Narcissus' (1897)*
  - o ***The Nigger of the "Narcissus": A Tale of the Forecastle.***
  - o Sometimes subtitled *A Tale of the Sea.*
  - o **Central character**: Afro-Caribbean man, **ill at sea.**
  - o Title controversy led to **altered US title** in **1897.**
  - o **2009** version titled **The N-Word of the Narcissus.**
  - o Life on **Narcissus** centers on **dying black sailor.**
  - o Crew includes **Captain Allistoun, Craik,** and **Donkin.**
  - o **Superstitious sailors cater** to **James Wait.**
  - o Sailors steal food, **rescue Wait** during storm.
  - o Wait causes **dissension**, nearly leading to **mutiny.**
  - o Novel explores **relationships under extreme circumstances.**
- ➤ *Heart of Darkness (1899)*
  - o **Heart of Darkness** (1899) is a **novella** by Conrad.
  - o Story of **Charles Marlow,** a sailor in **Africa.**
  - o The narrative style is **framed** storytelling.

- o **Heart of Darkness** uses a **third-person narrative framework**.
  - o **Unnamed narrator** introduces **Marlow** and tells **story**.
  - o Narrative shifts to **first-person** when Marlow **speaks**.
  - o **Frame narrative style** adds **complexity** and **interpretation layers**.
  - o **Critiques European colonial rule** and its impacts.
  - o Explores **power dynamics** and **morality** themes.
  - o Unnamed river **likely represents the Congo River**.
  - o **Congo Free State** ruled by **King Leopold II**.
  - o Marlow given a text by **Kurtz**, ivory trader.
  - o **Kurtz** has "gone native," central to Marlow's **mission**.
  - o Plot Summary:
  - o **Marlow**, the narrator, sails up the **Congo River**.
  - o Begins with **Marlow** telling his story to friends on the **Nellie**.
  - o **Marlow** is hired by the **Company** to find **Kurtz**.
  - o **Kurtz** is a remarkable agent, known for **ivory trading**.
  - o Marlow sees **European imperialism** and its **cruelty** firsthand.
  - o **"The horror! The horror!"** becomes an iconic phrase.
  - o Marlow encounters **enslaved Africans** suffering in **the jungle**.
  - o **Kurtz** is seen as a **god-like figure** by locals.
  - o Marlow observes the **greed** and **brutality** of Europeans.
  - o Marlow's journey symbolizes **descent into the unknown**.
  - o **The Manager** of the Central Station dislikes **Kurtz's fame**.
  - o **Kurtz's station** is filled with **skulls on stakes**.
  - o Marlow sees **Kurtz's dark influence** on his followers.
  - o **"Exterminate all the brutes!"** is in Kurtz's **report**.
  - o Marlow becomes disillusioned with **European "civilization"**.
  - o **Kurtz** falls ill, and **Marlow** tries to save him.
  - o Kurtz dies, whispering, **"The horror! The horror!"**
  - o Marlow meets **Kurtz's fiancée** and lies about his end.
  - o **Marlow** questions the true **nature of humanity**.
  - o The novel ends, leaving a sense of **moral ambiguity**.
- ➤ *Lord Jim (1900)*
  - o **Lord Jim** serialized in **Blackwood's Magazine** (1899-1900).
  - o Story begins with **crew abandoning passenger ship**.
  - o **Jim censured** for his **abandonment** of the ship.

- o Novel explores **Jim's redemption** and **self-acceptance** journey.
  - o **Jim**, a young sailor, seeks a **heroic life** at sea.
  - o Assigned to the **Patna** ship, carrying **pilgrims** to Mecca.
  - o When the ship hits an obstacle, **Jim jumps**, abandoning passengers.
  - o **"In an instant, he was a coward,"** haunted by guilt.
  - o Facing **court trial**, Jim loses his **sailor's certification**.
  - o **Marlow**, a sea captain, sympathizes with Jim's **torment**.
  - o Jim is given a new chance in **Patusan**, a remote village.
  - o Jim earns respect in Patusan as **"Lord Jim."**
  - o **"He was one of us"** — Marlow's view on Jim.
  - o In the end, Jim accepts **death for his honor**, restoring dignity.

- ➤ *The Inheritors (with Ford Madox Ford) (1901)*
- ➤ *Typhoon (1902, begun 1899)*
- ➤ *The End of the Tether (written in 1902; collected in Youth, a Narrative and Two Other Stories, 1902)*
- ➤ *Romance (with Ford Madox Ford, 1903)*
- ➤ *Nostromo (1904)*
  - o *Nostromo*, in full ***Nostromo: A Tale of the Seaboard.***
  - o **Nostromo**, an Italian sailor, trusted by Sulaco locals.
  - o **Charles Gould** prioritizes silver mine over country's stability.
  - o **Revolution** erupts, threatening Sulaco's future and peace.
  - o Gould hires **Nostromo** to protect silver from rebels.
  - o **Nostromo hides silver** but struggles with greed and temptation.
  - o **Trust decays** as Nostromo faces moral conflict and betrayal.
  - o **"No man matches money"** symbolizes wealth's destructive power.

- ➤ *The Secret Agent (1907)*
  - o **The Secret Agent** published by **Joseph Conrad** in **1907**.
  - o Set in **London, 1886**, follows **Mr. Adolf Verloc**.
  - o **Verloc** works as a **spy for unnamed country**.
  - o **Conrad** shifts from **seafaring tales** to **political themes**.
  - o Dedicated to **H. G. Wells**, explores **anarchism and espionage**.
  - o Examines **exploitation in Verloc's relationship** with **Stevie**.

- o **London's gloomy portrayal** influenced by **Dickens's Bleak House**.
- ➤ *Under Western Eyes (1911)*
    - o **Under Western Eyes** (1911) by **Joseph Conrad**.
    - o **Set in St. Petersburg, Russia, and Geneva**.
    - o Response to **themes in Dostoevsky's Crime and Punishment**.
    - o **Conrad disliked Dostoevsky's** work and influence.
    - o Interpreted as response to **Conrad's early life**.
    - o **Father** was a Polish **independence activist**.
    - o **Conrad left Poland** at age **sixteen**.
    - o Had **breakdown**, spoke to characters in **Polish**.
- ➤ *Chance (1913)*
- ➤ *Victory (1915)*
- ➤ *The Shadow Line (1917)*
- ➤ *The Arrow of Gold (1919)*
- ➤ *The Rescue (1920)*
- ➤ *The Nature of a Crime (1923, with Ford Madox Ford)*
- ➤ *The Rover (1923)*
- ➤ *Suspense (1925; unfinished, published posthumously)*

Question 1

Which among the following are true in the context of Chinua Achebe?
- A. He wrote Arrow of God and Things Fall Apart.
- B. His "Novelist as Teacher" is a seminal essay in the context of African Literature.
- C. The name of the tribe he depicted in Things Fall Apart is Igbo
- D. He is a Kenyan born American litterateur.
- E. He wrote the essay "An Abolition of English Department."

Choose the correct answer from the options given below:
1. A, C and D only.
2. A, B and E only.
3. A, B and C only.
4. B, C and D only.

Explanations:

Answer: 3. A, B and C only.

The following statements are true in the context of Chinua Achebe:

- ➢ He wrote Arrow of God and *Things Fall Apart*.
- ➢ His "Novelist as Teacher" is a seminal essay in the context of African Literature.
- ➢ The name of the tribe he depicted in Things Fall Apart is Igbo.
- ➢ He is a Nigerian-born African litterateur.
- ➢ He wrote the essay "An Image of Africa: Racism in Conrad's Heart of Darkness."

Question 2

Match List I with List II

List I	List II
A. Practical Criticism	I. John Crowe Ransom
B. The New Criticism	II. F.R. Leavis
C. The Well-Wrought Urn	III. I. A. Richards
D. The Great Tradition	IV. Cleanth Brooks

Choose the correct answer from the options given below:

1. A-II, B-I, C-III, D-IV
2. A-III, B-I, C-IV, D-II
3. A-III, B-IV, C-II, D-I
4. A-IV, B-III, C-II, D-I

Explanations

Answer: 2. A-III, B-I, C-IV, D-II

I. A. Richards wrote"Practical Criticism" (1929), and "The Philosophy of Rhetoric" (1936).

New Criticism was inspired by John Crowe Ransom's book "The New Criticism" (1941).

Cleanth Brooks' collection of essays, "*The Well Wrought Urn: Studies in the Structure of Poetry*" (1947).

R. Leavis wrote, "The Great Tradition" (1948), where he names Jane Austen, George Eliot, Henry James, and Joseph Conrad as the great English novelists, alongside Charles Dickens, Nathaniel Hawthorne, Herman Melville, and Edgar Allan Poe. He adds D.H. Lawrence to the pantheon later.

Question 3

Match List I with List II.

List I	List II
A. "A Simple Heart"	I. Joseph Conrad
B. "An Outpost of Progress"	II. Gustave Flaubert
C. "Six Feet of the Country"	III. R.K. Narayan
D. "A Horse and Two Goats"	IV. Nadine Gordimer

Choose the correct answer from the options given below :

1. (A)-(I), (B)-(IV), (C)-(III), (D)-(II)
2. (A)-(II), (B)-(I), (C)-(IV), (D)-(III)
3. (A)-(III), (B)-(II), (C)-(I), (D)-(IV)
4. (A)-(IV), (B)-(III), (C)-(II), (D)-(I)

Explanations:

Answer: 2. (A)-(II), (B)-(I), (C)-(IV), (D)-(III)

"Three Tales" is a collection by Gustave Flaubert, first published in 1877, featuring the stories "A Simple Heart," "Saint Julian the Hospitalier," and "Hérodias," exploring themes of devotion, legend, and historical intrigue.

Joseph Conrad's "An Outpost of Progress," written in July 1896 and inspired by his time in the Belgian Congo, appeared in Cosmopolis magazine in 1897 before being included in the 1898 collection "Tales of Unrest." The story reflects on colonial exploitation and moral decay.

Nadine Gordimer, a South African novelist and political activist, was awarded the Nobel Prize in Literature in 1991 for her profound writings that confronted moral and racial issues, especially against the backdrop of apartheid. Her significant works include "Burger's Daughter," and she was an influential member of the African National Congress, even advising Nelson Mandela during his 1964 trial. Her short story collections include "Face to Face" (1949), "The Soft Voice of the Serpent" (1952), and "Six Feet of the Country" (1956).

R. K. Narayan's "A Horse and Two Goats and Other Stories," published in 1970 with illustrations by his brother R. K. Laxman, comprises five stories, including the titular tale. This story humorously narrates a misunderstanding between an American tourist and Muni, an Indian goat-herder, highlighting the cultural gap and communication challenges between them.

Arrange the following literary texts in the chronological sequence:

> A. Middlemarch
> B. The Good Soldier
> C. Night and Day
> D. A Passage to India
> E. Heart of Darkness

Choose the correct answer from the options given below:

1. A,E,D,B,C
2. A,C,D,B,E
3. A,B,C,D,E
4. A,D,B,C,E

Explanations:
Answer: 3. A,B,C,D,E

- *Middlemarch*, by George Eliot, was serialized in 1871–72.
- *Heart of Darkness*, an 1899 novella by Joseph Conrad.
- *The Good Soldier*, a 1915 novel by Ford Madox Ford.
- *Night and Day*, Virginia Woolf's 1919.
- *A Passage to India*, published in 1924 by E.M. Forster,

Rudyard Kipling (1865-1936)

- **Rudyard Kipling** born in **Bombay** in **1865.**
- Father was a **British official** in India.
- **Educated in Devonshire,** wished to join **Army.**
- Abandoned **Army plans,** returned to **India.**
- Joined **Lahore Civil and Military Gazette.**
- Wrote **short stories** for **The Pioneer.**
- Early stories gained **worldwide attention.**
- Lived in **United States,** later settled in **England.**
- Awarded **Nobel Prize for Literature** in **1907.**

- ➤ Popularity **faded** over time, voice **fell silent**.
- ➤ Known primarily for **short story writing**.
- ➤ **Genius for terse narrative** and dramatic detail.
- ➤ Notable **style**, though cocksure and **individual**.
- ➤ **Plain Tales from the Hills** (1887) acclaimed.
- ➤ **Soldiers Three** (1888) among **enjoyable stories**.
- ➤ Less successful in **longer tales**.
- ➤ **The Light that Failed** (1891) **unsuccessful**.
- ➤ **Kim** (1901) rich in **observation** and **description**.
- ➤ **The Jungle Books** (1894, 1895) for **children**.
- ➤ Known poet of **Army life** and **Imperialism**.
- ➤ **South African War** (1899–1902) climaxed **patriotic poems**.
- ➤ **Mandalay** reveals **deeper springs of humanity**.
- ➤ **The Recessional** (1897) shows **poetical greatness**.

Notable Works

- ➤ *The City of Dreadful Night (1885), short story*
- ➤ *Departmental Ditties (1886), poetry*
- ➤ *Plain Tales from the Hills (1888)*
- ➤ *Soldiers Three (1888)*
- ➤ *The Story of the Gadsbys (1888)*
- ➤ *In Black and White (1888)*
- ➤ *Under the Deodars (1888)*
- ➤ *The Phantom 'Rickshaw and other Eerie Tales (1888) – including "The Man Who Would Be King"*
- ➤ *Wee Willie Winkie and Other Child Stories (1888)*
- ➤ *Barrack-Room Ballads (1892), poetry*
- ➤ *Many Inventions (1893)*
- ➤ ***The Jungle Book (1894)***
  - o *Total 14 Stories and Poems. Some of the famous stories are:*
  - o *"Mowgli's Brothers" (M) (short story)*
  - o *``"Kaa's Hunting" (M) (short story)*
  - o *"Road-Song of the Bandar-Log" (poem)*
  - o *"Tiger! Tiger!" (M) (short story)*
  - o *"Mowgli's Song That He Sang at the Council Rock When He Danced on Shere Khan's Hide" (poem)*
  - o *"The White Seal" (short story)*
  - o *"Lukannon" (poem)*
  - o ***"Rikki-Tikki-Tavi" (short story)***
  - o *"Darzee's Chaunt (Sung in Honour of Rikki-Tikki-Tavi)" (poem)*
  - o *"Toomai of the Elephants" (short story)*

- ➤ *The Second Jungle Book (1895)*
- ➤ *The Seven Seas (1896), poetry*
- ➤ *The Day's Work (1898)*
- ➤ *Stalky & Co. (1899)*
- ➤ *From Sea to Sea and Other Sketches, Letters of Travel (1899), non-fiction*
- ➤ *Just So Stories for Little Children (1902)*
- ➤ *The Five Nations (1903), poetry*
- ➤ ***Traffics and Discoveries (1904), 12 stories***
    - o ***"Wireless"** is a short story*
- ➤ ***Puck of Pook's Hill (1906)***
- ➤ *Novels*
    - o ***The Light that Failed (1891)***
    - o *The Naulahka: A Story of West and East (1892) (with Wolcott Balestier)*
    - o ***Captains Courageous (1896)***
    - o ***Kim (1901)***
- ➤ *Poetry collections*
    - o *Schoolboy Lyrics (1881)*
    - o ***Barrack-Room Ballads (1890)***
    - o *The Seven Seas (1896)*
    - o ***The Five Nations (1903)***
    - o *Songs from Books (1912)*
    - o *The Years Between (1919)*
    - o *Rudyard Kipling's Verse: Definitive Edition (1940)*

Famous Works from Exam's Persepective:

- ➤ *"Actions and Reactions"*
- ➤ ***"Baa Baa, Black Sheep"***
- ➤ ***"Barrack-Room Ballads"***
- ➤ ***"Captains Courageous"***
- ➤ *"Debits and Credits"*
- ➤ *"Departmental Ditties"*
- ➤ ***"Gunga Din" "***
- ➤ *Just So Stories"*
- ➤ ***"Kim"***
- ➤ *"Limits and Renewals"*
- ➤ *"Many Inventions"*
- ➤ ***The White Man's Burden: The United States and the Philippine Islands***
- ➤ *"Mary Postgate"*

- ➤ *"Plain Tales from the Hills"*
- ➤ ***The Last Suttee (1889)***
- ➤ ***"Puck of Pook's Hill"***
- ➤ *"Rewards and Fairies"*
- ➤ ***"The Day's Work"***
- ➤ *"The Light That Failed"*
- ➤ ***"The Man Who Would Be King"***
- ➤ *"The Naulahka"*
- ➤ ***"The Phantom Rickshaw"***
- ➤ *"Traffics and Discoveries"*

The Man Who Would Be King (1888)

- ➤ **"The Man Who Would Be King"** by **Rudyard Kipling**.
- ➤ Story of **two British adventurers** in **India**.
- ➤ They become **kings of Kafiristan** in **Afghanistan**.
- ➤ First published in **The Phantom Rickshaw** (1888).
- ➤ Also in **Wee Willie Winkie** (1895) collections.
- ➤ Adapted for **other media** multiple times.
- ➤ **Characters**: Daniel Dravot and Peachey Carnehan, British adventurers.
- ➤ **Setting**: Journey to **Kafiristan** to establish their own kingdom.
- ➤ **Plan**: They pose as gods to **gain power** over locals.
- ➤ **Success**: Dravot and Carnehan succeed initially, ruling as kings.
- ➤ **Downfall**: Dravot attempts to marry, **revealing his mortality**.
- ➤ **Tragic End**: Dravot is killed, and **Carnehan is tortured**.
- ➤ **Important Line**: "I was King once!" says a broken Carnehan.

The Jungle Book (1894)

- ➤ **The Jungle Book** (1894) by **Rudyard Kipling**.
- ➤ **Main characters** include animals like **Shere Khan**.
- ➤ **Mowgli**, a boy raised by **wolves in jungle**.
- ➤ Stories set in **Indian forest** around **Seonee**.
- ➤ **Abandonment and fostering** are central themes.
- ➤ Echoes **Kipling's childhood** experiences.
- ➤ **Triumph of protagonists** like **Rikki-Tikki-Tavi**.
- ➤ Themes of **law, freedom**, not **animal behavior**.
- ➤ Stories reflect **human archetypes in animal form**.
- ➤ Emphasis on **authority, obedience, jungle law**.
- ➤ Shows **freedom** to move between **worlds**.

- ➢ **"The White Man's Burden"** by **Rudyard Kipling**, **1899**.
- ➢ **Poem addresses** the **Philippine–American War** (1899–1902).
- ➢ **Encourages** U.S. **colonial control** over the **Philippines**.
- ➢ Originally written for **Queen Victoria's Diamond Jubilee**.
- ➢ Replaced by Kipling's **somber poem "Recessional"** (1897).
- ➢ Advocates for **American annexation** of the **Philippine Islands**.
- ➢ **Imperialist** theme, urging **American enterprise in empire**.
- ➢ Warns of **personal costs** in building an **empire**.
- ➢ **Phrase "white man's burden"** justifies **imperial conquest**.
- ➢ **Mission-of-civilization** linked to **manifest destiny**.
- ➢ **Ideology** reflects **early 19th-century expansion philosophy**.
- ➢ **"The White Man's Burden"**: Kipling urges **U.S. imperial responsibility**.
- ➢ Written as advice for the **U.S. colonizing the Philippines**.
- ➢ Describes colonized people as **"half-devil and half-child"** (line 8).
- ➢ Advocates for **"savage wars of peace"** to civilize others (line 17).
- ➢ Warns of the **burdens** of imperialism and **thankless toil**.
- ➢ Emphasizes the **moral duty** and **sacrifices** of colonizers.
- ➢ Reflects **Western views** of superiority, duty, and justification for empire.

Kim (1901)

- ➢ **Kim** by **Rudyard Kipling**, published in **1901**.
- ➢ Kipling's **final and most famous novel**.
- ➢ Follows an **Irish orphan's adventures** in **India**.
- ➢ **Orphan** becomes disciple of a **Tibetan monk**.
- ➢ Learns **espionage** from the **British secret service**.
- ➢ Notable for **nostalgic, colorful Indian culture**.
- ➢ Highlights **exotica** of **Indian street life**.
- ➢ **Kimball O'Hara ("Kim")**, an orphan, grows up in **Lahore**.
- ➢ He befriends a **Tibetan Lama** and becomes his **disciple**.
- ➢ Together, they embark on a **spiritual journey** across India.
- ➢ Kim meets **Mahbub Ali**, a horse trader and **British spy**.
- ➢ **British intelligence** recruits Kim, seeing his street smarts.
- ➢ **Colonel Creighton** sends Kim to school for spy training.
- ➢ Kim learns **espionage skills** while exploring **self-identity**.
- ➢ He navigates the **Great Game** between **Britain** and **Russia**.

- ➤ Kim faces inner conflict between **loyalty** and **spirituality**.
- ➤ The story symbolizes **duality** in British India and Kim's life.

Puck of Pook's Hill (1906)

- ➤ **Puck of Pook's Hill** by **Rudyard Kipling, published 1906.**
- ➤ Collection of **fantasy stories** in **English historical settings.**
- ➤ Counts as **historical** and **contemporary fantasy.**
- ➤ **Magical elements** depict **supernatural beings** in England.
- ➤ Stories told to **two children** in **Sussex.**
- ➤ Set near Kipling's **house, Bateman's,** in **High Weald.**
- ➤ Narrated by **Puck** or **historical figures** he summons.
- ➤ **Puck**: "the oldest Old Thing in **England.**"
- ➤ Stories vary from **historical novella** to **children's fantasy.**
- ➤ Examples include **A Centurion of the Thirtieth, Dymchurch Flit.**
- ➤ Each story **bracketed by a theme-related poem.**
- ➤ **Characters Dan and Una** accidentally summon **Puck**, the last fairy in England.
- ➤ **Puck**, known as **"Oldest Old Thing in England,"** tells tales.
- ➤ **Puck introduces historical characters** from England's past to the children.
- ➤ **Sir Richard Dalyngridge**, a Norman knight, tells of **battles and honor**.
- ➤ **Hugh the Saxon** shares stories of **Vikings and loyalty.**
- ➤ **Old Hobden**, the hedge-cutter, speaks of **land and its lore.**
- ➤ **Important line:** "For to admire and for to see, for to behold the world so wide."
- ➤ Stories explore **England's history, myths,** and **magic through adventure.**

"If—" (1910)

- ➤ Written circa 1895 as a **tribute** to **Leander Starr Jameson.**
- ➤ It is a literary example of **Victorian-era stoicism.**
- ➤ The poem, **first published in *Rewards and Fairies (1910).***
- ➤ The story "**Brother Square-Toes,**" is written as paternal advice to the poet's son, John.
- ➤ **Character:** The poem addresses **"you"** as a young person.
- ➤ **Key advice: "Keep your head when all about you"** are losing theirs.
- ➤ **Patience and honesty:** Value **patience and truthfulness** without seeking revenge.

- ➢ **Dreams and thoughts: "Dream, but not make dreams your master."**
- ➢ **Loss and resilience: Risk all on a toss, then start again** if you lose.
- ➢ **Strength: "Hold on"** when **"nothing in you"** wants to keep going.
- ➢ **Inclusivity and balance:** Walk with crowds, yet **"keep virtue"** and balance.
- ➢ **Outcome: "Yours is the Earth"** if you follow these virtues.

If you can keep your head when all about you
Are losing theirs and blaming it on you;
If you can trust yourself when all men doubt you,
But make allowance for their doubting too:
If you can wait and not be tired by waiting,
Or being lied about, don't deal in lies,
Or being hated don't give way to hating,
And yet don't look too good, nor talk too wise;

If you can dream—and not make dreams your master;
If you can think—and not make thoughts your aim,
If you can meet with Triumph and Disaster
And treat those two impostors just the same:
If you can bear to hear the truth you've spoken
Twisted by knaves to make a trap for fools,
Or watch the things you gave your life to, broken,
And stoop and build 'em up with worn-out tools;

If you can make one heap of all your winnings
And risk it on one turn of pitch-and-toss,
And lose, and start again at your beginnings
And never breathe a word about your loss:
If you can force your heart and nerve and sinew
To serve your turn long after they are gone,
And so hold on when there is nothing in you
Except the Will which says to them: 'Hold on!'

If you can talk with crowds and keep your virtue,
Or walk with Kings—nor lose the common touch,
If neither foes nor loving friends can hurt you,
If all men count with you, but none too much:
If you can fill the unforgiving minute
With sixty seconds' worth of distance run,

Yours is the Earth and everything that's in it,
And—which is more—you'll be a Man, my son!

QUESTIONS

Question 5

Match List - I with List - II.

List - I (Poem)	List - II (Poet)
A. To His Coy Mistress	I. Rudyard Kipling
B. The Scholar Gypsy	II. Andrew Marvel
C. Still I Rise	III. Matthew Arnold
D. If	IV. Maya Angelou

Choose the correct answer from the options given below :

    (1) A-II, B-III, C-IV, D-I
    (2) A-I, B-II, C-IV, D-III
    (3) A-III, B-II, C-IV, D-I
    (4) A-IV, B-III, C-I, D-II

Explanations:

Answer: (1) A-II, B-III, C-IV, D-I

    A. *To His Coy Mistress* – II. Andrew Marvell
    B. *The Scholar Gypsy* – III. Matthew Arnold
    C. *Still I Rise* – IV. Maya Angelou
    D. *If* – I. Rudyard Kipling

Question 6

In which short story does the narrator witness a consumptive young man named Mr Shaynor recreate "The Eve of St. Agnes" in a trance?

1. E.M. Forster's "The Eternal Moment"
2. Rudyard Kipling's "Wireless"
3. Somerset Maugham's "The Creative Impulse"
4. Aldous Huxley's "The Bookshop"

Explanations:

Answer: 2. Rudyard Kipling's "Wireless"

"Wireless" was first published in Scribner's Magazine in 1902 and later included in the collection "Traffics and Discoveries." It is a science fiction story that explores the concept of wireless communication, a revolutionary technology at the time.

Match List I with List II:

List I	List II
(A) O' Henry	(I) The Last Suttee
(B) Rudyard Kipling	(II) Beauty
(C) Oscar Wilde	(Il) At Verona
(D) Ralph Waldo Emerson	(IV) Hard to Forget

Choose the correct answer from the options given below:

1. (A)-(I), (B)-(III), (C)-(II), (D)-(IV)
2. (A)-(II), (B)-(IV), (C)-(III), (D)-(I)
3. (A)-(IV), (B)-(I), (C)-(III), (D)-(II)
4. (A)-(III), (B)-(I), (C)-(IV), (D)-(II)
5. **DROP**

Correct Explanation

William Sydney Porter (1862-1910), better known by his pen name O. Henry, was an American writer known primarily for his short stories, though he also wrote poetry and non-fiction. **His works include "The Gift of the Magi", "The Duplicity of Hargraves", and "The Ransom of Red Chief",** as well as the novel Cabbages and Kings. Porter's stories are known for their naturalist observations, witty narration and surprise endings. Some Postscripts: "Two Portraits", "A Contribution", "The Old Farm", "Vanity", "The Lullaby Boy", "Chanson de Bohême", **"Hard to Forget",** "Drop a Tear in This Slot", "Tamales"

Rudyard Kipling (1865–1936) wrote a verse called **The Last Suttee in 1889.**

The first version of *The Picture of Dorian Gray* was published as the lead story in the July 1890 edition of Lippincott's Monthly Magazine, along with five others.

AT VERONA is a poem written by Oscar Wilde. Opening line is given below:
"How steep the stairs within King's houses are For exile-wearied feet as mine to tread,
And O how salt and bitter is the bread"

Arrange the following poets in accordance with their years of birth.

    A.   Rudyard Kipling
    B.   Robert Browning
    C.   John Masefield
    D.   A.E. Housman
    E.   John Donne

Choose the correct answer from the options given below:

    1.   E, A, B, D, C
    2.   E, B, A, C, D
    3.   E, B, A, D, C
    4.   A, D, B, C, E

Explanations:
Ans: 3. E, B, A, D, C

Here are the poets in order of their years of birth, along with their life spans:

➤ John Donne (1572-1631)
➤ Robert Browning (1812-1889)
➤ Rudyard Kipling (1865-1936)
➤ A.E. Housman (1859-1936)
➤ John Masefield (1878-1967)

Question 9

Arrange the correct chronological sequence in which the following texts were published:

    A. Tess of the D'Urbervilles
    B. Kim
    C. The Old Wives Tale
    D. The Time Machine.
    E. A Portrait of the Artist as a Young Man

Choose the correct answer from the options given below

    1. A, D, B, C, E
    2. D, A, C, B, E
    3. B, D, A, C, E
    4. A, C, B, E, D

Explanations

Answer: 1. A, D, B, C, E

A. *Tess of the d'Urbervilles (1891)* is a novel by Thomas Hardy
D. *The Time Machine (1895)* is the first novel by H. G. Wells
B. *Kim* is a novel by Rudyard Kipling, published in 1901.
C. *The Old Wives' Tale* is a novel by Arnold Bennett, published in 1908.
E. *A Portrait of the Artist as a Young Man* is an autobiographical novel by James Joyce, serialised in The Egoist in 1914–15 and published in book form in 1916.

Question 10

Which of the following statements are true in the context of Rudyard Kipling?

    A. Kipling was born on 30 December 1865 in Bombay, India.
    B. Kipling was awarded Nobel Prize in 1907.
    C. The Jungle Books consist of four collections of stories
    D. Kipling originally used Shivalik hills as the background of The Jungle Book
    E. The Jungle Book was published in 1894.

Choose the correct answer from the options given below:

1. A, B and C only
2. B, C and D only
3. C, D and E only
4. A, B and E only

Explanations:

Answer: 4. A, B and E only

Rudyard Kipling: English novelist, poet, and journalist.

- **Born 30 December 1865, died 18 January 1936.**
- **He was born on 30 December 1865 in Bombay, in the Bombay Presidency of British India**
- Inspired by his birthplace, British India.
- Authored the Jungle Book duology, classic children's literature.
- Wrote "Kim" (1901) and "Just So Stories" (1902).
- Famous short story: "***The Man Who Would Be King***".
- Poems include "Mandalay" and "Gunga Din".
- "The White Man's Burden" reflects imperialist views.
- "If—" is celebrated for its motivational qualities.
- Henry James praised Kipling as a genius.
- **Won the Nobel Prize in Literature in 1907.**
- First English-language writer awarded the Nobel Prize.
- **At 41, youngest Nobel laureate in Literature in 1907.**
- "If—" likened to the message of The Gita.
- Criticized for his portrayal of India by R.K. Narayan.
- Shashi Tharoor called him a Victorian imperialist voice.
- ***The Jungle Book (1894)* is a collection of stories**
- Principal character Mowgli, raised by wolves in the jungle.
- **Stories predominantly set in Seoni, Madhya Pradesh.**
- **"The Second Jungle Book" includes eight further stories.**
- **Consists 7 Stories**
- **Story titles:**
    1. *Mowgli's Brothers*
    2. *Kaa's Hunting*
    3. *Tiger! Tiger!*
    4. *The White Seal*

5. *Rikki-Tikki-Tavi*
6. *Toomai of the Elephants*
7. *Her Majesty's Servants*

H.G. Wells (1865-1936)

- **H.G. Wells**: Acclaimed **scientific and social prophet**.
- Known for **science fiction** and **comic realism**.
- Born in **Bromley, Kent**, to a **shopkeeper** father.
- Mother worked at **Uppark**, where Wells read widely.
- Briefly apprenticed as a **draper** before teaching.
- Won a scholarship to **Normal School of Science**.
- Studied under **T.H. Huxley**, inspiring science fiction.
- Became a **socialist** and joined **Fabian Society**.
- *The Time Machine (1895)* predicted **future technologies**.
- Wrote about **class struggles** in comic contemporary novels.
- Married **Catherine Robbins** after first marriage failed.
- Explored **free love** themes in **Utopian novels**.
- Had affairs with **Dorothy Richardson** and **Rebecca West**.
- After **WWI**, advocated for a **world state**.
- Wrote **manifestos** like *The Outline of History*.
- Influenced **human rights** and the **United Nations**.
- Lived to see *World War Two*'s end.
- Significant role in shaping **peaceful global governance**.

Notable Works:

- *"A Modern Utopia"*
- *"Anticipations of the Reaction of Mechanical and Scientific Progress upon Human Life and Thought"*
- *"Experiment in Autobiography"*
- *"Kipps: The Story of a Simple Soul"*
- *"Love and Mr. Lewisham"*
- *"Mankind in the Making"*
- *"Mind at the End of Its Tether"*
- *"Mr. Britling Sees It Through"*
- *"The Food of the Gods"*
- *"The History of Mr. Polly"*
- *"The Invisible Man"*
- *"The Island of Doctor Moreau"*

- ➤ *"The New Machiavelli"*
- ➤ ***"The Outline of History"***
- ➤ *"The Science of Life"*
- ➤ *"The Shape of Things to Come"*
- ➤ ***"The Time Machine"***
- ➤ ***"The War of the Worlds"***
- ➤ *"The Work, Wealth, and Happiness of Mankind"*
- ➤ ***"Tono-Bungay"***

The Time Machine (1895)

- ➤ **The Time Machine** is a **science fiction novella.**
- ➤ **Published in 1895** by **H.G. Wells.**
- ➤ Popularized **time travel** via a **vehicle or device.**
- ➤ Term **"time machine"** coined by **Wells.**
- ➤ **Frame story** set in **Victorian England.**
- ➤ Focuses on **Time Traveller's journey** into **far future.**
- ➤ Commentary on **inequality** and **class divisions.**
- ➤ Projects **Eloi and Morlocks** as **future species.**
- ➤ Inspired by **News from Nowhere's** utopian themes.
- ➤ Wells' universe is **savage and brutal.**
- ➤ **The Time Traveller** builds a machine to explore **future eras.**
- ➤ **He travels to year 802,701 AD** and meets **Eloi**, peaceful people.
- ➤ Discovers **Morlocks**, who live underground and prey on Eloi.
- ➤ **Eloi represent weak future humanity; Morlocks**, brutal survivalists.
- ➤ Forms bond with **Weena**, an Eloi, who he tries to protect.
- ➤ "I grieved to think how brief the dream of the human intellect had been"—Time Traveller's reflection.
- ➤ Escapes **Morlocks**, returns to the present, but **disappears again.**
- ➤ The novel ends on uncertainty: **"The Time Traveller vanished three years ago."**

The Island of Doctor Moreau (1896)

- ➤ **The Island of Doctor Moreau**, 1896 **science fiction** novel.
- ➤ Written by **H.G. Wells** (1866–1946), English **author.**
- ➤ Narrated by **Edward Prendick**, a **shipwrecked man.**
- ➤ Prendick rescued and left on **Moreau's island.**
- ➤ **Doctor Moreau** creates **human-animal hybrids** via vivisection.
- ➤ Explores **pain, cruelty**, and **moral responsibility** themes.

- ➢ Questions **human identity** and interference with **nature**.
- ➢ Wells called it **"an exercise in youthful blasphemy."**

The Invisible Man (1897)

- ➢ **The Invisible Man** by **H.G. Wells** published **1897**.
- ➢ Story follows **scientist Griffin's** life and **death**.
- ➢ **Griffin** discovers how to make himself **invisible**.
- ➢ Uses **invisibility** for **nefarious acts**, including **murder**.
- ➢ **Killed** in the end; body becomes **visible** again.
- ➢ Themes include **madness, science, and moral decay**.

The War of the Worlds (1898)

- ➢ **The War of the Worlds** is a **science fiction novel**.
- ➢ **H.G. Wells** serialized it in **1897** in **UK/US**.
- ➢ **Hardcover published** by **William Heinemann** in **1898**.
- ➢ Written between **1895 and 1897**, detailing **alien conflict**.
- ➢ **First-person narrative** of unnamed **protagonist** in **Surrey**.
- ➢ **Martians invade** southern **England**, impacting **two brothers**.
- ➢ Highly **commented-on** in the **science fiction canon**.

Tono-Bungay (1909)

- ➢ **Serialized** in **English Review**; book in **1908**.
- ➢ Known as **Wells's successful social novel**.
- ➢ Inspired by **Dickens** and **Thackeray's** style.
- ➢ Narrated by **George Ponderevo, college dropout**.
- ➢ George assists **Uncle Edward** with **Tono-Bungay**.
- ➢ **Tono-Bungay**, a **worthless** yet **commercially successful medicine**.
- ➢ George critiques **society's gullibility** and **moral decay**.

Ann Veronica (1909)

- ➢ **Published** in **1909**, a **New Woman** novel.
- ➢ Follows **Ann Veronica Stanley** in **rebellion**.
- ➢ Challenges **patriarchal control** of **middle-class father**.
- ➢ Set in **Victorian London** with **Alpine excursion**.
- ➢ Explores **women's suffrage** movement vignettes.
- ➢ Highlights **1908 suffragette storm on Parliament**.
- ➢ **Addresses** the "contemporary New Woman problem."

- ➤ Inspired by **Wells's drapery trade experiences**.
- ➤ Follows **antihero Alfred Polly** in **Edwardian England**.
- ➤ Polly's **timid, directionless** character prevails.
- ➤ Finds **serenity despite bumbling** nature.
- ➤ Known for **"innate sense of epithet."**
- ➤ **Coins terms** like **"Shoveacious Cult"** humorously.
- ➤ **"Dejected angelosity"** for **Canterbury Cathedral ornaments**.

QUESTIONS

Question 11

Who among the following are called Edwardian Novelists?

A. George Eliot
B. Arnold Bennett
C. H. G. Wells
D. Edward Morgan Forster
E. Robert Louis Stevenson

Choose the correct answer from the options given below:

1. A, B and C
2. A, C and D
3. B, C and D
4. B, D and E

Explanations

Answer: 3. B, C and D

Victorian Novelists:

Victorian literature refers to English literature during the reign of Queen Victoria (1837–1901). The 19th century is considered by some to be the Golden Age of English Literature, especially for British novels. Famous novelists from this period include Charles Dickens, William Makepeace Thackeray, the three Brontë sisters, George Eliot, Thomas Hardy and Rudyard Kipling.

George Eliot (1819-1880) was an influential English Victorian novelist who revolutionised modern fiction with her method of psychological analysis. Among her notable works are "Adam Bede" (1859), "The Mill on the Floss" (1860), "Silas Marner" (1861), "Middlemarch" (1871–72), and "Daniel Deronda" (1876).

Robert Louis Stevenson (1850-1894) was a Scottish essayist, poet, and fiction author known for captivating novels like "Treasure Island" (1881), "Kidnapped" (1886), "Strange Case of Dr. Jekyll and Mr. Hyde" (1886), and "The Master of Ballantrae" (1889).

Edwardian Novelists:

The Edwardian era in the United Kingdom encompassed the reign of King Edward VII from 1901 to 1910, and it is often extended to the start of World War I, marking the end of the Victorian era.

> - **Arnold Bennett (1867-1931)**
> - **H.G. Wells (1866-1946)**
> - **E.M. Forster (1879-1970)**

John Galsworthy (1867-1933)

> - **John Galsworthy** was an English **novelist** and **playwright**.
> - Won the **Nobel Prize for Literature in 1932**.
> - Notable works include **The Forsyte Saga** and sequels.
> - **First published work**: *From the Four Winds* (1897).
> - Published early works under **pen name John Sinjohn**.
> - Used real name from **The Island Pharisees** onward.
> - **First novel, Jocelyn**, later refused to republish it.
> - **First play**, *The Silver Box*, became a success.
> - *The Silver Box* critiques **class-based justice**.
> - **The Man of Property** started the **Forsyte trilogy**.
> - Wrote both **plays and novels**, mainly appreciated in **plays**.
> - Addressed **class system** in his **social issue plays**.
> - Notable plays include **Strife (1909)** and **The Skin Game**.
> - **PEN International was founded in 1921 by Mrs. C. A. Dawson Scott, with John Galsworthy as its first president.**
> - Works align with **George Bernard Shaw's social themes**.

> ➤ **Galsworthy's plays** highlighted **early 20th-century issues**.

Notable Works:
- ➤ *"In Chancery"*
- ➤ *"Justice"*
- ➤ *"Strife"*
- ➤ *"The Forsyte Saga"*
- ➤ *"The Man of Property"*
- ➤ *"The Silver Spoon"*
- ➤ *"The White Monkey"*
- ➤ *"To Let"*

The Forsyte Saga (1922)

- ➤ **The Forsyte Saga** includes **three novels** and **two interludes**.
- ➤ Chronicles **three generations** of a **middle-class English family**.
- ➤ Published in **1922**, capturing **turn-of-century** England.
- ➤ First novel: **The Man of Property** (1906).
- ➤ First interlude: **"Indian Summer of a Forsyte"** (1918).
- ➤ Second novel: **In Chancery** (1920).
- ➤ Second interlude: **"Awakening"** (1920).
- ➤ Third novel: **To Let** (1921).
- ➤ **Soames Forsyte**, solicitor, married to **Irene**.
- ➤ **Irene loves** architect **Philip Bosinney**, rebels against Soames.
- ➤ **Soames rapes Irene**, ruins **Bosinney**, who dies tragically.

Strife (1909)

- ➤ *Strife* is a **three-act play** by **John Galsworthy**.
- ➤ **Galsworthy's third play** and most **successful**.
- ➤ Produced in **1909** at **Duke of York's Theatre**.
- ➤ Set during a **prolonged, unofficial factory strike**.
- ➤ **Trade union** and **directors** seek **strike resolution**.
- ➤ **Company chairman** confronts **strike leader** over hardships.
- ➤ **Strife** centers on a bitter **labor dispute** in a **factory**.
- ➤ **John Anthony**, factory chairman, refuses worker demands,
- ➤ His saying, **"Men must learn to obey."**
- ➤ **David Roberts**, the passionate workers' leader, insists, **"We'll starve together before we give in."**
- ➤ **The strike turns violent,** affecting both families and escalating tensions.

> The play ends in tragedy, leaving the **union defeated**, with **"no winners, only suffering."**

Justice (1910)

> *Justice* is a 1910 **play** by the British writer John Galsworthy.
> It was part of a campaign to improve conditions in British prisons.
> Winston Churchill attended an early play performance at the Duke of York's Theatre in London.
> **William Falder** forges a check to help **Ruth Honeywill**.
> **Ruth's influence** drives Falder's desperate act of forgery.
> **Falder's crime discovered**, leading to a harsh trial.
> Falder pleads, "I had no choice," but no leniency.
> Despite defense, **Falder is sentenced to harsh prison**.
> Prison conditions emphasize **Galsworthy's critique of justice**.
> **Ruth visits Falder**, urging him to find hope.
> After release, Falder faces **social stigma and struggles**.
> Falder, unable to cope, tragically ends his life.
> Galsworthy calls for **humanity and compassion in law**.

QUESTION

Question 12

Under whose presidency was PEN (an international association of poets, playwrights, editors, essayists and novelists) founded by Mrs. Dawson-Scott in 1921 ?

(1) John Galsworthy
(2) T.S. Eliot
(3) W.B. Yeats
(4) Ezra Pound

Explanations:
Answer: (1) John Galsworthy

PEN International was founded in 1921 by Mrs. C. A. Dawson Scott, with John Galsworthy as its first president.

Which two of the following are the interludes in John Galsworthy's *The Forsyte Saga* (1922)

    (A) To Let
    (B) Indian Summer of a Forsyte
    (C) Awakening
    (D) In Chancery

Choose the correct answer from the options given below:

1. (A) and (B) Only
2. (B) and (C) Only
3. (A) and (C) Only
4. (B) and (D) Only

Explanations:

Answer: **2.** (B) and (C) Only

The Forsyte Saga, first published under that title in 1922, is a series of three novels and two interludes published between 1906 and 1921 by the English author John Galsworthy, who won the Nobel Prize in Literature.

Interludes in John Galsworthy's The Forsyte Saga (1922):

(B) Indian Summer of a Forsyte.
(C) Awakening .

Extra Perk:

The Forsyte Saga is a series of novels written by John Galsworthy. Here is the chronological order of the novels:

- ➢ *The Man of Property (1906*
- ➢ *In Chancery (1920)*
- ➢ *To Let (1921)*

Apart from the main trilogy, there are two interludes:
- ➢ *"Indian Summer of a Forsyte" (1918).*
- ➢ *"Awakening" (1920)*

Arnold Bennett (1867-1931)

- **Enoch Arnold Bennett**: English author, known novelist.
- Wrote **34 novels, seven story volumes, 13 plays.**
- Kept a **daily journal** exceeding **a million words.**
- Contributed to **100+ newspapers** and periodicals.
- Worked in **Ministry of Information** during **WWI.**
- Wrote for **cinema** in the **1920s.**
- **Most financially successful British author** of his time.
- Born in **Hanley, Staffordshire Potteries.**
- Father intended him for the **legal profession.**
- **Moved to London** as a **clerk** at age **21.**
- Became **editor of women's magazine.**
- Became a **full-time author** in **1900.**
- Loved **French culture** and **French literature.**
- Moved to **Paris in 1902,** overcoming **shyness.**
- Married a **Frenchwoman** in **1907.**
- Returned to **England** in **1912.**
- Separated from **wife in 1921**, new partner later.
- Died in **1931 of typhoid** in **France.**
- Known for **"Five Towns" novels** on Potteries.
- Inspired by **Flaubert, Balzac** – detailed realism.
- Influenced by **George Moore's** realist style.
- His **criticism** was highly regarded.
- Successful play: **Milestones (1912)**, co-written.
- **The Great Adventure (1913)** adapted from **Buried Alive.**
- Significant novels: **Anna of the Five Towns, Clayhanger.**

Anna of the Five Towns (1902)

- **Published in 1902**, first novel set in **Potteries.**
- Details **provincial life** among self-made business classes.
- **Anna** and **Agnes** grow up under strict **father.**
- **Ephraim Tellwright**: wealthy miser and rigid **Methodist.**
- **Anna's inheritance** attracts **Henry Mynors' proposal.**
- Couple plans to live in **Titus Price's** home.
- Anna's suppressed **love for Willie**, ending in **tragedy.**

The Old Wives' Tale (1908)

- Published **1908**, follows **Constance** and **Sophia Baines**.
- Set between **1840-1905**, in **Burslem** and **Paris**.
- Constance stays, **Sophia** elopes with a **cad** husband.
- Sisters **reunited** as **old women**, changed by life.
- Contrasts **stability** and **change** in their personalities.
- Established **Bennett's reputation** as a great novelist.
- Regarded as one of **Bennett's finest works**.

The Clayhanger Family & Clayhanger (1910)

- Series published **1910-1918** in **Five Towns** setting.
- Commonly called **"trilogy"** but includes **four novels**.
- All novels set in **Staffordshire Potteries** region.
- **Clayhanger** (1910) introduces **family dynamics**.
- **Hilda Lessways** (1911) explores **Hilda's independent life**.
- **These Twain** (1915) follows **Hilda's and Edwin's** marriage.
- **The Roll-Call** (1918) depicts **new generation's struggles**.

QUESTIONS

Question 14

In "Mr Bennett and Mrs Brown", Virginia Woolf:

1. responds to E.M. Forster's remarks on the character in fiction.
2. criticises book buying preferences of the educated English class.
3. **Analyze the state of modern fiction by contrasting two generations of writers.**
4. presents modernity as a stable and coherent project uniting all artists.

Correct Explanations:

 In "Mr Bennett and Mrs Brown," a critical essay published in 1924, Virginia Woolf takes a deep dive into the state of modern fiction and the changing nature of the novel. Woolf contrasts the "materialists" of the Victorian era, like Arnold Bennett, with the new breed of modernist writers, such as James Joyce and Virginia Woolf herself, who were exploring new forms of expression and subject matter.

E. M. Forster (1879-1970)

- ➢ **Edward Morgan Forster**: English novelist, essayist, librettist, 20-time Nobel nominee.
- ➢ **Notable works**: *A Room with a View, Howards End, A Passage to India*.
- ➢ *A Passage to India* (1924) brought **Forster great success**.
- ➢ **Forster's themes**: Class, hypocrisy, and social criticism.
- ➢ Early novels reflected **Victorianism breaking into modernism**.
- ➢ Adopted themes of **independent women and social dynamics**.
- ➢ Style: **Freer, colloquial, moving from Victorian complexity**.
- ➢ **Social commentary** rooted in middle-class life observation.
- ➢ Forster explored **Mediterranean "paganism," earth connection**.
- ➢ **The Longest Journey** (1907) warned of isolation dangers.
- ➢ *Howards End*: Alliance between **liberal Schlegels, earthy Wilcoxes**.
- ➢ *Howards End's* ending: **Linking imagination and the earth**.
- ➢ Themes undermined by **World War I's impact**.
- ➢ Forster spent **wartime years in Alexandria, visiting India**.
- ➢ *A Passage to India's* **conflict of earth and imagination**.
- ➢ **Adela Quested** glimpses resolution between **cultures briefly**.
- ➢ **Fielding** and **Mrs. Moore** embody truthfulness, benevolence.
- ➢ Novel ends in **equilibrium, British-Indian tension unresolved**.
- ➢ Forster's essays, **short stories, and biographies published**.
- ➢ *Maurice* (1971), **a posthumous novel on homosexuality**.

Notable Work:

- ➢ *Where Angels Fear to Tread (1905)*
- ➢ *The Longest Journey (1907)*
- ➢ *A Room with a View (1908)*
- ➢ *Howards End (1910)*
- ➢ *A Passage to India (1924)*
- ➢ *Maurice (written in 1913–14, published posthumously in 1971)*

Where Angels Fear to Tread (1905)

- ➢ The title comes from Alexander Pope's **An Essay on Criticism** line: *"For fools rush in where angels fear to tread."*
- ➢ **Lilia Herriton** travels to **Italy** for a fresh start.
- ➢ In **Monteriano,** she meets and marries **Gino Carella**.
- ➢ The **Herriton family**, disapproving, tries to control Lilia's choices.
- ➢ **Philip Herriton** is sent to bring Lilia back.

> Lilia dies in childbirth, leaving a **son** with Gino.
> The Herritons plan to take the child from **Gino**.
> **Caroline Abbott** and Philip grow sympathetic toward Gino.
> Caroline questions if **taking the child** is truly right.
> In the end, the **child tragically dies** in an accident.
> Forster's message: "The danger of meddling in others' lives."

A Room with a View (1908)

> A young woman in the restrained culture of Edwardian-era England.
> Set in Italy and England
> **Lucy Honeychurch** visits Italy, seeking new experiences.
> Important Line: "She had an odd feeling in her heart."
> At **Pension Bertolini**, Lucy meets **George Emerson**.
> Returning to **England**, Lucy is engaged to **Cecil Vyse**.
> Realizing her love for George, Lucy breaks engagement.
> Important Event: She confronts her true feelings.
> Lucy and George return to Florence, finding freedom.
> Important Line: "Love is of the soul."

Howards End (1910)

> **Howards End** by **E.M. Forster**, published in **1910**.
> Story explores **relationships** between **Schlegels** and **Wilcoxes**.
> **Schlegels** are imaginative; **Wilcoxes** are pragmatic.
> **Margaret** forms a bond with **Ruth Wilcox**.
> Ruth wills **Howards End** to **Margaret** in a **note**.
> **Wilcox family** ignores Ruth's **wishes** after her death.
> **Margaret** inherits **Howards End** after marrying **Henry**.
> Margaret brings **Henry** to Howards End, now **broken**.

A Passage to India (1924)

> The novel is based on Forster's experiences in India.
> Deriving the title from Walt Whitman's 1870 poem *"Passage to India"* in Leaves of Grass.
> **Arrival**
>> Adela Quested and Mrs. Moore visit British India.
>> Dr. Aziz meets Mrs. Moore; they become friends.
> **Bridge Party**
>> A party is held to introduce Adela to locals.

- o Adela meets Fielding, who invites her to tea.
- ➢ **Fielding's Tea Party**
  - o Aziz, Fielding, Mrs. Moore, and Adela bond.
  - o Aziz invites the women to the Marabar Caves.
- ➢ **Marabar Caves**
  - o Mrs. Moore feels uneasy with the echo.
  - o Adela experiences confusion and an illusion of assault.
- ➢ **Aziz's Arrest**
  - o Aziz is accused of assault; racial tensions rise.
  - o Fielding believes Aziz is innocent, causing tension.
- ➢ **Moore Mystery**
  - o Mrs. Moore is apathetic and sent back to England.
  - o She dies during the voyage, leaving India divided.
- ➢ **Trial Scene**
  - o Adela realizes her mistake; Aziz is acquitted.
  - o The trial exposes deep British-Indian mistrust.
- ➢ **Aftermath**
  - o Adela leaves India, ending her engagement to Ronny.
  - o Aziz's friendship with Fielding becomes strained.
- ➢ **At Mau**
  - o Two years later, Fielding returns with his wife, Stella.
  - o Aziz dreams of Indian independence before true friendship.

Maurice (1971)

- ➢ **Maurice** is a novel by **E.M. Forster**.
- ➢ Tale of **homosexual love** in early **20th-century England**.
- ➢ Follows **Maurice Hall** from schooldays to **university**.
- ➢ **Written** in **1913–1914** and revised in **1932, 1959–1960**.
- ➢ Forster admired **poet, philosopher, socialist Edward Carpenter**.
- ➢ **Visit to Carpenter's home** inspired Maurice's creation.
- ➢ **Cross-class relationship** modeled after Carpenter and Merrill.
- ➢ Real-life model for **Maurice** and **Alec Scudder**.
- ➢ Forster shared novel with **select trusted friends**.
- ➢ Notable friends included **Sassoon, Strachey, and Carpenter**.
- ➢ **Published posthumously** in **1971** only.
- ➢ **Maurice** remains a **pioneering LGBTQ+ work** today.

Aspects of the Novel (1927) by E.M. Forster:

- ➢ Forster delivered lectures on the novel at Trinity College.

- ➢ Discusses seven universal aspects of the novel in his book.
- ➢ Uses classic texts to exemplify story, characters, plot, and more.
- ➢ Critics debate Forster's normative theory on novel-writing.
- ➢ W. Somerset Maugham learned to write novels like Forster.
- ➢ Virginia Woolf praised Forster's approach as non-authoritative.
- ➢ Forster portrayed as a casual friend to fiction.
- ➢ Woolf critiques the lack of definitive laws of fiction.

QUESTION

Question 15

Match List I with List II

List I (Essay)	List II (Essayist)
A. "The Tory Fox-Hunter"	I. Francis Bacon
B. "What I Believe"	II. Joseph Addison
C. "The Death of the Moth"	III. E.M.Forster
D. "Of Ambition"	IV. Virginia Woolf

Choose the correct answer from the options given below:
1. A -I , B -III , C -IV , D -II
2. A -III , B -IV , C -II , D -I
3. **A -II , B -III , C -IV , D -I**
4. A -IV , B -I , C -II , D -III

Correct Explanations:
- ➢ **"The Death of the Moth and Other Essays" is a collection of essays by Virginia Woolf.**
- ➢ **"What I Believe" is a humanist essay by E. M. Forster,** first published in 1938.
- ➢ **"Of Ambition" is an essay by Francis Bacon.**
- ➢ **"The Tory Fox Hunter" is an essay by Joseph Addison.**

Question 16

Match List I with List II

List (Novel)	List II (Writer)
A. A Handful of Dust	I. E. M. Forster
B. Brighton Rock	II. Evelyn Waugh

C. Howard's End	III. D. H. Lawrence
D. The Plumed Serpent	IV. Aldous Huxley
E. Those Barren Leaves	V. Graham Greene

Choose the correct answer from the options given below:

1. A- III; B-I; C-V; D-II; E-IV
2. A- I; B-IV; C-II; D-III; E-V
3. A- II; B-V; C-I; D-III; E-IV
4. A- V; B-II, C-IV, D-I; E-III

Correct Explanations:

A. "A Handful of Dust" by Evelyn Waugh: Published in 1934

B. "Brighton Rock" by Graham Greene: "Brighton Rock," first published in 1938

C. "Howard's End" by E.M. Forster: "Howard's End," published in 1910

D. "The Plumed Serpent" by D.H. Lawrence: Published in 1926,

E. "Those Barren Leaves" by Aldous Huxley: Published in 1925,

G. K. Chesterton (1874-1936)

- English critic and author of verse, essays, novels, and short stories.
- Known for his exuberant personality and rotund figure.
- Chesterton was educated at St. Paul's School.
- Later studied art at the Slade School and literature at University College, London.
- His writings to 1910 were of three kinds.
- **Notable Works:**
  - *The Defendant (1901),*
  - *Twelve Types (1902),*
  - *The Man Who Was Thursday (1908)*
  - *Heretics (1905).* In it, he expressed strongly pro-Boer views in the South African War.
  - *What's Wrong with the world (1910).*

The Man Who Was Thursday (1908)

- *The Man Who Was Thursday,* in full *The Man Who Was Thursday: A Nightmare.*
- An **allegorical novel** by G.K. Chesterton, published in **1908.**

- It relates the experiences of **Gabriel Syme**, a poet turned detective.
- He was shrouded, a nameless person hires to infiltrate a group of anarchists.
- Each named for a day of the week and all determined to destroy the world.
- **Gabriel Syme**, a poet-detective, infiltrates an **anarchist group** in London.
- Syme wins a **place on the Council** of anarchists, codenamed **Thursday**.
- **Council members**, each named after days, include **Sunday**, the mysterious leader.
- Syme realizes other members are also **undercover detectives**.
- In a tense **chase and confrontation**, Syme questions **Sunday's true identity**.
- Key line: **"We are all in revolt against revolution"** as they uncover Sunday's motives.
- Sunday is revealed as a **god-like figure**, testing their beliefs and resolve.
- The novel explores **faith, order vs. chaos**, and the **mystery of existence**.

English War Poets

- **Thomas Hardy** (1840–1928) wrote **significant war poems**.
- Poems relate to **Napoleonic Wars** and **Boer Wars**.
- **World War I** poems include *"Drummer Hodge"* and others.
- Hardy influenced **Rupert Brooke** and **Siegfried Sassoon**.
- Used **ordinary soldiers' viewpoint** and **colloquial speech**.
- **Wessex Poems** (1898) reflect **Napoleonic Wars' impact**.
- *The Dynasts* (1904–08) focuses on **Napoleonic War**.
- **British soldiers** wrote about **war experiences**.
- **Edward Thomas** and **Wilfred Owen** died in battle.
- **1985 Poet's Corner** memorial commemorates **16 Great War poets**.
    1. Richard Aldington,
    2. Laurence Binyon,
    3. Edmund Blunden,
    4. Rupert Brooke,
    5. Wilfrid Gibson,
    6. Robert Graves,
    7. Julian Grenfell,

8. Ivor Gurney,
9. David Jones,
10. Robert Nichols,
11. Wilfred Owen,
12. Herbert Read,
13. Isaac Rosenberg,
14. Siegfried Sassoon,
15. Charles Sorley,
16. Edward Thomas.

Edmund Blunden (1896-1974)

> ***Undertones of War*** (1928; new ed. 1956)
> About World War I

Rupert Brooke (1887-1915)

> **Rupert Brooke**, idealistic war **sonnet poet** of **WWI**.
> Known for **"The Soldier"** and **boyish good looks.**
> **W.B. Yeats** called him "the handsomest young man."
> Excelled in **cricket, football,** and **academics** at Rugby.
> **King's College** student, active in **Fabian Society**.
> Loved **rambling** in **Grantchester**; wrote **poem** about it.
> Published **Poems** in **1911**; gained **notoriety**.
> Traveled **U.S., Canada,** and **South Seas** (1913-14).
> Commissioned in **Royal Navy** at **WWI** outbreak.
> **Died of septicemia**, buried in **Skyros** olive grove.

The Soldier (1914)

> The poem is the fifth in a series of poems entitled 1914.
> Often contrasted with Wilfred Owen's 1917 antiwar poem "Dulce et Decorum est".
> Written with fourteen lines in a Petrarchan/Italian sonnet form.
> The poem is divided into an opening octet, and then followed by a concluding sestet.
> **Sonnet captures memoirs** of a **deceased soldier.**
> Declares **patriotism** through his **sacrifice** for **England.**
> **Sacrifice claims land** where his **body is buried.**
> **Doesn't follow Petrarchan form** of **predicament/resolution.**
> Atmosphere stays in **blissful state** of **English soldier.**

If I should die, think only this of me:
That there's some corner of a foreign field
That is for ever England. There shall be
In that rich earth a richer dust concealed;
A dust whom England bore, shaped, made aware,
Gave, once, her flowers to love, her ways to roam,
A body of England's, breathing English air,
Washed by the rivers, blest by suns of home.

And think, this heart, all evil shed away,
A pulse in the eternal mind, no less
Gives somewhere back the thoughts by England given;
Her sights and sounds; dreams happy as her day;
And laughter, learnt of friends; and gentleness,
In hearts at peace, under an English heaven.

Robert Graves (1895-1985)

- **Robert Graves** was an **English poet, novelist, scholar**.
- Wrote over **120 books**, including **I, Claudius**.
- Known for **autobiography** of **World War I** experiences.
- **Good-Bye to All That** reflects **war's grimness**.
- Began **writing poetry** at **Charterhouse School**.
- Served as **British officer** in **World War I**.
- **Wounded** in **1916**, deeply troubled for a **decade**.
- Experienced **mental conflict** and **unhappy marriage**.
- Found new **inspiration** with poet **Laura Riding**.
- Settled in **Majorca**, enabled by memoir's success.
- *I, Claudius* tells of **Julio-Claudian personalities**.
- Historical novels set in **Mediterranean civilizations**.
- **The Golden Fleece** inspired his study of **myths**.
- Wrote **The White Goddess**, a **controversial work**.
- Argues for **goddess worship** continuing into **Christian Era**.

I, Claudius (1934)

- **I, Claudius** is a **historical novel** by **Robert Graves**.
- Written as an **autobiography** of **Emperor Claudius**.
- Chronicles **Julio-Claudian dynasty** and **early Roman Empire**.

- ➤ Covers **Julius Caesar's** to **Caligula's assassinations**.
- ➤ **Events** based on works of **Suetonius** and **Tacitus**.

Good-Bye to All That (1929)

- ➤ **Good-Bye to All That**, **autobiography** by **Robert Graves** (1929).
- ➤ Written at age **34** as a "bitter leave-taking."
- ➤ **Title suggests** end of **old order** post-WWI.
- ➤ Addresses **patriotism, atheism, feminism, socialism, pacifism**.
- ➤ Explores **changes** in **traditional married life**.
- ➤ New **literary styles** reflect **Graves's experiences**.
- ➤ **Comic portrayal** of **British army officer** life in WWI.
- ➤ Covers **family history, childhood, schooling**, and **early marriage**.
- ➤ Reflects **"particular mode of living and thinking."**

David Jones (1895-1974)

- ➤ **David Jones** enlisted in **Royal Welch Fusiliers**.
- ➤ **In Parenthesis** drew from **wartime experiences**.
- ➤ Took **over a decade** to complete the work.
- ➤ Continued as an **artist and poet** lifelong.

Wilfred Owen (1893-1918)

- ➤ **Wilfred Owen**: English poet against **war's cruelty**.
- ➤ Known for **technical experiments in assonance**.
- ➤ Influential works published **posthumously**.
- ➤ Notable poems include **"Dulce et Decorum est"**.
- ➤ Other works: **"Insensibility," "Anthem for Doomed Youth"**.
- ➤ Also wrote **"Futility," "Spring Offensive," "Strange Meeting"**.
- ➤ Educated at **Birkenhead Institute, University of London**.
- ➤ Moved to **France** after illness in **1913**.
- ➤ Wrote **"Minor Poems—in Minor Keys"** collection.
- ➤ Early poems modeled on **John Keats**.
- ➤ Enlisted in **British army** in **1915**.
- ➤ **Trench warfare** experience matured Owen quickly.
- ➤ Later poems expressed **anger at war's brutality**.
- ➤ Wounded in **June 1917**, sent to **hospital**.
- ➤ Met **Siegfried Sassoon**, who influenced his work.
- ➤ **Sassoon** helped transform Owen's **poetic style**.
- ➤ Returned to **France in August 1918** as **commander**.

- ➤ Awarded **Military Cross** in **October 1918**.
- ➤ Killed **one week before Armistice Day**.

Strange Meeting (1919)

- ➤ **"Strange Meeting"** by **Wilfred Owen** reflects **WWI atrocities**.
- ➤ **Written in 1918**, published **posthumously in 1919**.
- ➤ **Narrated** by a soldier in the **underworld**.
- ➤ Meets **enemy soldier** he killed **the day before**.
- ➤ Considered **Owen's "most haunting and complex" poem**.
- ➤ **Pararhyme** is a distinct feature in Owen's poetry.
- ➤ **Entire poem** uses **pararhyming couplets** throughout.
- ➤ Example: **"And by his smile I knew that sullen hall..."**
- ➤ **Pararhyme links keywords** without detracting **solemnity**.
- ➤ **Absence of full rhyme** creates **discomfort, incompleteness**.
- ➤ **Discordant tone** matches **poem's disturbing mood**.
- ➤ Last of Owen's poems in **War Requiem**.
- ➤ Performed by **tenor, baritone**, and **chamber orchestra**.
- ➤ Full forces join on **"Let us sleep now..."**
- ➤ Line **"I am the enemy you killed, my friend"** inscribed on **memorial sculpture**.
- ➤ **Wilfred Owen Association memorial** at **Shrewsbury Abbey** in 1993.

Dulce et Decorum est (1920)

- ➤ **"Dulce et Decorum est"** by **Wilfred Owen, WWI poem**.
- ➤ **Title** from **Horace's Ode 3.2** means "sweet and fitting."
- ➤ **Full phrase**: pro patria mori – "to die for country."
- ➤ Known for **horrific imagery** and **war condemnation**.
- ➤ **Drafted at Craiglockhart**, October **1917**.
- ➤ **Revised** later at **Scarborough** or **Ripon**, early **1918**.
- ➤ Earliest manuscript dated **8 October 1917**.
- ➤ Addressed to **mother, Susan Owen**, as a **"gas poem"**.
- ➤ Describes **chlorine gas attack** on British soldiers.
- ➤ **One soldier** fails to **put on gas mask**.
- ➤ Speaker depicts **gruesome effects of gas**.
- ➤ War's reality counters **dulce et decorum est** belief.
- ➤ Owen **condemns war** and **mendacious platitudes**.
- ➤ Poem reveals **atrocities and soldier's experiences**.

Siegfried Sassoon (1886-1967)

- ➢ **Siegfried Sassoon**: English poet known for **antiwar poetry**.
- ➢ Praised for capturing **English country life** beautifully.
- ➢ Enlisted in **World War I**; twice **wounded**.
- ➢ Notable works: **The Old Huntsman** (1917), **Counterattack** (1918).
- ➢ Gained fame for **antiwar poetry** and **pacifism**.
- ➢ Awarded **Military Cross** yet spoke against **war**.
- ➢ Antiwar stance attributed initially to **shell shock**.
- ➢ **Confined** in a **sanatorium** due to his views.
- ➢ Met and influenced **Wilfred Owen** during confinement.
- ➢ Published **Owen's works** after Owen's **death**.
- ➢ Wrote **The Memoirs of George Sherston**, 3 volumes.
- ➢ Later **devotional poetry** in **Collected Poems** (1947).
- ➢ Final work, **The Path to Peace** (1960).

QUESTIONS

Question 17

Match List I with List II:

List I	List II
(A) "Faces along the bar/cling to their average day."	(I) Wilfred Owen
(B) "The awful daring of a moments surrender."	(II) T.S. Eliot
(C) "Bent double, like old beggars under sacks."	(III) Allen Ginsberg
(D) "I saw the best minds of my generation destroyed by madness."	(IV) W.H. Auden

Choose the correct answer from the options given below:

1. **(A)-(IV). (B)-(II). (C)-(I), (D)-(III)**
2. (A)-(III). (B)-(I), (C)-(IV), (D)-(II)
3. (A)-(I), (B)-(IV). (C)-(II). (D)-(III)
4. (A)-(II), (B)-(IV), (C)-(I), (D)-(III)

Correct Explanations:
A. **September 1, 1939 by W. H. Auden - 1907-1973:**

Stanza 5:

Faces along the bar Cling to their average day:
The lights must never go out,
The music must always play,
All the conventions conspire
To make this fort assume The furniture of home;

B. T.S. Eliot, The Waste Land

"The awful daring of a moment's surrender which an age of prudence
can never retract. by this, and only this, we have existed."

"Dulce et Decorum est" is a poem written by Wilfred Owen during World War I, published posthumously in 1920.

➤ The Latin title is taken from Ode 3.2 (Valor) of the Roman poet Horace and means "it is sweet and fitting".

➤ It is followed by pro patria mori, which means "to die for one's country".

Opening line of :Dulce et Decorum est"

Bent double, like old beggars under sacks,
Knock-kneed, coughing like hags, we cursed through sludge,
Till on the haunting flares we turned our backs,
And towards our distant rest began to trudge.

In the 1940's, Ginsberg, William S. Burroughs and Jack Kerouac were the founding fathers of what became known as "The Beat Gene**ration". His famous famous poem is entitled "Howl" (first published in 1956) and begins "I saw the best minds of my generation destroyed by madness"**

Read the following passage and answer the questions that follow:

WHEN I'M ALONE

'When I'm alone' - the words tripped off his tongue
As though to be alone were nothing strange.
'When I was young' he said, when I was young ..?
I thought of age, and loneliness, and change,
I thought how strange we grow when we're alone,

And how unlike the selves that meet, and talk,
And blow the candles out, and say good-night,
Alone ...The word is life endured and known.
It is the stillness where our spirits walk
And all but in most faith is overthrown.
SIEGFRIED SASSOON

Question 18

For the poet, 'Being alone is a condition conducive to

1. happiness of the self
2. becoming different from others
3. growing up in an unexpected way
4. thinking in a strange way

Explanations:

Answer: 3. growing up in an unexpected way

Question 19

For the speaker of the words 'When I'm alone, being alone is

1. The normal fate of a human being all his life
2. The normal fate of a human being when he is young
3. Not unlike being with others whom we meet
4. Not strange as a person should feel alone

Explanations:

Answer: 1. The normal fate of a human being all his life

Question 20

Which two of the following statements aptly captures the meaning of 'Alone' for thinking beings?

A. Meeting talking and bidding goodnight
B. Quietude and calmness of self
C. Life lived and understood
D. Becoming free from faith

Choose the correct answer from the options given below :

1. (A) and (B) Only
2. (C) and (A) Only
3. (B) and (C) Only

4. (D) and (B) Only

Explanations:
Answer: 3. (B) and (C) Only

The two statements that aptly capture the meaning of 'Alone' for thinking beings in the given passage are:

(B) Quietude and calmness of self
(C) Life lived and understood

DRAMA

J.M. Synge (1871-1909)

- ➢ **Edmund J.M. Synge**: Key figure in **Irish Literary Revival**.
- ➢ Came from **wealthy Anglo-Irish background**.
- ➢ Writings focused on **working-class Catholics** in Ireland.
- ➢ Explored **paganism** in rural Irish worldview.
- ➢ **Ill health** led to **schooling at home**.
- ➢ Early interest in **music**; studied at **Trinity College**.
- ➢ Moved to **Germany** in 1893 to study **music**.
- ➢ Abandoned music for **poetry** and **literary criticism**.
- ➢ Met **Yeats** in **Paris**, inspiring return to **Ireland**.
- ➢ **The Playboy of the Western World** sparked **riots**.
- ➢ Co-founded **Abbey Theatre** with **Yeats and Lady Gregory**.
- ➢ Other plays: **Riders to the Sea** and **The Tinker's Wedding**.
- ➢ Notable Works:
  - ○ *In the Shadow of the Glen, 1903*
  - ○ *Riders to the Sea, 1904*
  - ○ *The Well of the Saints, 1905*
  - ○ *The Aran Islands, 1907*
  - ○ *The Playboy of the Western World, 1907*
  - ○ *The Tinker's Wedding, 1908*
  - ○ *Poems and Translations, 1909*
  - ○ *Deirdre of the Sorrows 1910*
  - ○ *In Wicklow and West Kerry, 1912*

Riders to the Sea (1904)

- ➢ **Riders to the Sea** by **Irish playwright J.M. Synge**.
- ➢ Premiered by **Irish National Theater Society** in **1904**.
- ➢ **Helen Laird** starred as **Maurya** in **Molesworth Hall**.

- ➤ **One-act play** set in the **Aran Islands.**
- ➤ Features **poetic dialogue**, typical of **Synge's plays.**
- ➤ Central theme: **struggle against an impersonal sea.**
- ➤ Synge visited **Aran Islands** encouraged by **Yeats.**
- ➤ **Inspired by story** of washed-up body in **Donegal.**
- ➤ **Written in Hiberno-English** dialect of **Aran Islands.**
- ➤ Part of the **Irish Literary Revival.**
- ➤ Based on **stories collected** in **The Aran Islands.**
- ➤ Scenes include a **drowned man** identified by **clothing.**
- ➤ **Maurya** mourns her son **Michael**, lost at sea recently.
- ➤ **Cathleen** and **Nora**, her daughters, find **Michael's clothes.**
- ➤ Maurya fears the sea will take **Bartley**, her last son.
- ➤ Despite her warnings, Bartley rides to the mainland.
- ➤ Maurya laments, "They're all gone now, and there isn't anything more the sea can do to me."
- ➤ Bartley tragically dies in a **sea accident** soon after.
- ➤ Maurya accepts fate, saying, "No man at all can be living forever."
- ➤ The play portrays the **harshness of life** near the sea.

The Playboy of the Western World (1907)

- ➤ **A three-ac**t play first performed at the **Abbey Theatre, Dublin,** on 26 January 1907.
- ➤ It is set in **Michael James Flattery's public house** in County Mayo.
- ➤ Located on the west coast of Ireland) during the early 1900s.
- ➤ Christy Mahon, a young man running away from his farm, claiming he killed his father.
- ➤ **Christy Mahon** stumbles into **Flaherty's tavern** in Mayo.
- ➤ Claims he's **fleeing** after killing his **father.**
- ➤ **Flaherty praises** Christy's **boldness and bravery.**
- ➤ **Pegeen**, Flaherty's daughter, **falls in love** with Christy.
- ➤ Pegeen's **betrothed, Shawn Keogh, feels dismayed.**
- ➤ Christy becomes **town hero** due to his **storytelling.**
- ➤ Many women, including **Widow Quin**, are **attracted.**
- ➤ Christy impresses villagers with **donkey race victory.**
- ➤ Christy's **father Mahon** arrives, still **alive.**
- ➤ Town shuns Christy as a **liar and coward.**
- ➤ To regain **respect**, Christy attacks his **father again.**
- ➤ **Townsfolk prepare to hang** Christy for his **crime.**
- ➤ **Father survives** second attack and saves **Christy.**

➢ Pegeen laments: **"I've lost the only playboy..."**

QUESTION

What is the correct chronological sequence of famous dramatists in order of their birth?

A. William Congreve
B. John Dryden
C. William Wycherley
D. George Barnard Shaw
E. John Millington Synge

Choose the correct answer from the options given below :

(1) B, C, A, D, E
(2) A, C, B, E, D
(3) C, B, A, D, E
(4) E, B, C, A, D

Explanations:
Answer: (1) B, C, A, D, E

Here's the chronological order with both birth and death years:

1. **John Dryden** - born 1631, died 1700
2. **William Wycherley** - born 1641, died 1716
3. **William Congreve** - born 1670, died 1729
4. **George Bernard Shaw** - born 1856, died 1950
5. **John Millington Synge** - born 1871, died 1909

Question 22

Match List I with List II

List I	List II
A. Sean O'Casey	I. I'm Talking About Jerusalem
B. Dylan Thomas	II. The Winslow Boy

C. Terence Rattigan	III. Juno and the Paycock
D. Arnold Wesker	IV. In the Shadow of the Glen
E. J.M. Synge	V. Under Milk Wood

Choose the correct answer from the options given below:

1. A-II, B-I, C-III, D-V, E-IV
2. A-V, B-IV, C-II, D-I, E-III
3. **A-III, B-V, C-II, D-I, E-IV**
4. A-IV, B-II, C-III, D-V, E-I

Correct Explanations:

I. *"I'm Talking About Jerusalem"* is a play by Sir Arnold Wesker.
II. *"The Winslow Boy"* is a play by Terence Rattigan.
III. *"Juno and the Paycock"* is a play by Sean O'Casey.
IV. *"In the Shadow of the Glen"* is a play by J.M. Synge.
V. *"Under Milk Wood"* is a radio drama by Dylan Thomas.

Question 23

Arrange the following plays in their chronological sequence:

A. Sergeant Musgrave's Dance
B. The Playboy of the Western World
C. Look Back in Anger
D. Man and Superman

Choose the correct answer from the options given below:

1. D, B, A, C
2. B, D, A, C
3. **D, B, C, A**
4. B, D, C, A

Correct Explanations:

➢ *"Man and Superman"* is a four-act play by George Bernard Shaw, first performed in **1905**.
➢ *"The Playboy of the Western World"* is a three-act play by John Millington Synge, first performed in **1907**.

- ➤ *"Look Back in Anger"* is a three-act play by John Osborne, first performed in **1956**.
- ➤ *"Sergeant Musgrave's Dance"* is a play by John Arden, first performed in **1959**.

Sean O' Casey (1880-1964)

- ➤ **Sean O'Casey**: Renowned **Irish playwright** of **Dublin slums**.
- ➤ Known for **juxtaposing tragedy and comedy** uniquely.
- ➤ Born into **lower-middle-class Irish Protestant** family.
- ➤ **Father died** when **O'Casey was six**.
- ➤ Family grew **poorer**; limited **formal education**.
- ➤ **Self-educated** through extensive **reading**.
- ➤ Began working at **age fourteen** in **manual labor**.
- ➤ First play, **The Shadow of a Gunman**, in **1923**.
- ➤ **Abbey Theatre** performed and **supported** his work.
- ➤ Play reflects **revolutionary politics' impact on Dublin**.
- ➤ Followed by **Juno and the Paycock** (1924).
- ➤ **The Plough and the Stars** set during **1916 Easter Rising**.
- ➤ Themes of **Irish patriotism, tenement life, survival**.
- ➤ **Tragi-comedies** with contrasting **death** and **bravado**.
- ➤ **Juno and the Paycock** adapted into **Hitchcock film**.
- ➤ Focus on **heroic resilience** in characters like **Juno**.
- ➤ **Notable Works:**
    - ○ *The Shadow of a Gunman (1923)*
    - ○ *Juno and the Paycock (1924)*
    - ○ *The Plough and the Stars (1926)*
    - ○ *Within the Gates (1933)*
    - ○ *The Silver Tassie (1934)*
    - ○ *The Star Turns Red (1940)*
    - ○ *Red Roses for Me (1943)*
    - ○ *Behind the Green Curtains (1961)*

Juno and the Paycock (1924)

- ➤ **Juno and the Paycock** produced in **1924**, published **1925**.
- ➤ Set in **Dublin slums** during **Irish Civil War**.
- ➤ Chronicles fortunes of impoverished **Boyle family**.
- ➤ Reflects **strengths and shortcomings** of **Irish character**.
- ➤ **Violent death** contrasts with independence **struggles**.

- ➢ **Juno**, only working family member, holds them together.
- ➢ Husband **Jack Boyle** prefers drinking with **Joxer**.
- ➢ Family expects inheritance; **Jack borrows** heavily.
- ➢ **Inheritance** is divided among **Jack's cousins**.
- ➢ **Law student Bentham** drafted faulty will.
- ➢ **Bentham flees**, leaving **Mary pregnant** and helpless.
- ➢ Family left **destitute** after inheritance failure.
- ➢ **Son Johnny** killed by **Republican soldiers**.
- ➢ **Juno leaves** Jack to find better life.
- ➢ Jack **escapes reality** in **alcoholic haze**.

The Plough and the Stars (1926)

- ➢ **The Plough and the Stars** by **Sean O'Casey, 1926**.
- ➢ Set during the **Easter Rising** of **1916**.
- ➢ **Abbey Theatre premiere** sparked **nationalist rioting**.
- ➢ **Nora and Jack Clitheroe** try to survive **war**.
- ➢ **Nora** is pregnant; **Jack** fights and is **killed**.
- ➢ Nora's **baby stillborn**, leading to **mental breakdown**.
- ➢ **Bessie Burgess**, Protestant, becomes **Nora's caretaker**.
- ➢ **Bessie killed** by **sniper's bullet** at play's end.
- ➢ **Ireland under British rule**; rebellion is brewing.
- ➢ **Clitheroes live** in Dublin's **working-class tenement**.
- ➢ Jack was in the **Irish Citizen Army**.
- ➢ **Nora opposes** his return to **Nationalist cause**.
- ➢ **Friends and neighbors** support **rebellion**.
- ➢ **Powerful political idealism** impacts **ordinary lives**.
- ➢ Final play in O'Casey's **Dublin trilogy**.

George Bernard Shaw (1856-1950)

His Life

- ➢ **Mr. Shaw** was born in **Dublin** in **1856**.
- ➢ Son of a **retired civil servant**.
- ➢ **Educated** in Dublin, worked as **clerk at fifteen**.
- ➢ Moved to **London** in **1876** to try novel-writing.
- ➢ **Joined the Fabian Society** in **1884**.
- ➢ Actively participated in **socialistic work** with Fabians.
- ➢ Known for **witty, eloquent public speaking**.

- ➤ Began **journalism** in **1885**, covering various arts.
- ➤ Strong advocate of **Wagner's music** philosophy.
- ➤ Admired and promoted **Ibsen's dramatic works**.
- ➤ **Dramatic articles** in The Saturday Review, **1895–98**.
- ➤ Started writing and producing **his own plays**.
- ➤ Faced **public criticism** but persisted with **dramas**.
- ➤ Eventually gained **recognition** for his **dramatic works**.
- ➤ Shaw's plays now seen as **stimulating literature**.

His Novels

- ➤ **Shaw's career began** with **four rejected novels**.
- ➤ Published in **obscure, socialistic periodicals**.
- ➤ Best novels: **The Irrational Knot** and **Cashel Byron's Profession**.
- ➤ Republished as **"Novels of my Nonage"** in **1901**.
- ➤ **Shaw's style** shows **bold, dramatic character portraiture**.
- ➤ **Irreverent handling** of **treasured institutions**.
- ➤ Notable for **frigidity and barrenness of emotion**.
- ➤ Novels show a **crude socialism** approach.
- ➤ **Publishers likely feared socialism** in stories.
- ➤ **Readable** and **often amusing**, despite **early rejection**.

His Plays

- ➤ **Shaw** began as a **disciple of Ibsen**.
- ➤ Early work mimicked Ibsen's **cold, intellectual realism**.
- ➤ Lacked **humane, romantic idealism** of Ibsen's plays.
- ➤ **Widowers' Houses (1885)** focused on **slum-property**.
- ➤ Play was **hard, repulsive, lacking Shavian spirit**.
- ➤ **The Philanderer (1893)** showcased **technique mastery**.
- ➤ **Mrs. Warren's Profession** was **refused license** by censor.
- ➤ **Arms and the Man** ridiculed **war's "glories"** humorously.
- ➤ **Candida (1894)** explored **romantic sentimental comedy**.
- ➤ **Cæsar and Cleopatra (1898), serio-comic** and **picturesque**.
- ➤ **Man and Superman (1903)** was **audacious but lengthy**.
- ➤ **Heartbreak House (1917)** and **Back to Methuselah** showed **waning strength**.
- ➤ **Shaw's prefaces** often rivaled **importance of plays**.
- ➤ **Prefaces** tackled issues like **Shakespeare and early Christianity**.
- ➤ **Brilliant and incisive**, Shaw's prefaces defined his **prose**.

Notable Plays:

- *Mrs. Warren's Profession (1893)*
    - It is **a problem play**.
    - **Characters**: Mrs. Warren, Vivie, Crofts, Frank, Praed, brothel owner.
    - **Key Event**: Vivie discovers Mrs. Warren's brothel business.
    - **Important Line**: Mrs. Warren says, **"Not easy to earn honestly."**
    - **Vivie's Choice**: Vivie rejects her mother, chooses independence.
- *Arms and The Man (1894)*
    - Title comes from the opening words of **Virgil's Aeneid**.
    - **Characters**: **Raina**, Bluntschli, and Sergius in a love triangle.
    - **Plot**: Bluntschli hides in Raina's room, avoiding capture.
    - **Conflict**: Bluntschli's practicality challenges Raina's romantic war ideals.
    - **Resolution**: Raina chooses Bluntschli, embracing truth over fantasy.
- *Candida (1894)*
    - Part of his Plays Pleasant.
    - **Characters**: Candida, Reverend James Morell, and poet **Marchbanks**.
    - **Plot**: Marchbanks loves Candida, challenges Morell's devotion.
    - **Conflict**: Candida must choose between passion and stability.
    - **Resolution**: Candida chooses Morell, valuing stability and trust.
- *The Devil's Disciple (1896)*
    - The setting is in the Fall of 1777, during the Saratoga Campaign.
    - **Characters**: Richard, a rebellious hero; Judith; Rev. Anderson.
    - **Plot**: Richard sacrifices himself for Rev. Anderson's life.
    - **Twist**: Richard says, "I'm the devil's disciple," shocking townsfolk.
    - **Resolution**: British free Richard; he earns Judith's admiration.
- *Man and Superman (1902)*
    - **Man and Superman**, play by **George Bernard Shaw**.
    - **Published in 1903**, first performed in **1905**.
    - **Complete performance** only took place in **1915**.
    - Shaw subtitled it "**A Comedy and A Philosophy**."
    - Explores conflict between **spiritual man** and **biological woman**.
    - Incorporates Shaw's idea of the "**life force**."
    - Satirizes **relationship between the sexes**.
    - Act III, **"Don Juan in Hell,"** inspired by **Don Juan legend**.

- o **Characters**: John Tanner, Ann Whitefield, and Jack Malone.
- o **Plot**: Ann pursues Tanner, a reluctant philosopher and idealist.
- o **Tanner's Philosophy**: Advocates for freedom, opposes traditional marriage norms.
- o **Important Line**: "Life is the force that fights."
- o **Ann's Strategy**: Uses wit to manipulate Tanner's affections.
- o **Hell Scene**: Tanner debates morality with the Devil.
- o **Conflict**: Tanner resists Ann, fearing loss of freedom.
- o **Resolution**: Ann "wins" Tanner, proving Shaw's "Life Force."
- o **Theme**: Critique of romantic, societal expectations of love.
- o **Ending**: Tanner and Ann marry, fate overcoming philosophy.

➢ *Major Barbara (1905)*
- o **Characters**: Barbara, Andrew Undershaft, and Adolphus Cusins clash ideologically.
- o **Plot**: Barbara, a Salvation Army officer, rejects wealth.
- o **Conflict**: Undershaft's munitions wealth tests Barbara's moral beliefs.
- o **Resolution**: Barbara embraces Undershaft's view: "Poverty is the worst of crimes."

➢ *The Doctor's Dilemma (1906)*
- o It is a **problem play** about the **moral dilemmas** created by limited medical resources.
- o **Characters**: Dr. Ridgeon, artist Dubedat, and wife Jennifer.
- o **Plot**: Dr. Ridgeon must choose whom to save.
- o **Dilemma**: Ridgeon debates saving talented but immoral Dubedat.
- o **Resolution**: Ridgeon decides, highlighting flaws in medical ethics.

➢ *The Dark Lady of the Sonnets (1910)*
- o **Characters**: Features Shakespeare, Beefeater, Queen, and the Dark Lady.
- o **Setting**: Takes place at night outside the palace.
- o **Plot**: Shakespeare waits to meet the "Dark Lady."
- o **Queen's Entry**: Shakespeare mistakes the Queen for his muse.
- o **Humor**: The Queen humorously chastises Shakespeare's mistake.
- o **Monarch's Role**: Shaw critiques monarchy through Queen's dialogue.
- o **Shakespeare's Mission**: He advocates for a National Theatre establishment.

- o **The Dark Lady**: Represents Shakespeare's poetic inspiration and love.
    - o **Important Line**: "Will you patronize the players, Madam?"
    - o **Theme**: Blends history with comedy, supporting arts and reform.
- ➢ *Pygmalion (1912)*
    - o **Pygmalion** written by **George Bernard Shaw**, five acts.
    - o Premiered in **Vienna** in **German** language, **1913**.
    - o Performed in **England, 1914**, starred **Mrs. Patrick Campbell**.
    - o **Themes**: Love and class in a **humane comedy**.
    - o **Henry Higgins** takes bet to transform **Eliza Doolittle**.
    - o **Eliza**, a Cockney flower seller, undergoes **training**.
    - o Transforms into a **sensitive, refined young woman**.
    - o **Higgins** dismisses her as a **completed experiment**.
    - o **Eliza rejects** Higgins' **dehumanizing attitude**.
    - o **Shaw inspired** by phoneticians like **Henry Sweet**.
    - o **Greek myth** of **Pygmalion** influences Shaw's play.
    - o **Pygmalion** falls for his **living statue** in myth.
    - o **Victorian playwrights** used Pygmalion myth frequently.
    - o **W.S. Gilbert** wrote successful **Pygmalion and Galatea**.
    - o Shaw likely knew **musical Adonis** and **burlesque Galatea**.
    - o Shaw's **Pygmalion** adapted in **1938 film** version.
    - o **1956 musical** adaptation titled **My Fair Lady**.
    - o **1964 film** version of **My Fair Lady** released.
- ➢ *Heartbreak House (1917)*
    - o The "Russian manner" of the subtitle refers to the style of Anton Chekhov, which Shaw adapts.
    - o **Characters**: Ellie Dunn, Hesione Hushabye, Captain Shotover, Hector.
    - o **Plot**: Ellie arrives at Captain Shotover's eccentric home.
    - o **Themes**: Reflects moral and social decay in England.
    - o **Conflict**: Ellie's love contrasts with society's hollow values.
    - o **Important Line**: "The house is falling to pieces!"
- ➢ *Back to Methuselah (1918)*
- ➢ *Saint Joan (1923)*
    - o **Saint Joan** by **George Bernard Shaw** depicts **Joan of Arc**.
    - o Premiered in **1923**, after Joan's **canonization**.
    - o Reflects Shaw's belief in **trial participants' intentions**.
    - o Characters acted on what they **thought was right**.
    - o **Characters**: Joan, the Dauphin, Warwick, Cauchon, Dunois, and Inquisitor.

- o **Joan's Mission**: Joan inspires France to fight England.
- o **Important Line**: "I hear voices telling me to act."
- o **Victory**: Joan leads French to victory at Orleans.
- o **Dauphin's Crowning**: Joan ensures Dauphin is crowned at Reims.
- o **Conflict**: Joan's independence worries French and English leaders.
- o **Accusations**: Joan accused of witchcraft and heresy.
- o **Trial**: Joan refuses to deny her divine visions.
- o **Execution**: Joan burned as a heretic by the Church.
- o **Legacy**: Shaw shows Joan's martyrdom reshaping her legend.
- ➤ *The Apple Cart (1928)*
  - o It is a satirical comedy about several political philosophies.
  - o They are expounded by the characters, often in lengthy monologues.
  - o **Characters**: King Magnus, Prime Minister Proteus, Queen Jemima.
  - o **Plot**: King Magnus opposes government's attempt to limit monarchy.
  - o **Conflict**: Magnus challenges Proteus's power, asserting royal authority.
  - o **Climax**: Magnus threatens to abdicate, unsettling political stability.
  - o **Resolution**: King asserts control, "Don't upset the apple cart."

QUESTIONS

Question 24

Who is the author of the short play The Dark Lady of the Sonnets?'

1. Ben Jonson
2. George Bernard Shaw
3. Oscar Wilde
4. Oliver Goldsmith

Explanations:
Answer: 2. George Bernard Shaw

Question 25

The concept of " eugenics" finds its illustration predominantly in the writings of

    A. John Osborne
    B. George Bernard Shaw
    C. Eugene O'Neil
    D. Harold Pinter
    E. Arthur Miller

Choose the correct answer from the options given below;
1. A and B only
2. A and C only
3. **B and C only**
4. D and E only

Correct Explanations:
The concept predates the term; Plato suggested applying the principles of selective breeding to humans around 400 BC.

Question 26

Match List I with List II

LIST I	LIST II
A. You can't eat the orange and throw the peel away- a man is not a piece of fruit.	I. Man and Superman
B. Liberty means responsibility. That is why most men dread it.	II. A Doll's House
C. Nobody thinks, nobody cares. No beliefs, no convictions and no enthusiasm. Just another Sunday evening.	III. Death of a Salesman
D). Our home has been nothing but a playroom. I have been your doll-wife, just as at home I was papa's doll-child, and here the children have been my dolls.	IV. Look Back in Anger

Choose the correct answer from the options given below:

1. A-I, B-III, C-11, D-I
2. A-II, B-III, C-IV, D-I
3. A-I, B- IV, C-11, D-III
4. A-III, B-I, C-IV, D-11

Explanations:
Ans: A-III, B-I, C-IV, D-II

A. "You can't eat the orange and throw the peel away- a man is not a piece of fruit." The quote is by Arthur Miller from his play *"Death of a Salesman"* and spoken by the character Willy Loman. It expresses his belief that a person cannot be used up and then discarded like the peel of an orange.

B. *"Liberty means responsibility. That is why most men dread it."* **The quote is by George Bernard Shaw** and suggests that true freedom comes with the responsibility of making choices and being accountable for one's actions.

C. *"Nobody thinks, nobody cares. No beliefs, no convictions and no enthusiasm. Just another Sunday evening"* **is a quote from the play "Look Back in Anger" by John Osborne.**

D. *"Our home has been nothing but a playroom. I have been your doll-wife, just as at home I was papa's doll-child, and here the children have been my dolls."* **The quote is from Henrik Ibsen's play "A Doll's House"** and is spoken by the character Nora.

Question 27

Arrange the works in the chronological order of the staging/ publication of the following plays:

    A.   A Woman Killed with Kindness
    B.   John Bull's Other Island
    C.   The Double Dealer
    D.   The Shoemaker's Holiday
    E.   The Conscious Lovers

Choose the correct answers from the options given below:
1. B, D, C, A and E

2. D, A, C, E and B
3. C ,D, A,B and E
4. E, B, D, C and A

Explanations:

Ans: D, A, C, E and B

The chronological order of the staging of the plays is:

- ➢ *The Shoemaker's Holiday (1600)*
- ➢ *The Double Dealer (1693)*
- ➢ *A Woman Killed with Kindness (1603)*
- ➢ *The Conscious Lovers (1722)*
- ➢ *John Bull's Other Island (1904)*

Question 28

Which among the following texts is not based on the theme of disability?

1. Madeleine Ryan's A Room Called Earth
2. Gabrielle Zevin's Tomorrow, and Tomorrow, and Tomorrow
3. G.B. Shaw's Mrs. Warren's Profession
4. Julia Heaberlin's We are All the Same in the Dark

Explanations:

Answer: 3. G.B. Shaw's Mrs. Warren's Profession

"Mrs. Warren's Profession" is a provocative play by **George Bernard Shaw**, penned in 1893 and making its London stage debut in 1902. This work, grouped with "The Philanderer" and "Widowers' Houses" in Shaw's 1898 collection, **"Plays Unpleasant,"** <u>explores the life of a former prostitute</u> turned brothel owner struggling with her estranged daughter's judgments.

"Tomorrow, and Tomorrow, and Tomorrow," **a 2022 novel by Gabrielle Zevin,** weaves the tale of three friends who launch a flourishing video game enterprise. Marking Zevin's tenth novel and fifth aimed at an adult audience, the story begins in the 1980s with adolescents **Sam Masur and Sadie Green crossing paths in a <u>pediatric hospital</u>,** where Sadie's older sister is treated for leukemia and Sam recovers from surgeries necessitated by a tragic accident that claimed his mother's life.

"A Room Called Earth" **by Madeleine Ryan** offers an unforgettable narrative through the eyes of a <u>**uniquely insightful young woman.**</u> Her narrative provides a fresh perspective on existing in the world, challenging conventional norms with her distinctive outlook.

"We Are All the Same in the Dark" **by Julia Heaberlin** unravels the suspenseful tale of a small Texas town haunted by a legendary cold case. **The discovery of an <u>abandoned girl on the roadside</u> prompts a deep dive into the town's hidden past,** creating a riveting narrative that builds on the international success of Heaberlin's "Black-Eyed Susans."

Other Explantations:

These works each address aspects of disability, from learning disabilities and physical impairments to societal constructs of disability, highlighting the diverse narratives and challenges faced by individuals with disabilities.

"To Kill a Mockingbird" by Harper Lee - Explores prejudice through the eyes of three children towards a wrongly accused black man and their mysterious neighbor <u>with a learning disability,</u> Boo Radley.

"Of Mice and Men" by John Steinbeck - Highlights the friendship between George and Lennie, focusing on <u>Lennie's learning disability</u> and its exploitation in Depression-era America.

"The Sound and the Fury" by William Faulkner - Offers a unique perspective from Benji Compson, a character with <u>a significant learning disability</u>, challenging societal shame and family dynamics.

"Moby-Dick" by Herman Melville - Discusses disability through Captain Ahab's quest for revenge, emphasizing his <u>physical disability</u>.

"The Curious Incident of the Dog in the Night-time" by Mark Haddon - Gives insight into the autistic mind, promoting empathy and understanding.

"The Secret Garden" by Frances Hodgson Burnett - Features Colin, a boy who uses a wheelchair, and his transformation alongside a neglected garden.

"The First Man" by Albert Camus - Touches on Camus' relationship with his deaf and illiterate mother, reflecting on poverty and disability.

"The Giant's House" by Elizabeth McCracken - Tells the story of James Carlson Sweatt, whose extreme height is explored as both a disability and a unique trait.

"A Son of the Circus" by John Irving - Deals with the life of dwarfs in circus settings, discussing achondroplasia and societal perceptions of disability.

"Far From the Tree" by Andrew Solomon - Investigates the lives of families raising children with various disabilities, offering insights into acceptance and love.

Question 29

Match List I with List II

List I (Work)	List II (Character)
A. Charles Dickens' Martin Chuzzlewit	I. Abraham Durbeyfield -
B. G.B. Shaw's The Doctor's Dilemma	II. Harry
C. Thomas Hardy's Tess of d' Urbervilles	III. Sir Ralph Bloomfield Bonnington
D. T.S. Eliot's The Family Reunion	IV. Mrs Gamp

Choose the correct answer from the options given below:

1. A - IV, B - III, C - II, D - I
2. A - III, B -II, C -IV, D - I
3. A - III, B - II, C - I, D - IV
4. A - IV, B -III, C - I, D- II

Explanations:

Answer: 4. A - IV, B -III, C - 1, D- II

Martin Chuzzlewit (1844) is a novel by Charles Dickens. Using the pseudonym **"Boz,"** A notable character, **Sarah Gamp, provides dark humor as a drunken midwife and nurse.**

The Doctor's Dilemma **by George Bernard Shaw** is a four-act drama with an epilogue, debuted in London in 1906 and published in 1911. Complications arise when Ridgeon falls for Dubedat's loyal wife, Jennifer, introducing a twisted layer of personal and professional ethics, highlighted by characters like **Sir Ralph Bloomfield Bonington**.

Tess of the d'Urbervilles by Thomas Hardy, first serialized in 1891, tells the tragic story of Tess **Durbeyfield**, portrayed as a pure and virtuous woman crushed by the harsh morals of Victorian society.

The Family Reunion, a play by T. S. Eliot, combines elements of Greek tragedy and contemporary detective stories, using mostly blank verse to explore themes of guilt and redemption. The narrative centers around characters such as Amy, Lady Monchensey; Violet; Ivy; Charles and Gerald; Agatha; The Late Lord Monchensey; **Harry**; and Mary, detailing the protagonist's journey from overwhelming guilt towards a semblance of redemption.

CHAPTER 2

LITERATURE BETWEEN THE WAR

Introduction to the Rise of Modernism and Experimental Narratives

- Post-WWI literature explored themes of **disillusionment.**
- Shift towards **realism and rejection of romantic ideals.**
- Rise of Modernism marked by **experimental** forms.
- **Lost Generation** writers highlighted existential crisis.
- Focus on **individual alienation** and psychological depth.
- Influence of **Freudian psychology** on character portrayal.
- Use of **fragmented narrative and stream-of-consciousness.**
- Notable Modernists: T.S. Eliot, Virginia Woolf, James Joyce.
- Eliot's The Waste Land symbolized cultural decay.
- Woolf's works emphasized internal experience, isolation.
- Joyce's Ulysses revolutionized narrative structure.
- Rise of **political themes** in British literature.
- Growth of satirical works critiquing social norms.
- Auden and **Macspaunday** group addressed contemporary issues.
- Rise of regional literature and **local dialects.**
- D.H. Lawrence's focus on human nature, primal instincts
- George Orwell's works critiqued authoritarian regimes.
- Influence of existentialism on post-war literature.
- Themes of loss, trauma, and recovery post-WWI.
- Expansion of **women's voices** in literature.
- Increased exploration of class and economic struggles.
- Role of publishing houses like **Hogarth Press.**
- Impact of technology and industrialization on society.
- Writers experimented with form, language, and genre.
- Between-War literature paved way for **postmodernism.**

Bloomsbury group (1907-1930)

- **Bloomsbury Group**: Coterie of English writers and artists.
- Met from **1907 to 1930** in **Bloomsbury**, London.
- Gathered at homes of **Clive** and **Vanessa Bell.**

- ➢ Also met at **Virginia Woolf's** home with **Adrian.**
- ➢ Discussed **aesthetic** and **philosophical questions** regularly.
- ➢ Influenced by **G.E. Moore's Principia Ethica** (1903).
- ➢ Also inspired by **Principia Mathematica** by **Russell.**
- ➢ Sought definitions of **good, true, and beautiful.**
- ➢ Questioned ideas with "**comprehensive irreverence.**"
- ➢ Opposed **shams** with strong **agnostic spirit.**
- ➢ **Members of the Group:**
  - o Clive Bell, art critic
  - o Vanessa Bell, post-impressionist painter
- ➢ M. Forster, fiction writer
  - o Roger Fry, art critic, and post-impressionist painter
  - o Duncan Grant, post-impressionist painter
  - o John Maynard Keynes, economist
  - o Desmond MacCarthy, literary journalist
  - o Lytton Strachey, biographer
  - o Leonard Woolf, essayist and non-fiction writer
  - o Virginia Woolf, fiction writer, and essayist

Dorothy Richardson (1873-1957) & Pilgrimage (1915-1938)

- ➢ **Dorothy M. Richardson** born May 17, **1873**, in England.
- ➢ Known for **pioneering stream-of-consciousness fiction.**
- ➢ Grew up in **secluded** late Victorian **England.**
- ➢ **Parents separated** when she was **seventeen.**
- ➢ Worked in **teaching, clerical work,** and **journalism.**
- ➢ Married **artist Alan Elsden Odle** in **1917.**
- ➢ Known for sequence novel **Pilgrimage** (1915-1938).
- ➢ Pilgrimage volumes seen as **"chapters"** by Richardson.
- ➢ First volume: **Pointed Roofs** published in **1915.**
- ➢ **Backwater** followed in **1916; Honeycomb** in **1917.**
- ➢ Published **The Tunnel** in **1919; Interim** also **1919.**
- ➢ Next came **Deadlock** in **1921, Revolving Lights** in **1923.**
- ➢ **The Trap** appeared in **1925, Oberland** in **1927.**
- ➢ Published **Dawn's Left Hand** in **1931.**
- ➢ **Clear Horizon** came out in **1935.**
- ➢ **Dimple Hill** released in **1938,** completing series.
- ➢ **13 volumes** in total, including **posthumous volume.**

- ➢ **Pilgrimage** captures feminine **consciousness** and identity.
- ➢ Told through **Miriam Henderson**, a **New Woman**.

Virginia Woolf (1882-1941)

- ➢ **Virginia Woolf**, innovative **20th-century writer**.
- ➢ Known for **Mrs. Dalloway** and **To the Lighthouse**.
- ➢ Prolific in **essays, diaries, letters, biographies**.
- ➢ Captured **changing gender roles, class, technology**.
- ➢ Influenced by **Proust, Stravinsky, Post-Impressionists**.
- ➢ Explored **modernist themes**: subconscious, time, perception.
- ➢ **Stream of consciousness** reveals characters' inner lives.
- ➢ Focused on **marginal, ordinary minds** in daily life.
- ➢ In "The Art of Biography," Woolf questioned tradition.
- ➢ **Quote**: "The question now inevitably asks itself..."
- ➢ Refused **Companion of Honour** and honorary degrees.
- ➢ Wrote **A Room of One's Own** on women's rights.
- ➢ **Three Guineas** critiques society's view of women.
- ➢ **Flush** tells life of **Elizabeth Barrett Browning's spaniel**.
- ➢ **Orlando** fictionalizes friend **Vita Sackville-West's** life.
- ➢ Ran **Hogarth Press** with husband, **Leonard Woolf**.
- ➢ **Hogarth Press** published **T S Eliot, Freud, Forster**.
- ➢ Woolf connected to **Bloomsbury Set** of intellectuals.
- ➢ Born **Virginia Adeline Stephen** in **1882**.
- ➢ Father **Leslie Stephen** founded **Oxford Dictionary**.
- ➢ **Father knighted** for services to **literature**.
- ➢ Woolf's **mother, father, and brother died** early.
- ➢ Struggled with **mental health** throughout her life.
- ➢ **Committed suicide** in **1941**.
- ➢ **Woolf's legacy** endures in modern **literature**.
- ➢ **Edward Albee (1928-2016)** wrote a play *Who's Afraid of Virginia Woolf? (1962)*.

Notable Works

Novels

- ➢ *The Voyage Out (1915)*
- ➢ *Night and Day (1919)*
- ➢ *Jacob's Room (1922)*
- ➢ *Mrs Dalloway (1925)*

> *To the Lighthouse (1927)*
> *Orlando: A Biography (1928)*
> *The Waves (1931)*
> *The Years (1937)*
> *Between the Acts (1941)*

Short Story:

> *Two Stories (1917)*
> *Monday or Tuesday (1921)*
> *A Haunted House and Other Short Stories (1944)*
> *Mrs. Dalloway's Party (1973)*
> *The Complete Shorter Fiction (1985)*
> *A Woman's College from Outside*
> *Miss Pryme*
> *Moments of Being: 'Slater's Pins Have No Points'*
> *Monday or Tuesday*
> *Mrs Dalloway in Bond Street*
> *The Lady in the Looking-Glass: A Reflection*
> *The Legacy*
> *The Mark on the Wall*

Cross-genre

> *Flush: A Biography (1933)—Fictional "stream of consciousness" tale by Flush, a dog, but non-fiction in the sense of telling the story of the owner of the dog, Elizabeth Barrett Browning*

Biography

> *Roger Fry: A Biography (1940)*

Book length essays

> *A Room of One's Own (1929)*
> *On Being Ill (1930)*
> *Three Guineas (1938)*

Famous Essays

> ***A Room of One's Own***
> *The Art Of Fiction (**Note:** Also written by Henry James with the same title)*
> *The Art of Biography*
> ***The Leaning Tower***
> ***Modern Fiction (Essay)***
> ***Modern Letters***
> ***Mr. Bennett and Mrs. Brown (1924)***
> ***Notes on D. H. Lawrence***

> *The Novels of E. M. Forster*
> *The Novels of George Meredith*
> *The Novels of Thomas Hardy*
> *The Novels of Turgenev*
> *The Death of the Moth*
> *Women and Fiction*

Drama
> *Freshwater: A Comedy* edited by Lucio P. Ruotolo with drawings by Edward Gorey (first version 1923, revised and performed 1935, published 1976)

Translations
> *Stavrogin's Confession & the Plan of the Life of a Great Sinner*, from the notes of Fyodor Dostoevsky, translated in partnership with S. S. Koteliansky (1922)

Autobiographical writings
> *Moments of Being (1976) [2nd ed. 1985]*
> *The Platform of Time: Memoirs of Family and Friends, edited by S. P. Rosenbaum (London, Hesperus, 2007)*

Diaries and journals
> *A Writer's Diary (1953) - Extracts from the complete diary*
> *A Moment's Liberty: the shorter diary (1990)*
> *The Diary of Virginia Woolf (five volumes) - Diary of Virginia Woolf from 1915 to 1941*
> *Passionate Apprentice: The Early Journals, 1897-1909 (1990)*
> *Travels With Virginia Woolf (1993)* - Greek travel diary of Virginia Woolf, edited by Jan Morris

Prefaces *and contributions*
> *Introduction to Selections Autobiographical and Imaginative from the Works of George Gissing ed. Alfred C. Gissing (London & New York, 1929)*

Letters
> *Congenial Spirits: the selected letters (1993)*
> *The Flight of the Mind: Letters of Virginia Woolf vol 1 1888 - 1912 (1975)*
> *The Question of Things Happening: Letters of Virginia Woolf vol 2 1913 - 1922 (1976)*
> *A Change of Perspective: Letters of Virginia Woolf vol 3 1923 - 1928 (1977)*

- ➢ *A Reflection of the Other Person: Letters of Virginia Woolf vol 4 1929 - 1931 (1978)*
- ➢ *The Sickle Side of the Moon: Letters of Virginia Woolf vol 5 1932 - 1935 (1979)*
- ➢ *Leave the Letters Till We're Dead: Letters of Virginia Woolf vol 6 1936 - 1941 (1980)*
- ➢ *Paper Darts: The Illustrated Letters of Virginia Woolf (1991)*
- ➢ *Life as We Have Known It introductory letter (1931)*

> **Code**: *"Woolf begins a Voyage at Night with Jacob, meets Mr. Bennett and Mrs. Brown on the way, heads to the Lighthouse to meet Orlando, but the rough Waves delay them for Years, Between the Acts, longing for A Room of One's Own and Three Guineas."*

Notes on D.H. Lawrence May 18, 2021 by Virginia Woolf

"This then was the angle of approach, and it will be seen that it is an angle that shuts off many views and distorts others. But read from this angle, Sons and Lovers emerged with astonishing vividness, like an island from off which the mist has suddenly lifted. Here it lay, clean cut, decisive, masterly, hard as rock, shaped, proportioned by a man who, whatever else he might be—prophet or villain, was undoubtedly the son of a miner who had been born and bred in Nottingham. But this hardness, this clarity, this admirable economy and sharpness of the stroke are not rare qualities in an age of highly efficient novelists. The lucidity, the ease, the power of the writer to indicate with one stroke and then to refrain indicated a mind of great power and penetration. But these impressions, after they had built up the lives of the Morels, their kitchens, food, sinks, manner of speech, were succeeded by another far rarer, and of far greater interest. For after we have exclaimed that this coloured and stereoscopic representation of life is so like that surely it must be alive—like the bird that pecked the cherry in the picture—one feels, from some indescribable brilliance, sombreness, significance, that the room is put into order. Some hand has been at work before we entered. Casual and natural as the arrangement seems, as if we had opened the door and come in by chance, some hand, some eye of astonishing penetration and force, has swiftly arranged the whole scene, so that we feel that it is more exciting, more moving, in some ways fuller of life than one had thought real life could be, as if a painter had brought out the leaf or the tulip or the jar by pulling a green curtain behind it. But what is the green curtain that Lawrence has pulled so as to accentuate the colours? One never catches Lawrence—this is one of his most remarkable qualities—"arranging". "

QUESTIONS

Chronologically arrange the following texts in order of publication.

    A.   Betty Friedan's The Feminine Mystique
    B.   Simone de Beauvoir's The Second Sex
    C.   Virginia Woolf's A Room of One's Own
    D.   Germaine Greer's The Female Eunuch
    E.   Adrienne Rich's Of Woman Born

Choose the correct answer from the options given below :

    (1) A, B, C, D, E
    (2) C, B, A, D, E
    (3) D, C, B, A, E
    (4) B, C, A, D, E

Explanations:

Answer: (2) C, B, A, D, E

1. Virginia Woolf's *A Room of One's Own* – 1929
2. Simone de Beauvoir's *The Second Sex* – 1949
3. Betty Friedan's *The Feminine Mystique* – 1963
4. Germaine Greer's *The Female Eunuch* – 1970
5. Adrienne Rich's *Of Woman Born* – 1976

Arrange the following terms in the chronological order of emergence:

    A. Heresy of Paraphrase
    B. Stream of Consciousness
    C. Practical Criticism
    D. Defamiliarization

Choose the correct answer from the options given below:

    1. D, B, C, A
    2. B, D, A, C
    3. B, D, C, A

4. D, C, B, A

Explanations:

Answer: 3. B, D, C, A

- ➢ Stream of Consciousness (early 20th century)
- ➢ Defamiliarization (1910s-1920s)
- ➢ Practical Criticism (1920s)
- ➢ Heresy of Paraphrase (1920s)

Extra Perk:
Stream of Consciousness: Stream of Consciousness is a narrative technique that emerged in the early 20th century, particularly in the works of writers such a**s Virginia Woolf, James Joyce, and William Faulkner.**

Question 32

Arrange the following in the chronological order of publication:

- A. Crome Yellow
- B. Sons and Lovers
- C. Mrs Dalloway
- D. A Portrait of the Artist as a Young Man

Choose the correct answer from the options given below:
1. B, A, D, C
2. A, B, D, C
3. A, C, B, D
4. B, D, A, C

Explanations:

Answer: 4. B, D, A, C

- ➢ *Sons and Lovers by D.H. Lawrence (1913)*
- ➢ *A Portrait of the Artist as a Young Man by James Joyce (1916):*
- ➢ *Crome Yellow by Aldous Huxley (1921)*
- ➢ *Mrs Dalloway* by Virginia Woolf (1925)

Question 33

Which two texts among the following are linked to literary feminism?

- A. A Small Place
- B. The Yellow Wallpaper
- C. Emma

D. A Room of One's Own

Choose the correct answer from the options given below:

1. A and D only
2. C and D only
3. B and D only
4. A and C only

Explanations:
Answer: 3. B and D only

"The Yellow Wallpaper" by Charlotte Perkins Gilman and "A Room of One's Own" by Virginia Woolf are both important works in literary feminism.

Which two of the following are part of Virginia Woolf s collection of autobiographical essays?

A. "A Will to Word It"
B. "A Skcetch of the Past"
C. "A Faint Hue of the Past"
D. "Am I a Snob"

Choose the correct answer from the options given below:

1. (A) and (B) Only
2. (B) and (C) Only
3. (A) and (C) Only
4. (B) and (D) Only

Explanation:
Answer: 4. (B) and (D) Only

The two essays that are part of Virginia Woolf's collection of autobiographical essays are:

B. "A Sketch of the Past": In this essay, Woolf reflects on her childhood memories, family relationships, and the formation of her identity as a writer.

D. "Am I a Snob?": This essay explores Woolf's thoughts and contemplations on the concept of snobbery and her own position in relation to it.

Extra Perk:

A. "A Will to Word It": This essay explores Woolf's thoughts on the power of language and her own relationship with words, reflecting on the challenges and joys of writing.

C. "A Faint Hue of the Past": In this essay, Woolf delves into her memories and experiences, examining how the past influences and shapes the present, and offering glimpses into her personal reflections and observations.

Question 35

Erich Auerbach's Mimesis (1946) ends with a chapter on:

1. **Virginia Woolf's To the Lighthouse.**
2. Wyndham Lewis's The Apes of God.
3. James Joyce's Ulysses.
4. George Eliot's Middlemarch.

Correct Explanations:

Erich Auerbach's book Mimesis (1946) has been a landmark work in literary criticism. This book deals with the concept of "realism" in Western literature, tracing the development of this style from the time of the Old Testament to modernist writers. **The final chapter of the book is devoted to Virginia Woolf's novel To the Lighthouse.** In this chapter, Auerbach discusses the novel's unique style and structure, which he considers to be an innovative and powerful contribution to the development of modern literature.

Question 36

Arrange the following essays in chronological order of publication.

A. T. S. Eliot, "The Function of Criticism"
B. Edgar Allan Poe, "The Philosophy of Composition"
C. Henry James, "The Art of Fiction"
D. Virginia Woolf, "Modern Fiction"

Choose the correct answer from the options given below

1. C, B, A, D
2. C, B, D, A

3. B, C, D, A
4. **B, C, A, D**

Correct Explanations:

> Edgar Allan Poe's *"The Philosophy of Composition"* was published in **1846.**
> Henry James's *"The Art of Fiction"* was published in **1884.**
> T. S. Eliot's "The Function of Criticism" was published in **1923.**
> Virginia Woolf's *"Modern Fiction"* was published in **1925.**

Question 37

Virginia Woolf's Orlando opens in 1588, and Orlando, a sixteen-year-old boy, writes a poem called:
1. "The Evergreen Tree".
2. "The Poison Tree".
3. **"The Oak Tree".**
4. "The Magic Tree".

Correct Explanations:

In the opening of Virginia Woolf's novel "Orlando," the protagonist Orlando, who is a sixteen-year-old boy at the time, writes a poem titled **"The Oak Tree.".**

Question 38

In "Mr Bennett and Mrs Brown", Virginia Woolf:

1. responds to E.M. Forster's remarks on the character in fiction.
2. criticises book buying preferences of the educated English class.
3. **Analyze the state of modern fiction by contrasting two generations of writers.**
4. presents modernity as a stable and coherent project uniting all artists.

Correct Explanations:

In "**Mr Bennett and Mrs Brown**," a critical essay published in 1924, Virginia Woolf takes a deep dive into the state of modern fiction and the changing nature of the novel.

Match List I with List II

List I (Essay)	List II (Essayist)
A. "The Tory Fox-Hunter"	I. Francis Bacon
B. "What I Believe"	II. Joseph Addison
C. "The Death of the Moth"	III. E.M.Forster
D. "Of Ambition"	IV. Virginia Woolf

Choose the correct answer from the options given below:

1. A -I , B -III , C -IV , D -II
2. A -III , B -IV , C -II , D -I
3. **A -II , B -III , C -IV , D -I**
4. A -IV , B -I , C -II , D -III

Correct Explanations:
- ➢ **"The Death of the Moth and Other Essays"** is a collection of essays by Virginia Woolf, first published in 1942
- ➢ **"What I Believe"** is a humanist essay by E. M. Forster, first published in 1938
- ➢ **"Of Ambition"** is an essay by Francis Bacon
- ➢ **"The Tory Fox Hunter"** is an essay by Joseph Addison

Question 40

What is the correct sequence of the following feminist texts?

A. Sexual Politics
B. A World of Difference
C. The Female Imagination
D. Thinking About Women
E. A Room of One's Own

Choose the correct answer from the options given below :

1. (A). (B). (C). (D). (E)
2. **(E). (D). (A). (C), (B)**
3. (E). (B). (D), (A), (C)
4. (B). (C). (D), (E). (A)

Correct Explanations:

- *A Room of One's Own (1929)*
- *Thinking about Women* by Mary Ellmann in 1968
- *Sexual Politics* by Kate Millett in 1970
- *The Female Imagination:* A Literary and Psychological Investigation of Women's Writing By Patricia Meyer Spacks in 1976
- *A World of Difference* by Barbara Johnson in 1987

Question 41

Match List I with List II:

List I	List II
(A) To the Lighthouse	(I) 1913
(B) Sons and Lovers	(II) 1927
(C) Finnegans Wake	(III) 1939
(D) The Waste Land	(IV) 1922

Choose the correct answer from the options given below:

1. (A)-(I), (B)-(II), (C)-(IV), (D)-(III)
2. (A)-(IV), (B)-(II), (C)-(I), (D)-(III)
3. (A)-(III), (B)-(IV), (C)-(I), (D)-(II)
4. **(A)-(II). (B)-(I). (C)-(III). (D)-(IV)**

Correct Explanations:

- *To the Lighthouse*, a novel by Virginia Woolf was published in **1927**.
- *Sons and Lovers* is a semiautobiographical novel by D.H. Lawrence, published in **1913**.
- **Finnegans Wake (1939)** is an experimental novel by James Joyce.
- **The Waste Land**, a long poem by T.S. Eliot was published in **1922**.

Question 42

What is the correct chronological sequence of the following English non-fictional prose writers according to their years of birth?

A. Joseph Addison

B. Francis Bacon

C. Charles Lamb

D. Virginia Woolf

E. Matthew Amold

Choose the correct answer from the options given below:

1. A. D. C. B. E

2. B. A. C. E. D

3. C. A. D. E. B

4. D. C. B, A, E

Explanations

Answer: 2. B. A. C. E. D

- Sir Francis Bacon (1561-1626)
- Joseph Addison (1672-1719)
- Charles Lamb (1775-1834)
- Matthew Arnold (1822-1888)
- Virginia Woolf (1882-1941)

Question 43

Arrange the correct chronological sequence of the publication of the following texts:

A. Essay of Dramatic Poesy

B. A Room of One's Own

C. Culture and Anarchy

D. The Lives of the Poets

E. "Preface to the Lyrical Ballads"

Choose the correct answer from the options given below:

1. A, D, E, C, B

2. D, A, E, B, C

3. A, C, D, E, B

4. E, D, C, A, B

Explanations

Answer: 1. A, D, E, C, B

A. John Dryden's *Essay of Dramatick Poesy (1668)*.
D. *Lives of the Most Eminent English Poets* **(1779–81) by** Johnson.
E. *The Preface to Lyrical Ballads (1800)* by William Wordsworth.
C. *Culture and Anarchy: An Essay in Political and Social Criticism (1868)* by Matthew Arnold.
B. *A Room of One's Own (1929)* is an essay by Virginia Woolf.

Question 44

Which of the novelists have been correctly matched with their works?

    A. Thomas Hardy - The Return of the Native
    B. Charles Dickens - The History of Henry Esmond
    C. Virginia Woolf - Mrs. Dalloway
    D. George Eliot - Northanger Abbey
    E. Charlotte Bronte - The Professor

Choose the correct answer from the options given below:

    1. C, D and B
    2. A. C and E
    3. B. C and D
    4. C, D and E

Explanations:
Answer: 4. A. C and E

> ➤ *"The Return of the Native"* by Thomas Hardy (1878).

> ➤ *"The History of Henry Esmond"* by William Makepeace Thackeray (1852).
> ➤ *"Mrs. Dalloway"* by Virginia Woolf (1925).
> ➤ *"Northanger Abbey"* by Jane Austen (1817).
> ➤ *"The Professor"* by Charlotte Bronte (1857).

Question 45

Given below are two statements:

Statement (1): A Room of One's Own is a feminist essay about women's education, exclusion and writing by Virginia Woolf.
Statement (II): In Other Worlds is a collection of essays written by Edward W. Said on contemporary ideas such as psychoanalysis and social theory.

In the light of the above statements, choose the most appropriate answer from the options given below:

(1) Both Statement (I) and Statement (II) are true
(2) Both Statement (I) and Statement (II) are false
(3) Statement (I) is true but Statement (II) is false
(4) Statement (I) is false but Statement (II) is true

Explanations:

Answer: (3) Statement (I) is true but Statement (II) is false

The correct answer is (3) Statement (I) is true but Statement (II) is false.

Statement (I) correctly describes "A Room of One's Own" by Virginia Woolf as a feminist essay addressing women's education, exclusion, and writing.

A Room of One's Own is a significant essay penned by **Virginia Woolf, first published in 1929. This work originated from two lectures delivered by Woolf in 1928 at Newnham** College and Girton College, the pioneering women's colleges at Cambridge University. Notably relevant to UGC NET English, the essay passionately **addresses the status of women, particularly women artists,** asserting that a woman must possess financial independence and a dedicated space to write.

Woolf contends that centuries of prejudice, coupled with financial and educational disparities, have impeded women's creative pursuits. She vividly illustrates this point through the hypothetical scenario of a gifted but uneducated sister of **William Shakespeare, Judith Shakespeare,** tragically restrained by societal expectations. Woolf celebrates the achievements of women who defied these limitations, **citing examples such as Jane Austen, George Eliot, and the Brontë sisters—Anne, Charlotte, and Emily.**

Question 46

"All writers since Chaucer have come from the middle class ... have had good, at least expensive education...."

Where has Virginia Woolf explained it?

> 1. Mrs. Dalloway
> 2. To the Lighthouse
> 3. The Leaning Tower
> 4. A Room of One's Own

Explanations:
Answer: 3. The Leaning Tower

"The Moment" is a collection that, while not solely comprising the latest of Virginia Woolf's works, unites previously uncollected essays, reflecting the tone and themes familiar to readers of "The Common Reader." This compilation includes critiques on a range of literary figures and works, from "The Faery Queen" to Scott and Lockhart, alongside a selection of Woolf's less overtly poetic essays. **However, the collection's significance is particularly underscored by essays like "The Leaning Tower" and "The Artist and Politics," penned in Woolf's final years.** These pieces delve into the profound effects of war on her delicate sensibility, hinting at a growing awareness of external realities impacting her literary exploration. Specifically, "The Leaning Tower," presented in 1940, articulates Woolf's perspective on the evolving state of literature amid societal upheaval.

Question 47

Which among the following is not true about E.P. Thompson's The Making of the Working Class?

> A. Studies the development of working class consciousness
> B. Defines class as a relationship not as a social structure
> C. It is the first systematic study of the history of working class
> D. It critiques Virginia Woolf's A Room of One's Own
> E. Reinforces the idea that race and ethnicity are the forms of collective identity

Choose the most appropriate answer from the options given below:

1. A and B only
2. C and D only
3. E and D only
4. B and D only

Explanations:

Answer: 3. E and D only

The Making of the English Working Class is a seminal social history of England authored by E.P. Thompson, a historian of the New Left. The book focuses on the development of the English artisan and **working-class communities from 1780 to 1832.**

Thompson attempts to add a humanist element to social history, being critical of those who turn the people of the working class into an inhuman statistical block. Thompson uses the term "working class", rather than "classes", throughout **the book to emphasize the growth of a working-class consciousness**.

Thompson's theories on working-class consciousness are at the core of his work, and the working class's agency was manifested by its core values of **solidarity, collectivism, mutuality, political radicalism and Methodism**.

Question 48

Arrange the following texts chronologically based on the date of publication:

A. Frankenstein by Mary Shelley
B. A Room of One's Own by Virginia Woolf
C. Maria by Mary Wollstonecraft
D. The Female Eunuch by Germaine Greer
E. The Return of the Soldier by Rebecca West

Choose the correct answer from the options given below

1. C,B,A,D,E
2. C,A,E, D,B
3. C,B,E,A,D

4.   A,E,B,C,D

Explanations:
Answer: 2. C,A,E, D,B

> ➤ *Maria: or, The Wrongs of Woman (1798)* is Mary Wollstonecraft.
> ➤ *Frankenstein; or, The Modern Prometheus*, Gothic horror novel by Mary Wollstonecraft Shelley that was first published in 1818.
> ➤ *The Return of the Soldier* is the debut novel of English novelist Rebecca West, first published in 1918.
> ➤ *A Room of One's Own,* essay by Virginia Woolf, published in 1929.
> ➤ *The Female Eunuch* is a 1970 book by Germaine Greer.

Question 49

Arrange the following literary texts in the chronological sequence:

A. Middlemarch
B. The Good Soldier
C. Night and Day
D. A Passage to India
E. Heart of Darkness

Choose the correct answer from the options given below:

1.   A,E,D,B,C
2.   A,C,D,B,E
3.   A,B,C,D,E
4.   A,D,B,C,E

Explanations:
Answer: 3. A,B,C,D,E

> ➤ *Middlemarch,* by George Eliot, was serialized in 1871–72.
> ➤ *Heart of Darkness,* a 1899 novella by Joseph Conrad.
> ➤ *The Good Soldier,* a 1915 novel by Ford Madox Ford.
> ➤ *Night and Day,* Virginia Woolf's 1919.
> ➤ *A Passage to India,* published in 1924 by E.M. Forster.

James Joyce (1882-1941)

His Life and Literary Career

- **James Joyce** born on **February 2, 1882**, in Rathgar.
- Raised in a **middle-class, Catholic family**.
- Family's **prosperity dwindled**, moving to **North Dublin**.
- Attended **Jesuit school**, studied **philosophy and languages**.
- Moved to **Paris in 1902** for medical school.
- Shifted focus from medicine to **writing**.
- Returned to **Dublin** in **1903**, met **Nora Barnacle**.
- Joyce and Nora **lived abroad** from 1905 onward.
- Lived in **Italy**, **Switzerland**, and **Paris**.
- Returned to **Zurich in 1940**, died **1941**.
- Published *Chamber Music* in **1907**, age **twenty-five**.
- Wrote *Dubliners*, published in **1914** after delays.
- Concerns over **libel** delayed Dubliners' **publication**.
- Characters in **Dubliners** inspired by **real people**.
- Published *A Portrait of the Artist in 1916*.
- Wrote play *Exiles*, published in **1918**.
- Famous for *Ulysses* **(1922)** and *Finnegans Wake* **(1939)**.
- Developed **stream-of-consciousness prose style**.
- Focused on **Irish political and cultural themes**.
- **Ireland sought independence** from **Great Britain**.
- **Charles Stewart Parnell** proposed the **Home Rule Bill**.
- Parnell dubbed **"Uncrowned King of Ireland"**.
- Affair with **Kitty O'Shea** ruined Parnell's **career**.
- **Parnell died in 1891**, when Joyce was nine.
- **Irish cultural revival** followed Parnell's **death**.
- Revival promoted **Irish literature and language**.
- Encouraged pride in **Irish identity** and **heritage**.
- **Ireland splintered** into factions post-Parnell's **death**.
- Conflicts among **Protestants, Catholics, Conservatives, Nationalists**.
- **Joyce explored Irish politics and religion** in writings.
- Though abroad, Joyce retained **interest in Ireland**.
- Articulated **Irish experiences** through his **masterpieces**.

Notable Works

Novel Series

Stephen Dedalus
> *Stephen Hero (precursor to A Portrait; written 1904–06, published posthumously 1944)*
> *A Portrait of the Artist as a Young Man (novel, 1916)*
> *Ulysses (novel, 1922)*

Finnegan
> *Finn's Hotel (Ithys Press, 2013)*
> *Finnegans Wake (1939, restored 2012)*

Short Stories
> *Dubliners (short-story collection, 1914)*
> *The Cat and the Devil (London: Faber and Faber, 1965)*
> *The Cats of Copenhagen (Ithys Press, 2012)*

Poetry collections
> *Chamber Music (poems, Elkin Mathews, 1907)*
> *Giacomo Joyce (written 1907, published by Faber and Faber, 1968)*
> *Pomes Penyeach (poems, Shakespeare and Company, 1927)*
> *Collected Poems (poems, Black Sun Press, 1936, which includes Chamber Music, Pomes Penyeach and other previously published works)*

Play
> *Exiles (play, 1918)*

Code: Stephen, the Hero from Dubliners, is Portrayed as an Artist, Exiled with Ulysses and Finnegans.

Dubliners (1914)

> **Dubliners**, by **James Joyce**, written **1904–07**, published **1914**.
> **Three stories** published as **Stephen Dedalus** inspired **Dubliners**.
> **Dubliners** features a **well-defined structure** with **recurring symbols**.
> First **three stories** narrated in **first person** portray **children**.
> Next **four stories** focus on **young adults**, third-person narration.
> Following **four stories** explore **mature middle-aged life**.
> Next **three stories** examine **politics, art, and religion**.
> Final story, **"The Dead,"** considered a **world masterpiece**.

The Portrait of the Artist as a Young Man (1916)

> **A Portrait of the Artist** is Joyce's **first novel**.
> A **Künstlerroman** tracing Stephen Dedalus' **awakening**.

- ➤ Dedalus' surname refers to **Daedalus**, Greek **craftsman**.
- ➤ Stephen **rebels against Catholic** and **Irish conventions**.
- ➤ Culminates in Stephen's **self-exile** to **Europe**.
- ➤ Novel uses techniques later expanded in **Ulysses**.
- ➤ Began as **Stephen Hero**, a 63-chapter **autobiography**.
- ➤ Joyce condensed it into a **five-chapter modernist novel**.
- ➤ Abandoned **strict realism** for **free indirect speech**.
- ➤ **Ezra Pound serialized** it in **The Egoist magazine**.
- ➤ Published in **1916** by **B. W. Huebsch, New York**.
- ➤ Secured Joyce's position in **literary modernism**.
- ➤ **Plot:**
  - ○ **Stephen Dedalus** grows up in **19th-century Ireland**.
  - ○ Casts off **social, familial, religious constraints** for art.
  - ○ Raised with strong **Catholic faith** and **Irish identity**.
  - ○ Attends strict religious school **Clongowes Wood College**.
  - ○ Initially **lonely and homesick**, later finds his place.
  - ○ **Family tensions** rise after **Parnell's death**.
  - ○ Furious **political argument** disrupts **Christmas dinner**.
  - ○ **Father's financial incompetence** sinks family into **debt**.
  - ○ **Moves to Dublin**, leaves **Clongowes** due to poverty.
  - ○ Attends prestigious school **Belvedere**, excels in **writing**.
  - ○ Experiences **shame and guilt** after visiting a **prostitute**.
  - ○ Engages in **sins** like masturbation, gluttony, and **lust**.
  - ○ Fiery **sermons** about **sin, judgment, and hell** affect him.
  - ○ Resolves to lead a life of **Christian piety**.
  - ○ Becomes a model of **Catholic abstinence** and **self-denial**.
  - ○ **Director suggests priesthood**, but Stephen **declines**.
  - ○ Finds priestly life incompatible with **sensual beauty**.
  - ○ Observes **girl wading**, has epiphany about **beauty**.
  - ○ **Love for beauty** shouldn't cause **shame**, he decides.
  - ○ Vows to **live life to the fullest**.
  - ○ Resolves to escape **family, religion, and nation**.
  - ○ Joins **university**, develops strong **friendships**.
  - ○ **Close bond** with **Cranly**, shares artistic theories.
  - ○ Explores **artistic independence** through conversations.
  - ○ Seeks liberation from **friends' and family's expectations**.
  - ○ **Determines to leave Ireland**, pursues **artistic freedom**.
  - ○ Identifies with **mythical Daedalus**, aims to "fly" high.
  - ○ Strives to overcome **obstacles** through **artistic creation**.
  - ○ Embraces **individualism** to achieve his **artistic vision**.

- o Stephen's journey reflects Joyce's own **artistic awakening**.

Ulysses (1922)

- ➢ **Ulysses**, a **modernist novel** by **James Joyce**.
- ➢ **Serialized in The Little Review** from **1918-1920**.
- ➢ **Published in Paris** by **Sylvia Beach** in **1922**.
- ➢ Called **"a demonstration and summation** of modernism."
- ➢ Chronicles **Leopold Bloom's day** in **Dublin, 16 June 1904**.
- ➢ Draws **parallels with Homer's Odyssey** characters and themes.
- ➢ Explores **modernism, Dublin, and Ireland's British relations**.
- ➢ Features **stream of consciousness**, experimental **prose**, allusions.
- ➢ Attracted controversy, including **obscenity trial in 1921**.
- ➢ Fans celebrate **16 June as Bloomsday** worldwide.
- ➢ **Characters**: Leopold Bloom, Molly Bloom, Stephen Dedalus, Buck Mulligan.
- ➢ **Setting**: One day, June 16, 1904, in Dublin.
- ➢ **Stephen**: Struggles with guilt over his mother's death.
- ➢ **Leopold Bloom**: Wanders Dublin, avoiding his wife Molly.
- ➢ **Molly**: Plans an affair with Hugh "Blazes" Boylan.
- ➢ **Themes**: Identity, adultery, guilt, and modernist experimentation.
- ➢ **"Telemachus"**: Opens with Stephen's morning quarrel with Mulligan.
- ➢ **"Calypso"**: Bloom prepares breakfast, contemplates his wife's affair.
- ➢ **"Proteus"**: Stephen muses on life and philosophical questions.
- ➢ **"Hades"**: Bloom attends Paddy Dignam's funeral, reflects on mortality.
- ➢ **"Sirens"**: Musical episode, Bloom observes Boylan's seduction attempts.
- ➢ **"Cyclops"**: Bloom faces xenophobia, anti-Semitism at a pub.
- ➢ **"Circe"**: Nightmarish hallucinations in the brothel; surreal chaos.
- ➢ **"Penelope"**: Molly's soliloquy reveals her inner thoughts, desires.
- ➢ **Important Line**: "Yes I said yes I will Yes."

Finnegan's Wake (1939)

- ➢ **Finnegans Wake** is a novel by **James Joyce**.
- ➢ Called **"a work of fiction** with deconstruction."
- ➢ Known for its **experimental style** and **difficulty**.
- ➢ Written in **Paris** over **seventeen years**.
- ➢ Published in **1939** as Joyce's **final work**.
- ➢ Written in an **idiosyncratic language**, blending **neologisms**.

- ➢ Combines **English words, puns**, and **multiple languages**.
- ➢ Recreates **sleep and dreams** through its techniques.
- ➢ Joyce attempted to combine **aesthetic ideas** and **references**.
- ➢ Joyce stated, **"Every syllable can be justified."**
- ➢ Features **stream of consciousness, free dream associations**.
- ➢ **Unread by general public** due to its **complexity**.
- ➢ **Title**: Finnegan's Wake revolves around Tim Finnegan's fall.
- ➢ **Theme**: Cyclical nature of life, death, and rebirth.
- ➢ **Structure**: A dream-like narrative defying linear storytelling.
- ➢ **Main Character**: HCE represents Everyman and universal humanity.
- ➢ **Humphrey Chimpden Earwicker (HCE)**
- ➢ **ALP**: Anna Livia Plurabelle, symbolizing rivers and femininity.
- ➢ **Children**: Shaun and Shem embody oppositional sibling archetypes.
- ➢ **Language**: Dense wordplay blending multiple languages and puns.
- ➢ **Fall**: HCE accused of indecency, causing his symbolic fall.
- ➢ **Letter**: ALP writes a letter defending HCE's reputation.
- ➢ **Wake**: Tim Finnegan's wake echoes themes of Irish folklore.
- ➢ **Dream**: Narrative set in HCE's fragmented subconscious dreams.
- ➢ **Cycles**: Time loops endlessly, no definitive start or end.
- ➢ **Key Line**: "A way a lone a last a loved."
- ➢ **Influence**: Work inspired modernist experimentation in literature.
- ➢ **Ending**: ALP merges into the river, restarting the cycle.
- ➢ *Finnegans Wake* by James Joyce ends with the word **"the."**

QUESTIONS

Question 50

Match List I with List II

List I (Character)	List II (Novel)
A. Winston Smith	I. Sons and Lovers
B. Paul Morel	II. Ulysses
C. 'whiskey priest'	III. Nineteen Eighty-four
D. Leopold Bloom	IV. Decline and Fall
E. Paul Pennyfeather	V. The Power and the Glory

Choose the correct answer from the options given below:

1. **A-III, B-I, C-V, D-II, E-IV**

2. A-I, B-V, C-II, D-III, E-IV
3. A-IV, B-III, C-V, D-II, E-I
4. A-V, B-I, C-IV, D-II, E-III

Correct Explanations:

A. **Winston Smith** is a character in the novel *"Nineteen Eighty-Four"* by George Orwell.

B. **Paul Morel** is a character in the novel *"Sons and Lovers"* by D.H. Lawrence.

C. The **"whiskey priest"** is a character in the novel *"The Power and the Glory"* by Graham Greene..

D. **Leopold Bloom** is a character in the novel *"Ulysses"* by James Joyce.

E. **Paul Pennyfeather** is a character in the novel *"Decline and Fall"* by Evelyn Waugh.

Question 51

Which among the following are examples of the Künstlerroman?

A.   The Portrait of a Lady
B.   David Copperfield
C.   Tom Jones
D.   A Portrait of the Artist as a Young Man

Choose the correct answer from the options given below:
1.   A and C only
2.   **B and D only**
3.   A and B only
4.   C and D only

Correct Explanations:

Both "A Portrait of the Artist as a Young Man" by James Joyce and "David Copperfield" by Charles Dickens are considered examples of the Künstlerroman, a type of novel that focuses on the growth and development of an artist or writer.

In "A Portrait of the Artist as a Young Man," Joyce presents the story of Stephen Dedalus, a young man who struggles to find his artistic voice in the face of societal pressures and religious expectations.

Similarly, "David Copperfield" chronicles the life of the titular character, who starts out as a young boy with a passion for reading and writing.

Other Explanations:
"The Portrait of a Lady" by Henry James and "Tom Jones" by Henry Fielding are not typically considered examples of Künstlerroman, although they do feature protagonists who undergo personal growth and transformation throughout the course of the narrative.

"Tom Jones," on the other hand, **is a picaresque novel** that follows the adventures of the titular character as he travels through England in search of love and fortune.

D. H. Lawrence (1885-1930)

Life and Literary Career

> - **David Herbert Lawrence** born **September 11, 1885**, Eastwood, England.
> - Known more as **novelist**, first-published as **poet**.
> - Early poems influenced by **Ezra Pound** and **Imagism**.
> - Rejected Pound's circle, pursued **independent poetry**.
> - Poetry reflects **inner force**, stark and **immediate**.
> - Celebrated for works on **plants** and **animals**.
> - Poems criticize **puritanism** and **societal hypocrisy**.
> - Lawrence viewed **sex**, **subconscious**, **nature** as cures.
> - Prolific but controversial, facing **censorship cases**.
> - Famously censored for **Lady Chatterley's Lover (1928)**.
> - **Poetry collections**: *Look! We Have Come Through* (1917).
> - **Birds, Beasts, and Flowers (1923)** shows his **nature themes**.
> - *Pansies (1929)* banned in **England** upon release.
> - Persecuted in **WWI** due to wife's **German ties**.
> - Traveled widely searching for a **new homeland**.
> - Formed a **group of admirers** in **Taos, New Mexico**.
> - **Tuberculosis** ended his life in **France (1930)**.
> - Died at **forty-four**, leaving a **literary legacy**.

Notable Works

Novels

> *The White Peacock (1911)*
> *The Trespasser (1912)*
> *Sons and Lovers (1913)*
> *The Rainbow (1915)*
> *Women in Love (1920)*
> *The Lost Girl (1920)*
> *Aaron's Rod (1922)*
> *Kangaroo (1923)*
> *The Boy in the Bush (1924), coauthored with M.L. (Mollie or Molly) Skinner*
> *The Plumed Serpent (1926)*
> *Lady Chatterley's Lover (1928)*
> *The Escaped Cock (1929), republished as The Man Who Died*

Code: "The White Peacock trespassed with My Sons and Lovers while watching the Rainbow. Women fell in Love but lost their Girl. Aaron spotted a Kangaroo, and the Boy saw a Serpent. Lady Chatterley's Lover escaped."

Short-story collections

> *The Prussian Officer and Other Stories (1914)*
> *England, My England and Other Stories (1922)*
> *The Fox, The Captain's Doll, The Ladybird (1923)*
> *St Mawr and Other Stories (1925)*
> *The Woman who Rode Away and Other Stories (1928)*
> *The Rocking-Horse Winner (1926)*
> *The Virgin and the Gipsy and Other Stories (1930)*

Poetry collections

> *Love Poems and others (1913)*
> *Amores (1916)*
> *Look! We have come through! (1917)*
> *New Poems (1918)*
> *Bay: a book of poems (1919)*
> *Tortoises (1921)*
> *Birds, Beasts and Flowers (1923)*
> *The Collected Poems of D H Lawrence (1928)*
> *Pansies (1929)*
> *Nettles (1930)*
> *The Triumph of the Machine (1930)*

- ➢ **Famous Poems**
    - ○ "Snake"
    - ○ "Piano"
    - ○ "Love on the Farm"
    - ○ "Self-Pity"
    - ○ "The Ship of Death"
    - ○ "Bavarian Gentians"
    - ○ "The Rain"
    - ○ "The White Horse"
    - ○ "The Song of the Man Who Has Come Through"
    - ○ "Last Words to Miriam"

Plays

- ➢ *The Daughter-in-Law (1913)*
- ➢ *The Widowing of Mrs. Holroyd (1914)*

Non-fiction books and pamphlets

- ➢ Movements in European History (1921)
- ➢ D. H. Lawrence's essay ***"Why the Novel Matters"*** explores the significance of the novel as a literary form.
- ➢ Studies in Classic American Literature (1923)
    - ○ Lawrence's responses to writers like Walt Whitman, Herman Melville and Edgar Allan Poe also shed light on his craft.

Sons and Lovers (1913)

- ➢ **Sons and Lovers** is a **1913 novel** by **D. H. Lawrence.**
- ➢ Protagonist **Paul Morel** faces **emotional conflicts** and relationships.
- ➢ Explores **mother's demands** and influences of **two lovers.**
- ➢ Published by **Duckworth, London,** and **Kennerley, New York.**
- ➢ Initially received **lukewarm reception**, with **obscenity allegations.**
- ➢ Now regarded as a **masterpiece** and **Lawrence's finest work.**
- ➢ Reflects **Lawrence's life** and his **attachment to mother.**
- ➢ Mother's death in **1910** deeply influenced Lawrence's writing.
- ➢ **Met Frieda Richthofen,** conceived **The Rainbow** and **Women in Love.**
- ➢ Later novels emphasized **sexual maturity** and **complex relationships.**
- ➢ **Setting**: Focused on a Nottinghamshire coal-mining village.
- ➢ **Main Character**: Paul Morel, torn between love and duty.
- ➢ **Family**: Mrs. Morel dominates Paul, shaping his life.

- ➢ **Father**: Walter Morel, a miner, is emotionally detached.
- ➢ **Conflict**: Paul's devotion to his mother hinders relationships.
- ➢ **Love Interest**: Paul falls for Miriam, a pure-hearted girl.
- ➢ **Paul's Struggle**: Torn between Miriam and his mother's control.
- ➢ **Clara**: Paul has a passionate affair with Clara Dawes.
- ➢ **Themes**: Explores love, class, family, and emotional struggles.
- ➢ **Important Line**: "She hated her husband for his commonness."
- ➢ **Paul's Growth**: Struggles to assert independence from his mother.
- ➢ **Tragedy**: Mrs. Morel's death profoundly impacts Paul.
- ➢ **Paul's Decision**: Chooses loneliness over fulfilling relationships.
- ➢ **Ending**: Paul faces life alone, searching for purpose.
- ➢ **Legacy**: Explores human psyche and emotional complexities.

The Rainbow (1915)

- ➢ **The Rainbow**, by **D.H. Lawrence**, published in **1915**.
- ➢ Officially **banned**, labeled **obscene**, unsold copies **confiscated**.
- ➢ Follows three generations of the **Brangwen family** (1840-1905).
- ➢ **Tom Brangwen's marriage** to Lydia Lensky **breaks down**.
- ➢ **Anna's marriage** to Tom's nephew Will **gradually fails**.
- ➢ Focuses on Ursula, a **schoolteacher**, their **eldest child**.
- ➢ Ursula **rejects marriage** after affair with **Anton Skrebensky**.
- ➢ **Rainbow symbolizes hope** for Ursula's **future**.
- ➢ Ursula's story continues in **Women in Love**.
- ➢ **Generations**: The novel spans three Brangwen family generations.
- ➢ **Characters**: Tom Brangwen marries Lydia, a Polish widow.
- ➢ **Themes**: Focuses on love, individuality, and personal growth.
- ➢ **Marriage**: Anna, Lydia's daughter, marries Will Brangwen.
- ➢ **Conflict**: Anna and Will's passionate yet turbulent relationship.
- ➢ **Ursula**: Daughter Ursula explores education and independence.
- ➢ **Education**: Ursula struggles with conformity in school and life.
- ➢ **Love**: Ursula's complex affair with Anton Skrebensky ends.
- ➢ **Important Line**: "She wanted so much more—always more."
- ➢ **Ending**: Ursula envisions hope and renewal under the rainbow.

Women in Love (1920)

- ➢ **Women in Love (1920)** by **D.H. Lawrence** is a sequel.
- ➢ Follows **Brangwen sisters, Gudrun and Ursula's lives**.
- ➢ **Gudrun**, an artist, loves **industrialist Gerald Crich**.

- ➤ Contrasts with **Ursula's love** for **Rupert Birkin**.
- ➤ **Intense attraction** exists between **Gerald and Rupert**.
- ➤ Explores **British society** before **World War I**.
- ➤ Characters inspired by **Lawrence, Frieda, Mansfield, Murry**.
- ➤ Concludes in **Tyrolean Alps** with emotional depth.
- ➤ **Characters**: Ursula, Gudrun, Gerald, and Rupert explore relationships.
- ➤ **Plot**: Sisters Ursula and Gudrun find contrasting love stories.
- ➤ **Theme**: Examines love, industrialism, and modern societal struggles.
- ➤ **Ursula-Rupert**: A relationship seeking spiritual and emotional union.
- ➤ **Gudrun-Gerald**: A destructive, passionate, and doomed love affair.
- ➤ **Conflict**: Rupert struggles between freedom and commitment with Ursula.
- ➤ **Tragedy**: Gerald's obsession with control leads to his demise.
- ➤ **Famous Line**: "What is love if it's not free?"
- ➤ **Setting**: Industrial Midlands reflects change and human disconnect.
- ➤ **Ending**: Ursula and Rupert envision hope beyond societal norms.

Lady Chatterley's Lover (1928)

- ➤ **Lady Chatterley's Lover** by **D.H. Lawrence**, published **1928**.
- ➤ First **English edition** published in **Florence** and **Paris**.
- ➤ Expurgated version appeared in **England, 1932**.
- ➤ Full text published in **New York (1959)** and **London (1960)**.
- ➤ **Landmark obscenity trial**: Regina v. Penguin Books, Ltd.
- ➤ Trial justified **taboo sexual terms** in the novel.
- ➤ Reflects **Lawrence's belief** in natural **passionate love**.
- ➤ Story about **Constance Reid** (Lady Chatterley).
- ➤ Husband, **Sir Clifford**, paralysed from **Great War injury**.
- ➤ **Constance's affair** with **gamekeeper Oliver Mellors**.
- ➤ **Class difference** central to the novel's **motif**.
- ➤ Constance realises she needs **body, not just mind**.
- ➤ Love seen as physical, beyond intellectual **connection**.
- ➤ **haracters**: Lady Constance Chatterley, Sir Clifford, and Mellors.
- ➤ **Plot**: Lady Chatterley feels trapped in passionless marriage.
- ➤ **Conflict**: Clifford's paralysis leads to emotional disconnection.
- ➤ **Affair**: Constance bonds with Mellors, estate gamekeeper.
- ➤ **Themes**: Love, class, nature, and physical intimacy explored.
- ➤ **Important Line**: "Ours is essentially a tragic age."

- ➢ **Clifford's Dependence**: Symbolizes industrialization's dehumanizing effects.
- ➢ **Society's Judgment**: Affair challenges rigid societal norms.
- ➢ **Resolution**: Constance and Mellors dream of future together.
- ➢ **Legacy**: Novel's frankness caused censorship, legal challenges.

QUESTIONS

Question 52

What is the correct chronological sequence of the following books of D.H. Lawrence?

    A. Lady Chatterley's Lover
    B. Sons and Lovers
    C. The Rainbow
    D. The White Peacock
    E. The Plumed Serpent

Choose the correct answer from the options given below :

    (1) A, B, D, C, E
    (2) D, B, C, E, A
    (3) B ,D, E, C, A
    (4) E, A, B, C, D

Explanations:
Answer: (2) D, B, C, E, A

Novels
- *The White Peacock (1911)*
- *The Trespasser (1912)*
- *Sons and Lovers (1913)*
- *The Rainbow (1915)*
- *Women in Love (1920)*
- *The Lost Girl (1920)*
- *Aaron's Rod (1922)*
- *Kangaroo (1923)*
- *The Boy in the Bush (1924), coauthored with M.L. (Mollie or Molly) Skinner*

- *The Plumed Serpent (1926)*
- *Lady Chatterley's Lover (1928)*
- *The Escaped Cock (1929)*, republished as *The Man Who Died*

> **Code**: "The White Peacock trespassed with My Sons and Lovers while watching the Rainbow. Women fell in Love but lost their Girl. Aaron spotted a Kangaroo, and the Boy saw a Serpent. Lady Chatterley's Lover escaped."

Question 53

Which famous English poet, at an early age announcing his admiration for D. H. Lawrence, excitedly wrote to his friend, "I have been reading Sons and Lovers and feel ready to die. If Lawrence had been killed after writing that book he'd still be England's greatest novelist"?

1. Virginia Woolf
2. WH Auden
3. Dylan Thomas
4. Philip Larkin

Explanations:

Answer: 4. Philip Larkin

On 20 March 1942, at the age of nineteen, Philip Larkin expressed his excitement to his friend Jim Sutton about his admiration for D. H. Lawrence. In his letter, Larkin proclaimed his admiration for Lawrence's novel "Sons and Lovers," stating that if Lawrence had died after writing that book, he would still be considered England's greatest novelist.

A few years later, Larkin's own aspirations as a fiction writer began to materialise with the publication of his novels "Jill" in 1946 and "A Girl in Winter" in 1947. These works showcased Larkin's awareness of the diverse range of Modernist experimentation found in the writings of Lawrence, as well as contemporaries such as Virginia Woolf and Katherine Mansfield. The Modernist fiction of the early decades of the twentieth century inspired Larkin to move beyond realistic portrayal and venture into a symbolist approach, exploring intangible subjects such as obscure dreams and desires.

Other Explanations:
Notes on D.H. Lawrence May 18, 2021 by Virginia Woolf

"This then was the angle of approach, and it will be seen that it is an angle that shuts off many views and distorts others. But read from this angle, Sons and Lovers emerged with astonishing vividness, like an island from off which the mist has suddenly lifted. Here it lay, clean cut, decisive, masterly, hard as rock, shaped, proportioned by a man who, whatever else he might be—prophet or villain, was undoubtedly the son of a miner who had been born and bred in Nottingham. But this hardness, this clarity, this admirable economy and sharpness of the stroke are not rare qualities in an age of highly efficient novelists. The lucidity, the ease, the power of the writer to indicate with one stroke and then to refrain indicated a mind of great power and penetration. But these impressions, after they had built up the lives of the Morels, their kitchens, food, sinks, manner of speech, were succeeded by another far rarer, and of far greater interest. For after we have exclaimed that this coloured and stereoscopic representation of life is so like that surely it must be alive—like the bird that pecked the cherry in the picture—one feels, from some indescribable brilliance, sombreness, significance, that the room is put into order. Some hand has been at work before we entered. Casual and natural as the arrangement seems, as if we had opened the door and come in by chance, some hand, some eye of astonishing penetration and force, has swiftly arranged the whole scene, so that we feel that it is more exciting, more moving, in some ways fuller of life than one had thought real life could be, as if a painter had brought out the leaf or the tulip or the jar by pulling a green curtain behind it. But what is the green curtain that Lawrence has pulled so as to accentuate the colours? One never catches Lawrence—this is one of his most remarkable qualities—"arranging". "
W. H. Auden on Lawrence

The transformation Lawrence underwent after his death was remarkable. During his lifetime, he was viewed as an outsider, a figure who stood apart from society and challenged its norms with his provocative ideas. He was seen as a disruptor, casting figurative bombs into the herd. However, following his passing, Lawrence experienced a resurrection of sorts, assuming the role of a Byronic hero. **W. H. Auden captured this phenomenon by recounting how women, travelling great distances to reach the memorial chapel dedicated to Lawrence in Taos, stood in awe, contemplating what it would have been like to be intimate with him.**

Raymond Williams on Lawrence

In England, a young Philip Larkin held Lawrence in extraordinarily high
regard, attributing to him an abundance of genius and even a divine quality.
**The critic Raymond Williams noted that after the war, Lawrence became
a figure of immense fascination and desire, to the point of caricature**.
Lawrence had become the embodiment of what many aspired to be.

Question 54

**The following lines are from one of the poems of D. H. Lawrence. Identify
the poem?**

*"And so, I missed my chance with one of the lords Of life
And I have something to expiate;
A pettiness."*

1. Bat
2. Snake
3. Mosquitoe
4. Cypresses

Explanations:

*"A snake came to my water-trough
On a hot, hot day, and I in pyjamas for the heat,
To drink there.*

*In the deep, strange-scented shade of the great dark carob tree
I came down the steps with my pitcher
And must wait, must stand and wait, for there he was at the trough
        before me.*

——————

——————

*For he seemed to me again like a king,
Like a king in exile, uncrowned in the underworld,
Now due to be crowned again.*

***And so, I missed my chance with one of the lords
Of life.***

And I have something to expiate:
A pettiness." Snake BY D. H. LAWRENCE

Other Explanations

D.H. Lawrence, the renowned English writer, is known for his significant contributions to poetry. Here is a list of some of his famous poems:

- **"Snake"** - A powerful and symbolic poem exploring human fear and fascination towards nature.
- **"Piano"** - A nostalgic and lyrical poem that delves into themes of memory, music, and longing.
- "Love on the Farm" - A sensual and passionate poem celebrating the primal and natural aspects of love.
- **"Self-Pity"** - A poignant and introspective poem that reflects on the experience of feeling sorry for oneself.
- **"The Ship of Death"** - A haunting and existential poem that delves into the themes of mortality and the afterlife.
- **"Bavarian Gentians"** - A vivid and vividly descriptive poem that captures the beauty and transience of life.
- **"The Rain"** - A sensory and atmospheric poem that explores the transformative power of rain.
- **"The White Horse"** - A metaphorical and mystical poem that reflects on the spiritual journey of the self.
- **"The Song of the Man Who Has Come Through"** - A reflective and philosophical poem that delves into themes of personal growth and transformation.
- **"Last Words to Miriam"** - A poignant and emotional poem that explores the complexities of love and relationships.

Question 55

Penguin Books were prosecuted for obscenity and later acquitted for publishing a novel of D. H. Lawrence that makes a frank description of sex and an uncompromising use of four-letter words. Which of the following is the title of the novel?

1. Sons and Lovers
2. The White Peacock
3. Lady Chatterley's Lover
4. Women in Love

Explanations:

Answer: **3.** Lady Chatterley's Lover

Lady Chatterley's Lover, his last novel published in 1928, explores the passionate relationship between a working-class man and an upper-class woman. The book faced widespread censorship and was banned in various countries due to its explicit sexual content and the use of then-taboo language. **An unexpurgated edition was not published openly in the United Kingdom until 1960, following a watershed obscenity trial against the publisher Penguin Books,** which won the case and quickly sold three million copies.

Sons and Lovers, published in 1913, delves into the complex emotional conflicts experienced by the protagonist, Paul Morel. The novel explores his relationships with a domineering mother and two contrasting lovers, shaping his journey towards adulthood. Initially receiving a lukewarm critical reception and facing allegations of obscenity, it is now regarded as a masterpiece by many critics. The novel was originally published by **Gerald Duckworth and Company Ltd. in London** and **Mitchell Kennerley Publishers** in New York.

The White Peacock, Lawrence's first novel published in 1911, underwent multiple revisions before its final form. Inspired by Maurice Greiffenhagen's painting 'An Idyll,' the novel weaves a tale of love and longing. The early versions had the working title of Laetitia. The novel was published by **Heinemann in the UK and Duffield & Co. in the US**.

Women in Love, published in 1920, serves as a sequel to Lawrence's earlier novel The Rainbow. It follows the lives of the Brangwen sisters, Gudrun and Ursula, as they navigate relationships and confront societal expectations. The novel was published by **Thomas Seltzer**.

Question 56

What is not true about D.H. Lawrence's Sons and Lovers?

A. Sons and Lovers is a semi-autobiographical novel.
B. It is a psychological study of the familial and love relationships of a working-class English family.

C. The film adaptation of the novel was directed by Jack Cardiff.
D. The storyline traces three generations of Brangwen family.
E. The novel narrates the story of Paul Morel whose love for his beloved overshadows the affectionate bond with his mother.

Choose the correct answer from the options given below:

1. (A) and (C) Only
2. (B) and (D) Only
3. (D) and (E) Only
4. (C) and (E) Only

Explanations:
Answer: 3. (D) and (E) Only
The Rainbow is a novel by British author D. H. Lawrence, first published by Methuen & Co. in 1915. **It follows three generations of the Brangwen family living in Nottinghamshire**

Sons and Lovers," **a semiautobiographical novel** by D.H. Lawrence **published in 1913,** marks his emergence as a mature novelist with its in-depth **psychological portrayal of a working-class English family's** intricate familial and romantic relationships.

Sons and Lovers is a 1960 British period drama **film directed by Jack Cardiff and adapted by Gavin Lambert and T. E. B.** Clarke from the semi-autobiographical 1913 novel of the same name by D. H. Lawrence.

Question 57

Identify the correct order of the publication of D.H. Lawrence's works:

A. Rainbow
B. Kangaroo
C. Women in Love
D. Sons and Lovers
E. The Widowing of Mrs. Holroyd

Choose the correct answer from the options given below:

1. D,E,A,C, B

2. B,C,D,E,A
3. A,B,C,D,E
4. A,E,C,B,D

Explanations:
Answer: 1. D,E,A,C, B
List of Woeks

- *The White Peacock (1911)*
- *The Trespasser (1912)*
- ***Sons and Lovers (1913)***
- ***The Widowing of Mrs. Holroyd (1914) (PLAY)***
- ***The Rainbow (1915)***
- ***Women in Love (1920)***
- *The Lost Girl (1920)*
- *Aaron's Rod (1922)*
- ***Kangaroo (1923)***
- *The Boy in the Bush (1924), coauthored with M.L. (Mollie or Molly) Skinner*
- *The Plumed Serpent (1926)*
- *Lady Chatterley's Lover (1928)*
- *The Escaped Cock (1929), republished as The Man Who Died*

Ezra Pound (1885-1972)

Life and Literary Career:

- **Ezra Pound** shaped **modernist poetry** aesthetics.
- Facilitated work exchange between **British and American writers**.
- Advanced contemporaries like **Yeats**, **Frost**, and **T. S. Eliot**.
- Promoted **Imagism**, inspired by **Chinese and Japanese poetry**.
- Imagism stressed **clarity**, **precision**, and **economy of language**.
- Pound: "Compose in the sequence of the musical phrase."
- Spent fifty years on epic poem **The Cantos**.
- Born in **Hailey, Idaho**, on **October 30, 1885**.
- Studied at **University of Pennsylvania**, graduated from **Hamilton College**.
- Taught at **Wabash College**, then traveled abroad.
- Fascinated by **Japanese and Chinese poetry**.
- Married **Dorothy Shakespear** in **1914**.
- Became **London editor** of **Little Review** in 1917.

- ➤ Moved to **Italy in 1924**, involved in **Fascist politics**.
- ➤ Arrested for **treason** after **WWII** broadcasts.
- ➤ Declared mentally ill, confined to **St. Elizabeths Hospital**.
- ➤ Awarded **Bollingen Prize** for **Pisan Cantos (1948)**.
- ➤ Released in 1958, returned to **Italy**.
- ➤ Died in **Venice**, November 1, 1972, as semi-recluse.
- ➤ Legacy marked by **politics** and **poetic achievements**.

Notable Works:

- ➤ *"Guide to Kulchur"*
- ➤ *"Homage to Sextus Propertius"*
- ➤ *"Hugh Selwyn Mauberley"*
- ➤ *"Lustra"*
- ➤ *"Personae"*
- ➤ *"Ripostes"*
- ➤ *"The Cantos"*
- ➤ *"The Pisan Cantos"*
- ➤ *"Trachinian Women"*

In a Station of the Metro (1913)

- ➤ **"In a Station of the Metro"** published April **1913**.
- ➤ Poem depicts a **Paris metro station moment**.
- ➤ Faces described using **"equation," not description**.
- ➤ Considered a quintessential **Imagist poem**.
- ➤ Reprinted in **Lustra** (1917) and **Personae** (1926).
- ➤ Regarded as the first **English haiku**.
- ➤ Lacks **traditional 3-line, 17-syllable haiku structure**.
- ➤ Contains only **fourteen words, no verbs**.
- ➤ Example of **verbless poetry** in **Modernist style**.
- ➤ Pound influenced **Imagist poetry**, later embraced **Vorticism**.
- ➤ **Imagism** moved away from **verbose Victorian literature**.
- ➤ Pound: "Sort of American stuff...ridiculed in Paris."
- ➤ Poem **breaks pentameter**, uses **visual spacing**.
- ➤ Original version had **different word spacing**.
- ➤ Found in **Poetry magazine's** April 1913 edition.
  In a Station of the Metro
  The apparition of these faces in the crowd:
  Petals on a wet, black bough.

The Cantos (1917-1969)

- **The Cantos** by **Ezra Pound** is incomplete, **116 cantos.**
- Written mainly between **1915–1962**, early work **abandoned.**
- Published cantos date from **1922 onwards.**
- **Book-length work**, considered **challenging modernist poetry.**
- Themes include **economics, governance,** and **culture.**
- Features **Chinese characters** and non-English quotations.
- Requires **scholarly commentary** for deeper understanding.
- Broad **historical references** with abrupt **transitions.**
- Includes **Mediterranean culture, East Asia,** and **Italy.**
- Refers to **Provence, 17th century England,** and **Africa.**
- Many references **lack explanation**, challenging casual readers.
- Early cantos reflect **Homer, Ovid,** and **Dante's influence.**
- **The Pisan Cantos** admired, written during **incarceration.**
- **Won Bollingen Prize** in **1949** for **Pisan Cantos.**
- Focused later on **conveying messages over techniques.**

Hugh Selwyn Mauberley (1920)

- **Hugh Selwyn Mauberley (1920)** is by **Ezra Pound.**
- Regarded as a **turning point** in Pound's career.
- Name "Selwyn" possibly honors **Selwyn Image.**
- Resembles **T. S. Eliot's Prufrock** in personality.
- Pound described it as "condense a [Henry] James novel."
- **Opening section** critiques **culture's corruption** in modern society.
- Fictional **Mauberley** appears in the **second section.**
- Represents **failings of contemporary artists.**
- Pleads for **form and style** as **authentic meaning.**

Question 58

Which one of these essays by Ezra Pound defines an Image as 'that which presents an intellectual and emotional complex in an instant of time"?

1. "A Retrospect"
2. "The Renaissance"
3. "The Tradition"
4. "How to Read"

Explanations:

Answer: **1.** "A Retrospect,"

In his essay "A Retrospect," Ezra Pound provides an influential and defining definition of an Image. He describes an Image as something that captures a complex combination of intellectual and emotional elements within a single moment or instant of time.

Extra Perk:

"A Retrospect": In his essay "A Retrospect," Ezra Pound reflects on the state of contemporary poetry and outlines his principles for a new poetic movement..

"The Renaissance": "The Renaissance" is an essay by Ezra Pound in which he explores the literary and cultural achievements of the Renaissance period..

"The Tradition": In "The Tradition," Ezra Pound examines the concept of literary tradition and its impact on modern poetry. He challenges the notion that tradition should be seen as an unchanging and stagnant force, advocating instead for a dynamic engagement with the past..

"How to Read": In "How to Read," Ezra Pound offers guidance on how to approach and appreciate literature. He emphasizes the importance of close reading, attentive observation, and engagement with the text.

Question 59

Arrange the following in the chronological order of publication:

    (A) The Pisan Canw
    (B) Ballad of Reading Goal
    (C) Mourn not for Adonais
    (D) First step up Parnassus
    (E) The Complaint of Troilus

Choose the correct answer from the options given below:

1. (E), (D), (E), (C), (A)
2. (C), (A), (E), (D), (E)
3. (B), (C), (A), (E), (D)
4. (E), (D), (C), (B), (A)

Explanations:

Answer: Dropped

The correct chronological order of publication for the given works is as follows:

(D) First Step up Parnassus (1820) by Thomas Love Peacock
(C) Mourn not for Adonais (1821) by Percy Bysshe.
(A) The Pisan Cantos (1948) by Ezra Pound.
(E) The Complaint of Troilus (1952) by Geoffrey Hill.
(B) Ballad of Reading Gaol (1898) by Oscar Wilde.

Who among the following declared in 1920 that "there is no longer any intellectual life in England'"

1. Dorothy Richardson
2. Virginia Woolf
3. Ezra Pound
4. T.S. Eliot

Explanations:
Answer: 3. Ezra Pound

The Imagist Movement in Poetry

The Imagist movement, initially termed 'imagistes' and later Anglicized to 'imagists,' made a significant mark on modern poetry with the publication of four anthologies between 1914 and 1917. Distancing themselves from the sentimentality and romanticism of the 19th century, the Imagists, including notable poets like Ezra Pound, H.D., Richard Aldington, Amy Lowell, Marianne Moore, and William Carlos Williams, sought to revitalize poetry by rejecting clichés and embracing clarity, conciseness, and the essence of subjects. Although not all poets affiliated with the movement explicitly identified as Imagists, many aligned with its goals of adopting the best poetic practices from the past. Their principles emphasized directness in subject portrayal, the necessity of each word, and the preference for irregular musical rhythms over a uniform beat. Ezra Pound's 1913 article "A Few Don'ts by an Imagiste" and his poem "In a Station of the Metro" exemplify the Imagist approach, presenting complex intellectual and emotional experiences in singular moments, thereby laying the groundwork for what many consider the start of modern poetry.

Ezra Pound had gone from London to Paris, declaring with a flounce that there was 'no longer any intellectual life in England'. It was 1920.

Wyndham Lewis (1882-1957)

- **Wyndham Lewis** founded the **Vorticist movement** in England.
- Studied **painting in Paris** before returning to **London**.
- Championed **Expressionism** and **Cubism** among British artists.
- Created **geometric artworks** influenced by machines, architecture.
- **Vorticism** derived from viewing life as a **vortex**.
- Published **Blast**, a journal attacking **Victorian values**.
- Featured **Imagist poetry** and **radical graphic design**.
- Served as **WWI artillery officer**, then **war artist**.
- Shifted to **portraiture** and focused on **writing**.
- Published **books, short stories, essays** post-war.
- Early support for **Nazism** complicates legacy, despite **art**.

Vorticism (1912-1915)

- **Vorticism**: Flourished in **England (1912–15)**.
- Founded by **Wyndham Lewis**, linked to **industrialization**.
- Opposed **19th-century sentimentality**, embraced machine energy.
- Promoted a **cult of sheer violence**.
- Vorticist art was **abstract, sharp-planed compositions**.
- Influenced by **Cubism** and **Futurism** movements.
- Key contributors: **Ezra Pound** and **Jacob Epstein**.
- Unified **visual arts** and **literary expression**.

T.S. Eliot (1888-1965)

Life and Literary Career

- **T. S. Eliot** born in **St. Louis**, September **26, 1888**.
- Lived in **St. Louis** for first **eighteen years**.
- Attended **Harvard University** for undergraduate and **master's degrees**.
- Left the **United States** for the **Sorbonne** in **1910**.
- Returned to **Harvard** for a doctorate in **philosophy**.
- Settled in **England** in **1914**, married **Vivienne Haigh-Wood**.
- Worked in **London** as a **teacher**, then at **Lloyd's Bank**.
- Influenced by **Ezra Pound**, who recognized his **genius**.
- **"The Love Song of J. Alfred Prufrock"** published in **1915**.
- First book **Prufrock and Other Observations**, published **1917**.
- **The Waste Land (1922)** became his most **influential work**.

- ➤ Dominated **poetry** and **criticism** from **1930 to 1960**.
- ➤ Inspired by **English metaphysical poets** and **French symbolists**.
- ➤ Articulated **disillusionment** of post-**World War I generation**.
- ➤ Rejected **Victorian values**, innovated **poetic technique**.
- ➤ Converted to **orthodox Christianity** in the **late 1930s**.
- ➤ Major later works: **Ash Wednesday** (1930), **Four Quartets** (1943).
- ➤ Important criticism: **The Sacred Wood** (1920), others followed.
- ➤ Significant verse dramas: **Murder in the Cathedral, The Family Reunion**.
- ➤ Became a **British citizen** in **1927**, joined **Faber & Faber**.
- ➤ Published **younger poets**, became **director** of the firm.
- ➤ Ended unhappy marriage in **1933**, remarried **Valerie Fletcher**.
- ➤ Won **Nobel Prize for Literature** in **1948**.
- ➤ Died in **London** on January **4, 1965**.
- ➤ **Poetry reflected** cultural, social, and **religious conservatism**.
- ➤ **Avant-garde poet**, reshaped modern **literary taste**.
- ➤ Left a profound **legacy** in poetry and **criticism**.
- ➤ Impacted both **English literature** and younger **generations**.

Major Works:

Poetry:

- ➤ *The Love Song of J. Alfred Prufrock (1917)*
- ➤ *Gerontion (1920)*
- ➤ *The Waste Land (1922)*
- ➤ *The Hollow Men (1925)*
- ➤ *Ariel Poems (1927–1954) [Journey of the Magi (1927)]*
- ➤ *Ash Wednesday (1930)*
- ➤ *Old Possum's Book of Practical Cats (1939)*
- ➤ *Four Quartets (1945)*

Prose:

- ➤ *The Sacred Wood (1920)*
- ➤ *Tradition and the Individual Talent (1920)*
- ➤ *"Hamlet and His Problems" (1920)*
- ➤ *The Use of Poetry and the Use of Criticism (1933),*
- ➤ *After Strange Gods (1934),*
- ➤ *Notes Towards the Definition of Culture (1940)*

Plays:

- ➤ *Sweeney Agonistes (published in 1926, first performed in 1934)*
- ➤ *The Rock (1934)*

> *Murder in the Cathedral (1935)*
> *The Family Reunion (1939)*
> *The Cocktail Party (1949)*
> *The Confidential Clerk (1953)*
> *The Elder Statesman (first performed in 1958, published in 1959)*

"Lovely Gentlemen Waste Hollow Ashes, Possums Follow Quartets."

- **Love Song**: *The Love Song of J. Alfred Prufrock (1917)*
- **Gentlemen**: *Gerontion (1920)*
- **Waste**: *The Waste Land (1922)*
- **Hollow**: *The Hollow Men (1925)*
- **Ashes**: *Ash Wednesday (1930)*
- **Possums**: *Old Possum's Book of Practical Cats (1939)*
- **Follow Quartets**: *Four Quartets (1945)*

Fist Major Essay Collection The Sacred Wood, included Tradition and the Individual Talent (1920) and "Hamlet and His Problems" (1920) In the middle phase we have The Use of Poetry and the Use of Criticism (1933),
The Last Major Essay Notes Towards the Definition of Culture (1940)

Note: **All the plays are after major poems.**
First play Sweeny and the Second Play The Rock.
The last play *The Elder Statesman (1958)*

Code to Remember plays

After Murder in the Cathedral, The Family Reunited for a Cocktail Party, but the Confidential Clerk Ruined Everything.

The Love Song of J Alfred Prufrock (1917)

> **"Prufrock"**, first published poem by **T.S. Eliot**.
> Written in **February 1910**, published in **1915**.
> **Ezra Pound** instigated its publication in **Poetry Magazine**.
> Included in **Prufrock and Other Observations** (1917).
> Marked shift from **Romantic verse to Modernism**.
> Influenced by **Dante**, the **Bible**, and **Shakespeare**.
> References **Andrew Marvell** and **French Symbolists**.
> Uses **stream of consciousness** technique in narration.

- ➢ Described as a **"drama of literary anguish"**.
- ➢ A **dramatic interior monologue** of an urban man.
- ➢ **Epitomizes frustration** of the modern individual's **impotence**.
- ➢ Explores **isolation, indecision, and modern disillusionment**.
- ➢ **Prufrock** feels haunted by lost **youth** and **happiness**.
- ➢ "I have **measured out my life with coffee spoons**."
- ➢ Laments **lost opportunities** and lack of **spiritual progress**.
- ➢ Haunted by **unattained carnal love** and longing.
- ➢ Themes include **regret, decay, and mortality awareness**.
- ➢ Reflects **weariness**, embarrassment, and **sexual frustration**.
- ➢ **"Prufrock"** symbolizes **modern disillusionment** and despair.
- ➢ Became one of **Modernism's most recognized voices**.

Gerontion (1920)

- ➢ **"Gerontion" by T.S. Eliot**, published in **1920**.
- ➢ Title means **"little old man"** in **Greek**.
- ➢ A **dramatic monologue** by an elderly narrator.
- ➢ Reflects **Europe** post-**World War I** perspectives.
- ➢ Originally considered as **preface to The Waste Land**.
- ➢ **Ezra Pound** convinced Eliot against this inclusion.
- ➢ Themes of **religion, sexuality**, and **modernist concerns**.
- ➢ Opens with an **epigraph** from **Measure for Measure**:
  "Thou hast nor youth nor age."
- ➢ **"Us" and "I"** suggest an elderly **speaker's reflections**.
- ➢ **Lines 53-58** echo themes from **Prufrock**.
- ➢ Describes a **household** with a **boy and woman**.
- ➢ Mentions a **Jewish landlord** and **European residents**.
- ➢ Transitions to **abstract spiritual malaise reflections**.
- ➢ Ends with:
  "Thoughts of a dry brain in a dry season."
- ➢ **"Dry brain"** refers to the **narrator's aging mind**.
- ➢ **Hugh Kenner** compares voices to **The Waste Land**.
- ➢ Suggests multiple **voices** express **Gerontion's impressions**.
- ➢ Poem resembles **Jacobean play** style, fragmented structure.
- ➢ Lacks a **formal plot** but delivers vivid imagery.
- ➢ Highlights **Eliot's modernist techniques** and **narrative methods**.

The Waste Land (1922)

- ➢ **The Waste Land** by **T. S. Eliot**, published **1922**.

- ➢ Regarded as a **central modernist work** of poetry.
- ➢ First appeared in **The Criterion** and **The Dial**.
- ➢ **Book form** publication in **December 1922**.
- ➢ Famous lines: **"April is the cruellest month"**.
- ➢ **"I will show you fear in dust"**.
- ➢ Sanskrit mantra: **"Shantih shantih shantih"**.
- ➢ Combines **Holy Grail legend** with British society.
- ➢ References **Ovid, Dante, Shakespeare**, and **Upanishads**.
- ➢ **Shifts between satire, prophecy,** and dissonant voices.
- ➢ **Themes of disillusionment** dominate the poem's tone.
- ➢ **Abrupt speaker and time shifts** throughout sections.
- ➢ Divided into **five sections**, each exploring themes.
  1. **"The Burial of the Dead"**
  2. **"A Game of Chess"**
  3. **"The Fire Sermon"**
  4. **"Death by Water"**
  5. **"What the Thunder Said"**
- ➢ **Allusions** blend **Western canon** with Eastern philosophy.

I. The Burial of the Dead

- ➢ **Theme**: Death and rebirth are central motifs here.
- ➢ **Opening Line**: "April is the cruellest month, breeding..."
- ➢ **Contrast**: Spring, often a symbol of life, linked to suffering.
- ➢ **Madame Sosostris**: A clairvoyant introduces Tarot imagery.
- ➢ **Important Tarot Cards**: "The Hanged Man," "The Drowned Phoenician Sailor."
- ➢ **London Fog**: "Unreal City, under the brown fog of a winter dawn."
- ➢ **Disillusionment**: Post-WWI trauma echoes in fragmented voices.
- ➢ **Memory**: "I will show you fear in a handful of dust."
- ➢ **Death of Religion**: References to Ezekiel and Ecclesiastes.
- ➢ **Tone**: Bleak, fragmented, introducing a chaotic modern world.

II. A Game of Chess

- ➢ **Setting**: Lavish room contrasts with tense, intimate relationships.
- ➢ **Key Line**: "The chair she sat in, like a burnished throne."
- ➢ **Women's Voices**: Highlights failed communication and marital breakdown.

- ➤ **Lamentation**: "My nerves are bad tonight. Yes, bad."
- ➤ **Lil's Story**: Gossip reflects lower-class struggles and moral decay.
- ➤ **Refrain**: "HURRY UP PLEASE IT'S TIME" suggests time running out.
- ➤ **Symbolism**: Chess symbolizes manipulative human interactions.
- ➤ **Fragmentation**: Juxtaposition of high and low cultures intensifies disarray.
- ➤ **Eliot's Modernity**: Combines classical allusions with modern speech.
- ➤ **Tone**: Anxiety and existential dread dominate.

III. The Fire Sermon

- ➤ **Theme**: Lust and spiritual emptiness dominate this part.
- ➤ Meditates on **death and self-denial**.
- ➤ Influenced by **Augustine of Hippo** and **Eastern religions**.
- ➤ **Key Line**: "The river sweats oil and tar..."
- ➤ **Setting**: Thames River, symbolizing decay and pollution.
- ➤ **Tiresias**: The blind prophet unites past, present, and future.
- ➤ **Encounter**: Tiresias narrates a seduction devoid of passion.
- ➤ **Music**: Song references reinforce cultural fragmentation.
- ➤ **Decay**: "Sweet Thames, run softly, till I end my song."
- ➤ **Critique**: Modern society's spiritual barrenness highlighted.
- ➤ **Religious Allusion**: Buddha's Fire Sermon urges liberation from desires.
- ➤ **Tone**: Deeply melancholic and detached.

IV. Death by Water

- ➤ **Phlebas**: A drowned sailor reflects on life's vanity.
- ➤ **Theme**: Life's transient nature and inevitability of death.
- ➤ **Key Line**: "Consider Phlebas, who was once handsome and tall."
- ➤ **Water Symbolism**: Ambiguous – life-giving and destructive.
- ➤ **Warnings**: "O you who turn the wheel..." calls for reflection.
- ➤ **Universal Message**: Death comes for all, regardless of status.
- ➤ **Transition**: Prepares for the spiritual focus in the final section.
- ➤ **Imagery**: Ocean's depths symbolize forgotten ambitions.
- ➤ **Allusion**: Echoes the drowning in "The Tempest."
- ➤ **Tone**: Calm yet hauntingly reflective.

V. What the Thunder Said

- **Theme**: Spiritual desolation and hope for redemption.
- **Setting**: Desert landscape symbolizes barrenness of modern life.
- **Key Line**: "Here is no water but only rock..."
- **Religious Allusion**: References to Christ and Eastern philosophy.
- **Thunder's Voice**: "DA" signifies "Give, Sympathize, Control."
- **Imagery**: Cities crumble; echoes of a dying civilization.
- **Resurrection Hope**: "Who is the third who walks always beside you?"
- **Ending Line**: "Shantih shantih shantih" – peace transcending understanding.
- **Allusions**: Upanishads, Dante, and the Bible converge.
- **Tone**: Climactic, moving from despair to tentative renewal.

Key Notes

- **Structure**: Fragmented, reflective of post-WWI disillusionment.
- **Style**: Combines mythological, religious, and modernist imagery.
- **Legacy**: Defined modernism and remains one of 20th-century's iconic poems.

Ariel Poems (1927–1954) [Journey of the Magi (1927)]

- **Historical Context**: Published during the interwar period (1927).
- **Commission**: Written as part of the Ariel Poems series.
- **Religious Reflection**: Focused on Eliot's Christian conversion (1927).
- **Theme**: Transformation, faith, and spiritual struggle.
- **Perspective**: Narrated by one of the Magi.
- **Key Line**: "A cold coming we had of it..."
- **Tone**: Reflects hardship, doubt, and spiritual renewal.
- **Imagery**: Harsh journey contrasts with divine purpose.
- **Historical Setting**: Represents Biblical journey of the Magi.
- **Symbolism**: Winter suggests death; birth of Christ rebirth.
- **Characters**: The Magi represent seekers of faith.
- **Religious Allusions**: Combines Nativity with spiritual ambiguity.

- ➤ **Modernist Approach**: Merges religious myth with personal faith.
- ➤ **Repetition**: "This Birth was / Hard and bitter agony..."
- ➤ **Legacy**: A pivotal poem in Eliot's religious journey.

Ash Wednesday (1930) by T.S. Eliot

- ➤ **Conversion**: Written after Eliot's conversion to Anglicanism in 1927.
- ➤ **Theme**: Represents Eliot's spiritual struggle and new faith.
- ➤ **Cultural Shift**: Marked Eliot's shift to Christian themes.
- ➤ **Historical Context**: Depression era, rise of spiritual questioning.
- ➤ **Opening**: Expresses despair, "Because I do not hope to turn."
- ➤ **Repentance**: Speaker seeks God's mercy through humility.
- ➤ **Imagery**: Contrasts "dust" with celestial visions of heaven.
- ➤ **Journey**: Explores the path from despair to faith.
- ➤ **Refrain**: "Lady, three white leopards sat under a juniper-tree."
- ➤ **Ending**: Acceptance of salvation, "Suffer us not to mock ourselves."
- ➤ **Tone**: Reflective, seeking peace through divine guidance.

Old Possum's Book of Practical Cats (1939) by T.S. Eliot

- ➤ **For Children**: Written as light verse for family entertainment.
- ➤ **Character Inspiration**: Based on Eliot's observations of cats.
- ➤ **War Context**: Published during early WWII tensions.
- ➤ **Popularity**: Inspired the Broadway musical *Cats* in 1981.
- ➤ **Theme**: Explores quirky, endearing personalities of cats.
- ➤ **Famous Lines**: "The naming of cats is a difficult matter."
- ➤ **Characters**: Jellicle Cats, Old Deuteronomy, and Rum Tum Tugger.
- ➤ **Plot**: Narrates adventures and traits of various cats.
- ➤ **Best-Known Poems**: "Macavity: The Mystery Cat," "Mr. Mistoffelees."
- ➤ **Macavity**: A mischievous, mysterious "Napoleon of Crime."
- ➤ **Mr. Mistoffelees**: A magical cat with extraordinary powers.
- ➤ **Rum Tum Tugger**: A rebellious, flamboyant feline.
- ➤ **Old Deuteronomy**: Wise, revered leader of Jellicle Cats.
- ➤ **Jennyanydots**: A domestic cat with organizational talents.
- ➤ **Gus**: A theatrical cat reminiscing about glory days.
- ➤ **Mungojerrie and Rumpleteazer**: Mischievous cat duo known for mischief.
- ➤ **Bustopher Jones**: A well-dressed, sophisticated "cat about town."

> ➤ **Skimbleshanks**: A meticulous Railway Cat with responsibilities.
> ➤ **Grizabella**: A tragic, nostalgic figure, remembered from *Cats*.

Four Quartets (1943)

> ➤ **Four Quartets**: Four poems by **T. S. Eliot**.
> ➤ **Burnt Norton** published in **1936's Collected Poems**.
> ➤ Other three poems written during **World War II**.
> ➤ **Titles: East Coker, The Dry Salvages, Little Gidding**.
> ➤ First published as series by **Faber and Faber**.
> ➤ Published separately between **1940 and 1942**.
> ➤ Collected in **1943** by **Eliot's New York publisher**.
> ➤ Common theme: **time, universe, and the divine**.
> ➤ Blends **Anglo-Catholicism** with **Eastern and Western traditions**.
> ➤ References: **Bhagavad-Gita, Pre-Socratics, Julian of Norwich**.
> ➤ Critics call it Eliot's **last great work**.
> ➤ **George Orwell** criticized its overt **religiosity**.
> ➤ Recognized for its **philosophical and mystical depth**.
> ➤ **Each poem** comprises **five sections**.
> ➤ **Later poems** synthesize themes from **earlier sections**.
> ➤ **Sections connect** to **The Waste Land** structure.
> ➤ Helped Eliot **structure larger poems** with difficulty.
> ➤ According to C.K. Stead, the structure is based on:
>   1. The movement of time, in which brief moments of eternity are caught.
>   2. Worldly experience, leading to dissatisfaction.
>   3. Purgation in the world, divesting the soul of the love of created things.
>   4. A lyric prayer for, or affirmation of the need of, intercession.
>   5. The problem of attaining artistic wholeness, which becomes an analogue for and merges into the problem of achieving spiritual health.
> ➤ Four Quartets are:
>   1. Burnt Norton
>   2. East Coker,
>   3. The Dry Salvages,
>   4. Little Gidding

Burnt Norton

> ➤ Burnt Norton, located in Cotswold Hills, Gloucestershire.
> ➤ Eliot visited Burnt Norton during summer 1934.

- ➢ Poem set in house's rose garden, exploring time.
- ➢ Opening lines from Murder in the Cathedral (1935).
  "Time present and time past
  Are both perhaps present in time future,
  And time future contained in time past."

East Coker
- ➢ **"East Coker"** written in **strong-stress metre**, five sections.
- ➢ Explores **cyclical patterns**, **history**, and **spiritual renewal**.
- ➢ Named after **Somersetshire hamlet**, Eliot's ancestral home.
- ➢ Eliot's ancestors immigrated to **America** in **1660s**.
- ➢ **Visited site** in **1937**, inspiring poem's imagery.
- ➢ Poem's tone is **bleak**, featuring **deserted streets**.
  "For us, there is only the trying. The rest is not our business."

The Dry Salvages
- ➢ Written in **strong-stress "native" metre**, five sections.
- ➢ **"The Dry Salvages"** rhymes with **"assuages"**, themes of **time/history**.
- ➢ Title refers to **rocks near Cape Ann, Mass.**
- ➢ Eliot visited **Cape Ann** during his **childhood**.
- ➢ Features **Atlantic Ocean** and **Mississippi River imagery**.
- ➢ Reflects **Christian doctrines**, especially the **Incarnation**.
- ➢ Explores **contradictory concepts** understood **partially**.
- ➢ Concerns human **experience** and **spiritual response**.
  "But to apprehend
  The point of intersection of the timeless
  With time, is an occupation for the saint."

Little Gidding
- ➢ **Little Gidding** delayed due to **Eliot's declining health**.
- ➢ Finished in **September 1942** after early **dissatisfaction**.
- ➢ Central theme: **time and humanity's place within it**.
- ➢ Poem unites generations and **Western civilisation**.
- ➢ Discusses **WWII**: choice between **bombing** or **Holy Spirit**.
- ➢ **God's love redeems** humanity through **purgation by fire**.
- ➢ **"All shall be well"** from **Julian of Norwich**.
- ➢ Eliot parallels **poetry** with work on **soul and society**.

Murder in the Cathedral (1935)

- ➢ **"Murder in the Cathedral"** is a **poetic drama.**
- ➢ Written by **T.S. Eliot**, performed in **1935.**
- ➢ Set in **December 1170**, about **Thomas Becket.**
- ➢ Describes the **martyrdom of Canterbury's archbishop.**
- ➢ **Characters**: Thomas Becket, Chorus, Priests, and Four Tempters.
- ➢ **Setting**: Canterbury Cathedral, during Archbishop Becket's final days.
- ➢ **Plot**: Becket returns from exile, facing imminent threats.
- ➢ **Tempters' Persuasion**: Temptations include power, safety, and false martyrdom.
- ➢ **Becket's Resolve**: Chooses martyrdom for spiritual over worldly glory.
- ➢ **Important Line**: "The last temptation is the greatest treason."
- ➢ **Chorus' Role**: Reflects fear and conflict of common people.
- ➢ **Becket's Death**: Knights kill him, fulfilling his martyrdom prophecy.

The Family Reunion (1939)

- ➢ **The Family Reunion** by **T.S. Eliot** written in **blank verse.**
- ➢ Combines **Greek drama** and **detective play elements.**
- ➢ Explores **hero's journey** from **guilt to redemption.**
- ➢ Initially **unsuccessful in 1939**, later **revived successfully.**
- ➢ Hero reflects Eliot's **estrangement from first wife.**
- ➢ **Characters**: Harry, Agatha, Amy, Mary, and Downing family members.
- ➢ **Plot Start**: Harry returns to Wishwood for mother's birthday.
- ➢ **Conflict**: Haunted by guilt over his wife's death.
- ➢ **Theme**: Explores sin, guilt, and spiritual redemption.
- ➢ **Amy's Desire**: Hopes Harry continues family legacy at Wishwood.
- ➢ **Agatha's Revelation**: Unveils dark secrets about family history.
- ➢ **Harry's Struggle**: Wrestles with inner demons and responsibility.
- ➢ **Turning Point**: Harry renounces Wishwood and seeks spiritual path.
- ➢ **Important Line**: "Only through time is time conquered."
- ➢ **Resolution**: Harry leaves, embracing freedom and spiritual renewal.

The Cocktail Party (1949)

- ➢ **The Cocktail Party**, a play by **T. S. Eliot.**
- ➢ Based on **Alcestis** by **Euripides, Ancient Greek playwright.**
- ➢ Eliot's **most popular play**, remembered alongside **Murder in the Cathedral.**

- ➢ Written in **1948** while at **Princeton's Institute for Advanced Study**.
- ➢ **Characters**: Edward, Lavinia, Celia, and an enigmatic Unidentified Guest.
- ➢ **Plot Begins**: Lavinia leaves Edward before their cocktail party.
- ➢ **Key Event**: Edward seeks guidance from the Unidentified Guest.
- ➢ **Conflict**: Edward learns Lavinia knows of his affair.
- ➢ **Resolution Starts**: Lavinia returns, agreeing to rebuild their marriage.
- ➢ **Celia's Path**: Chooses spiritual martyrdom over worldly desires.
- ➢ **Key Line**: "What we know matters less than love."
- ➢ **Marriage Restored**: Edward and Lavinia embrace a practical union.
- ➢ **Celia's Fate**: Faces death, symbolizing spiritual transcendence.
- ➢ **Themes**: Redemption, human frailty, and spiritual self-discovery.

The Confidential Clerk (1953)

- ➢ The Confidential Clerk is a comic verse play by T. S. Eliot.
- ➢ **Characters**: Sir Claude, Colby, Lucasta, Mrs. Guzzard, Eggerson involved.
- ➢ **Plot**: Sir Claude hires Colby as his confidential clerk.
- ➢ **Conflict**: Colby doubts his legitimacy as Claude's secret heir.
- ➢ **Mrs. Guzzard**: Her revelations shake Claude and Colby's assumptions.
- ➢ **Lucasta**: Learns secrets about her own uncertain parentage.
- ➢ **Identity Crisis**: Both Colby and Lucasta question their true origins.
- ➢ **Important Line**: "We are all seeking to belong somewhere."
- ➢ **Resolution**: Colby rejects inheritance, choosing independence over privilege.
- ➢ **Theme**: Explores identity, family secrets, and existential belonging.
- ➢ **Message**: Happiness found in truth and rejecting false illusions.

Tradition And The Individual Talent (1920)

- ➢ First appeared in **1919**.
- ➢ Later appeared in ***The Sacred Wood: Essays on Poetry and Criticism (1920)***.
- ➢ Tradition and the Individual Talent is divided into **three parts**:
  1. The concept of "Tradition,"
  2. The Theory of Impersonal Poetry,
  3. The conclusion.
- ➢ **Eliot emphasizes the importance of history** in poetry.

- ➢ **Poetry should be "impersonal," separate** from the writer.
- ➢ Eliot's **"historical sense" connects pastness** and presence.
- ➢ Past works of art form an **evolving order**.
- ➢ **"The past should be altered by the present."**
- ➢ **Poets must know** both **recent and distant past**.
- ➢ Eliot stresses knowing the **"mind of Europe."**
- ➢ Poets must **"self-sacrifice"** to the **awareness of history.**
- ➢ This **self-sacrifice erases the poet's personality.**
- ➢ The poet's mind is a **"receptacle"** for emotions.
- ➢ Intense concentration creates a **new "art emotion."**
- ➢ True art is not about the **artist's life.**
- ➢ Art reflects **synthesis, depth, and comprehensive study.**
- ➢ **"Poetry is not a turning loose of emotion."**
- ➢ **"Escape from personality" counters Romantic excesses.**
- ➢ Eliot's **impersonal poet resembles Keats' "chameleon poet."**
- ➢ Critical study shifted focus to **poetry, not poets.**
- ➢ **"Tradition and the Individual Talent" shaped criticism.**
- ➢ Critics challenge Eliot's **canonical works** standards.
- ➢ Essay remains a **key text** in modern criticism.

The concept of "Tradition."

- ➢ **Eliot defines Tradition** and its role in **poetry.**
- ➢ **Tradition** is often "seldom... appear[s] except in censure."
- ➢ Eliot emphasizes **Tradition** as a **literary criticism** component.
- ➢ Gives **Tradition** a **special and complex meaning**.
- ➢ Describes **Tradition** as a "simultaneous order."
- ➢ **Past and present** are fused in **Tradition.**
- ➢ Literature of **Europe** starts from **Homer onward.**
- ➢ Eliot calls **Tradition** the "mind of Europe."
- ➢ **Talent** is thought to be **innate genius.**
- ➢ **Conventional wisdom** emphasizes **inborn talent** in arts.
- ➢ **Eliot believed talent** comes from **thorough poetry study.**
- ➢ Claimed **"Tradition"** shapes poetic **talent and depth.**
  "cannot be inherited, and if you want it, you must obtain it by great labour."

The Theory of Impersonal Poetry

- ➢ Poetry should be **"impersonal,"** distinct from **writer's personality.**
- ➢ **Tradition** demands the poet's continual **surrender.**

- ➢ Artistic creation is a process of **depersonalization**.
- ➢ Poet acts as a **catalyst** in artistic **creation**.
- ➢ **Feelings** and **emotions** are synthesized into **artistic images**.
- ➢ Greatness lies in **synthesis**, not raw **emotion**.
- ➢ Poetry is an **"escape from emotion,"** says Eliot.
- ➢ Essay emphasizes history's **importance** in **poetry**.
- ➢ Eliot aims to achieve **two key ideas**.
- ➢ The **"impersonal poet"** links to Keats' **"chameleon poet."**
- ➢ **Eliot** views poetry as **objective, not subjective**.

Hamlet and His Problems (1919)

- ➢ **Essay critically assesses Hamlet**, by T.S. Eliot.
- ➢ First published in **The Sacred Wood** (1920).
- ➢ Later appeared in **Selected Essays** (1932).
- ➢ Eliot claimed **Hamlet is "an artistic failure."**
- ➢ Popularized the **objective correlative** to evoke emotion.
- ➢ Example of **New Criticism** in literary analysis.
- ➢ Main issue lies in **the play**, not **Hamlet**.
- ➢ **Critical success** comes from Hamlet's appeal to critics.
- ➢ **Creative critics project themselves** onto **Hamlet's character**.
- ➢ Eliot accused **Goethe** of turning Hamlet into **Werther**.
- ➢ Eliot criticized **Coleridge** for making Hamlet **Coleridgean**.
- ➢ Critiques by **Goethe and Coleridge** were **misleading**.
- ➢ Praised **J.M. Robertson** and **Elmer Edgar Stoll**.
- ➢ Robertson focused on **historical interpretation of Hamlet**.
- ➢ Eliot emphasized critiques with **broader play scope**.
- ➢ Named three **sources inspiring Shakespeare's Hamlet**.
  1. Thomas Kyd's The Spanish Tragedy,
  2. The Ur-Hamlet,
  3. A version of the play was performed in Germany during Shakespeare's lifetime.
- ➢ The essay is pivotal for **objective analysis**.
- ➢ Influences **modern criticism** with **new literary methods**.
- ➢ **Delay occurred** from avoiding the **king's guards**.
- ➢ **Eliot agrees** Hamlet's motive centers on **mother's guilt**.
- ➢ **Revenge motive poorly combined** with **source material**.
- ➢ **Eliot introduced the term: Objective Correlative**.
- ➢ **Objective Correlative** systematically **represents emotions**.
- ➢ "The artistic **'inevitability' lies** in this complete adequacy..."

"The artistic 'inevitability' lies in this complete adequacy of the external to the emotion....",

- ➤ **Contrast to Hamlet**, lacks adequate **emotion-external match**.
- ➤ **Hamlet's emotional expression** fails in the **surroundings**.
- ➤ Audience struggles to **localize Hamlet's emotions** effectively.

Objective correlative

- ➤ **Objective correlative** expresses emotion using **objects, situations**.
- ➤ Evokes **specific sensory experience** for the **audience**.
- ➤ Helps readers understand a character's **emotional state**.
- ➤ Eliot critiques Hamlet's lack of **objective correlative**.
- ➤ Hamlet's **confusion** results from unexpressed **complex emotions**.
- ➤ Hamlet's **disgust for Gertrude** lacks clear representation.
- ➤ Neither **Hamlet nor Shakespeare** objectifies these **feelings**.
- ➤ This obstacle delays Hamlet's **revenge and plot**.
- ➤ Eliot: Hamlet's **bafflement stems from Shakespeare's shortcoming**.
- ➤ Finding an objective correlative would change **Hamlet's plot**.
- ➤ Eliot praises Shakespeare's **use in other works**.
- ➤ Example: **Macbeth's Lady Macbeth sleepwalking** scene mentioned.
- ➤ Shakespeare's sensory details reveal **Lady Macbeth's mental state**.
- ➤ Eliot highlights **effective sensory impressions** in **Macbeth**.
- ➤ **Objective correlative's absence** weakens **Hamlet's emotional impact**.

The Metaphysical Poets (1921)

- ➤ **Eliot's article** reviews Grierson's **Metaphysical Lyrics** anthology.
- ➤ Explores **value and significance** of **metaphysical poets**.
- ➤ Metaphysical poets were a distinct **English movement**.
- ➤ Eliot compares them with **French Symbolist poets**.
- ➤ **Defining metaphysical poetry** is difficult due to differences.
- ➤ Samuel Johnson's **criticism influenced metaphysical poetry's reputation**.
- ➤ Johnson described metaphysical poetry as **"heterogeneous ideas yoked by violence"**.
- ➤ Eliot argues **heterogeneous ideas** appear in other poetry.
- ➤ **Johnson's own poem** unites heterogeneous elements similarly.
- ➤ Eliot highlights **Johnson's hypocrisy** criticizing metaphysical poets.
- ➤ Eliot examines **George Herbert's complex syntax** and simplicity.

- ➤ Herbert shows **fidelity to thought and feeling**.
- ➤ **Union of thought and feeling** is Eliot's main theme.
- ➤ Metaphysical poetry developed through **John Donne's analytic mode**.
- ➤ Donne influenced by **Elizabethan verse drama contemporaries**.
- ➤ **Shakespeare and Chapman** influenced by **Montaigne's essays**.
- ➤ **Montaigne invented the modern essay form**.
- ➤ Eliot contrasts the poetry of the **French writers Jean Racine and Charles Baudelaire with that of John Milton and John Dryden**.
- ➤ Montaigne influenced **Shakespeare's soliloquies**, e.g., "To be or not to be".
- ➤ Soliloquies show **characters arguing with themselves**.
- ➤ Eliot notes **reason and feeling linked** in verse drama.
- ➤ Thought is a **sensory, not purely rational experience**.
- ➤ Eliot's thesis is the **"dissociation of sensibility"**.
- ➤ Dissociation began in **17th-century English poetry**.
- ➤ Metaphysical poets maintained **sensory connection in thought**.
- ➤ **Donne's style contrasts Shakespeare's emotive soliloquies**.
- ➤ Herbert's poetry balances **complexity with emotional clarity**.
- ➤ Eliot admires metaphysical poets' **innovative techniques**.
- ➤ Eliot refutes Johnson's **dismissal of metaphysical style**.
- ➤ Metaphysical poets united **ideas, emotions, and intellectual rigor**.

Dissociation of sensibility

- ➤ **Dissociation of Sensibility** coined by **T.S. Eliot in 1921**.
- ➤ Used in the essay **"The Metaphysical Poets."**
- ➤ Describes changes in **English poetry** post-Metaphysical era.
- ➤ Metaphysical poets felt **"thought as immediately as odour."**
- ➤ Eliot emphasized **"direct sensuous apprehension of thought."**
- ➤ Fusion of **thought and feeling** lost by later poets.
- ➤ Later poetry had **elevated language** and **cruder emotions**.
- ➤ Eliot saw loss as **natural poetry development**.
- ➤ **Mechanism of sensibility** changed in **later poetry**.

  "constantly amalgamating disparate experience"

  "difference between the intellectual and the reflective poet"

  "possessed a mechanism of sensibility which could devour any kind of experience"

  "[the] poets revolted against the ratiocinative, the descriptive; they thought and felt by fits, unbalanced; they reflected"

  "[a] thought to Donne was an experience; it modified his sensibility"

"more mature"

"wear better"

"cryptically that he thought it might have been caused by the same factors as those which brought about the Civil War"

"The difference is not a simple difference of degree between poets. It is something which had happened to the mind of England between **the time of Donne or Lord Herbert of Cherbury** and the time of **Tennyson and Browning**; it is the difference between the **intellectual poet and the reflective poet.** Tennyson and Browning are poets, and they think; but they do not feel their thought as immediately as the odour of a rose. **A thought to Donne was an experience; it modified his sensibility.** When a poet's mind is perfectly equipped for its work, it is constantly **amalgamating disparate experience;** the ordinary man's experience is chaotic, irregular, fragmentary. The latter falls in love, or reads Spinoza, and these two experiences have nothing to do with each other, or with the noise of the typewriter or the smell of cooking; m the mind of the poet these experiences are always forming new wholes. We may express the difference by the following theory: The poets of the seventeenth century, the successors of the dramatists of the sixteenth, possessed a mechanism of sensibility which could devour any kind of experience. They are simple, artificial, difficult, or fantastic, as their predecessors were; no less nor more than Dante, Guido Cavalcanti, Guinicelli, or Cino. In the seventeenth century a dissociation of sensibility set in, from which we have never recovered; and this dissociation, as is natural, was aggravated by the influence of the two most powerful **poets of the century, Milton and Dryden.** Each of these men performed certain poetic functions so magnificently well that the magnitude of the effect concealed the absence of others. The language went on and in some respects improved; the **best verse of Collins, Gray, Johnson, and even Goldsmith** satisfies some of our fastidious demands better than that of Donne or Marvell or King. But while the language became more refined, the feeling became more crude. The feeling, the sensibility, expressed in the **"Country Churchyard"** (to say nothing of Tennyson and Browning) is cruder than that in the "Coy Mistress." The second effect of the influence of Milton and Dryden followed from the first, and was therefore slow in manifestation. The sentimental age began early in the eighteenth century, and continued. The poets revolted against the ratiocinative, the descriptive; they thought and felt by fits, unbalanced; they reflected. **In one or two passages of Shelley's "Triumph of Life," in the second "Hyperion"** *there are traces of a struggle toward unification of sensibility.* But Keats and Shelley died, and Tennyson and Browning ruminated.After this brief exposition of a theory - too brief, perhaps, to carry conviction - we may ask, what would have been the fate of the 'metaphysical' had the current of poetry descended in a direct line from them, as it descended in a direct line to them ? **They would not, certainly, be classified as metaphysical.** *The possible interests of a poet are unlimited; the more intelligent he is the better; the more intelligent he is the more likely that he will have interests: our only condition is that he turn them into poetry, and not merely meditate on them poetically. A philosophical theory which has entered into poetry is established, for its truth or falsity in one sense ceases to matter, and its truth in another sense is proved. The poets in question have, like other poets, various faults. But they were, at best, engaged in the task of trying to find the verbal equivalent for states of mind and feeling. And this means both that they are more mature, and that they wear better, than later poets of certainly not less literary ability.It is not a permanent necessity that poets should be interested in philosophy, or in any other subject. We can only say that it appears likely that poets in our civilization, as it exists at present, must be difficult. Our civilization comprehends great variety and complexity, and this variety and complexity, playing upon a refined sensibility, must produce various and complex results. The poet must become more and more comprehensive, more allusive, more indirect, in order to force, to dislocate if necessary, language into his meaning.* **(A brilliant and extreme statement of this view, with which it is not requisite to associate oneself, is that of M. Jean Epstein, "La Poesie d'aujourd-hui.")** *Hence we get something which looks very much like the conceit - we get, in fact, a method curiously similar to that of the 'metaphysical poets', similar also in its use of obscure words and of simple phrasing."*

The Function of Criticism (1923)

- ➢ **'The Function of Criticism'**, essay by **T. S. Eliot**.
- ➢ Follows ideas from **'Tradition and the Individual Talent'**.
- ➢ Focuses on the **role of the critic**, not creation.
- ➢ Explores **comparisons between creative and critical work**.
- ➢ Begins by quoting his essay: **"a problem of order"**.
- ➢ **Criticism's function** relates to **order**, Eliot asserts.
- ➢ Greatest artists **"surrender" to a shared artistic community**.

- ➢ **Second-rate artists** emphasize their **individuality excessively.**
- ➢ Like insecure people, they constantly **assert themselves.**
- ➢ Great artists draw on and **involve others' work.**
- ➢ **Criticism** should be **"autotelic"**, with a specific purpose.
- ➢ **Art exists** for enjoyment and contemplation.
- ➢ **Criticism corrects public taste**, explains art effectively.
- ➢ Refers to **John Middleton Murry's Classicism vs Romanticism.**
- ➢ **Classicism** values belief in an **Outside Authority.**
- ➢ **Romantic view** relies on the **Inner Voice.**
- ➢ Eliot terms **Inner Voice as "Whiggery".**
- ➢ Whiggery dismisses **principles** in art **appraisal.**
- ➢ **Tradition trusts "accumulated wisdom of time".**
- ➢ Artists must perform **critical labour** on their own work.
- ➢ Tasks include **rewriting, correcting, testing, and sifting.**
- ➢ **Whiggery ignores** the critical effort behind art.
- ➢ Good critics need a **"highly developed sense of fact".**
- ➢ Best criticism helps readers **appreciate and understand art.**
- ➢ **Critics** should present **facts**, not subjective opinions.
- ➢ Criticism has a purpose; **art is self-justifying.**
- ➢ **Inner Voice approach** lacks clear critical **principles.**
- ➢ Criticism values **tradition**, not subjective **impressions.**
- ➢ Creative work inherently involves **critical processes.**
- ➢ Eliot emphasizes **criticism's disciplined, factual approach.**

Inner Voice:

- ➢ **Inner Voice** represents reliance on personal, subjective judgment.
- ➢ Rejects **Outside Authority**, trusting individual instincts in art.
- ➢ Eliot terms it **"Whiggery,"** dismissing traditional principles.
- ➢ Promotes **self-reliance** but risks lacking critical rigor.
- ➢ Contrasts with valuing **tradition** and **accumulated wisdom.**

The Use of Poetry and the Use of Criticism (1933)

Notes Towards the Definition of Culture (1940)

The Frontiers of Criticism (1956)

- ➢ **"The Frontiers of Criticism"** lecture by **T. S. Eliot**, 1956.
- ➢ Delivered at the **University of Minnesota**, 1956.
- ➢ Reprinted in **On Poetry and Poets**, 1957.

- ➢ Defines boundaries of **literary criticism** versus **history**.
- ➢ Distinguishes **literary criticism** from **historical studies of literature**.
- ➢ Responds to the rise of **New Critical perspective**.
- ➢ Analyzes **Eliot's own poetic works**, rare in criticism.
- ➢ Poets and critics now often in **separate camps**.
- ➢ Essay reflects **Eliot's evolving critical thought**, 1919-1956.
- ➢ Combines perspectives of **poet and literary critic**.
- ➢ Essay shows **Eliot's influence** on the **New Critics**.
- ➢ Eliot says, **"failed to see"** ties to **New Criticism (106)**.
- ➢ Essay proclaims principles **similar to New Critics'**.
  - ○ *the idea of the circumstances surrounding a work's creation as irrelevant (112)*
  - ○ *the "danger . . . of assuming that there must be just one interpretation of the poem as a whole, [and] that it must be right" (113)*
  - ○ *the lack of a need to assess the author's intent (113–14)*
  - ○ *the unimportance of the "feelings" of the reader (114)*
  - ○ *the limitation of literary criticism to the study of the literary object, i.e., the work itself (116)*

T.S. Eliot's Contributions to Literary Criticism and New Criticism

- ➢ Eliot influenced the New Criticism school significantly.
- ➢ Described his criticism as a "by-product" of poetry.
- ➢ Critic William Empson acknowledges Eliot's deep influence.
- ➢ "Tradition and the Individual Talent" emphasizes art's historical context.
- ➢ Introduced the concept of art in a "simultaneous order."
- ➢ The Waste Land exemplifies his theory of tradition.
- ➢ **"Hamlet and His Problems" discusses the "objective correlative" concept.**
- ➢ Advocated for non-subjective judgment of poetry.
- ➢ Eliot's classical ideals shaped New Criticism's approach.
- ➢ Criticized Romantic poets, especially Shelley, for their emotion.
- ➢ Argued that good poems escape from emotion.
- ➢ Believed contemporary poets must embrace difficulty.
- ➢ Revived interest in metaphysical poets through critical essays.
- ➢ Praised metaphysical poets for blending psychological and sensual experience.

- ➢ **Introduced "unified sensibility," likened to metaphysical poetry.**
- ➢ The Waste Land reflects Eliot's programmatic criticism approach.
- ➢ Advocated poets write criticism to advance personal interests.
- ➢ Later focused on writing for the theatre.
- ➢ Explored drama aesthetics in essays like "Poetry and Drama."
- ➢ The Waste Land reflects despair over World War I.

QUESTIONS

Question 61

Who among the following are the two great masters of the French language that T. S Eliot contrasts with Dryden and Milton in The Metaphysical Poets'?

A. Francois Villon
B. Jean Racine
C. Charles Baudelaire
D. Arthur Rimbaud

Choose the correct answer from the options given below:

1. A and C only
2. A and D only
3. B and C only
4. B and D only

Explanations:
Answer: 3. B and C only

In "The Metaphysical Poets," T.S. Eliot contrasts the poetry of the French writers Jean Racine and Charles Baudelaire with that of John Milton and John Dryden. Eliot praises Racine and Baudelaire for their use of language and their ability to express complex emotions and ideas with simplicity and precision. He contrasts them with Milton and Dryden, whom he sees as more concerned with the expression of moral or political values in their poetry.

Eliot's comparison can be found in the following excerpt from "The Metaphysical Poets":

"The French writers, the great masters of the language, have been more concerned with the form of language than with its content. They have been occupied with devising rhetorical devices to convey states of mind, rather than with the exploration of states of mind. They have been concerned, not so much

*with expressing themselves as with expressing human nature. **The greatest of them, Racine and Baudelaire, have a much closer affinity with the metaphysical poets than has Dryden or Milton**.*"

Arrange the following critical works in their chronological order of publication:

- A. "Preface to Lyrical Ballads"
- B. "A Defence of Rhyme"
- C. "Life of Cowley"
- D. "The Frontiers of Criticism"

Choose the correct answer from the options given below:

1. A, C, B and D
2. B, A, C and D
3. B, C, A and D
4. C, A, D and B

Explanations:

Answer: 3. B, C, A and D

- ➤ Samuel Daniel (1562–1619)'s ***A Defence of Rhyme (1603)***.
- ➤ ***"Life of Cowley"***: by Samuel Johnson and first published in **1779**.
- ➤ ***"Preface to Lyrical Ballads"***: by William Wordsworth and originally published in **1800**.
- ➤ ***"The Frontiers of Criticism"*** is a lecture given by T. S. Eliot at the University of Minnesota in **1956**.

Which two of the following plays are mentioned in T.S. Eliot's "Tradition and Individual Talent'?

- (A) Agamemnon
- (B) Antigone
- (C) Othello
- (D) Dr. Faustus

Choose the correct answer from the options given below:

1. (A)and (D) Only
2. (A) and (C) Only
3. (B) and (C) Only

4.   (B) and (D) Only

Explanations:

Answer: 2. (A)and (D) Only

T.S. Eliot does mention the plays "Agamemnon" and "Othello" in his essay "Tradition and the Individual Talent." The passage given below highlights Eliot's discussion on the transmutation of emotion in art.

""Great variety is possible in the process of transmutation of emotion: the murder of Agamemnon, or the agony of Othello, gives an artistic effect apparently closer to a possible original than the scenes from Dante. In the Agamemnon, the artistic emotion approximates to the emotion of an actual spectator; in Othello to the emotion of the protagonist himself. But the difference between art and the event is always absolute; the combination which is the murder of Agamemnon is probably as complex as that which is the voyage of Ulysses. In either case there has been a fusion of elements. ""

Question 64

In "The Function of Criticism", T.S. Eliot attacked J. Middleton Murry and similar critics for being devotees of what he called:

1.   **"the Inner Voice".**
2.   "the Romantic Impulse".
3.   "the Symbol Hunt".
4.   "the Muse's Mystery".

Correct Explanations:

T.S. Eliot did criticise J. Middleton Murry and other similar critics for being devotees of what he called "the Inner Voice" in his essay "The Function of Criticism." Eliot argued that this approach to criticism relied too heavily on subjective impressions and personal reactions, rather than on objective standards of excellence and a rigorous analysis of the work itself. He believed that true criticism should be grounded in a deep knowledge and understanding of the literary tradition and should aim to judge a work's artistic merits based on those standards rather than simply relying on personal taste.

Question 65

How does T.S. Eliot sum up the peculiar quality of Marvell's " Horatian Ode"?

1. Description
2. **'telescoping of images and multiplied associations (UGC Key)**
3. 'a tough reasonableness beneath a slight lyric grace
4. 'a contrast of ideas, different in degree but the same in principle

Correct Explanations:

T.S. Eliot sums up the peculiar quality of Marvell's "Horatian Ode" as "a tough reasonableness beneath a slight lyric grace". The description "telescoping of images and multiplied associations" is actually how Eliot characterises the metaphysical poets in general, not specifically Marvell's "Horatian Ode". The third option, "a contrast of ideas, different in degree but the same in principle", is a description of the method of the metaphysical poets as well.

T.S. Eliot indeed wrote about Marvell's "Horatian Ode." Still, he did not describe its peculiar quality as a "telescoping of images and multiplied associations." Rather, Eliot referred to the poem as having "a unity of sensibility, a profound and delicate sensibility." Here is the full quote:

"Marvell's Horatian Ode has a unity of sensibility, a profound and delicate sensibility, which is nowhere else to be found in the literature. It is a quality which cannot be explained in the abstract, which is dependent upon a particular sensitive apprehension of life. It is this quality which makes the poem a classic."

Question 66

Match List I with List II

List I (Writer)	List II (Book)
A. Homi Bhabha	I. Reading the Popular
B. T S Eliot	II. The Location of Culture
C. Roland Barthes	III. Notes towards the Definition of Culture
D. John Fiske	IV. Image-Music-Text

Choose the correct answer from the options given below:

1. A - IV, B - II, C - III, D - I
2. A - III, B - II, C - I, D - IV
3. A - I, B - II, C - IV, D - III
4. **A - II, B - III, C - IV, D - I**

Correct Explanations:

These are all book titles written by prominent cultural theorists. They are:

I. *"Reading the Popular"* by John Fiske.
II. *"The Location of Culture"* by Homi K. Bhabha.
III. *"Notes towards the Definition of Culture"* by T.S. Eliot.
IV. *"Image-Music-Text"* by Roland Barthes.

Question 67

Arrange the following terms in their chronological sequence of appearance:

    A.   dissociation of sensibility
    B.   unreliable narrator
    C.   theatre of cruelty
    D.   egotistical sublime

Choose the correct answer from the options given below

    1.   D, A, B, C
    2.   D, A, C, B
    3.   D, B, A, C
    4.   B, D, A, C

Correct Explanations:

D. According to the Romantic English poet John Keats (1795-1821), artists of fixed opinions suffered from "egotistical sublime," obsessing over singular truths to the point that they were unable to produce characters and storylines that convincingly diverged from their personal world views.

A. Dissociation of sensibility is a literary term first used by T. S. Eliot in his essay "The Metaphysical Poets" (1921).

C. The Theatre of Cruelty (1931-1936) is a form of theatre generally associated with Antonin Artaud. Artaud, who was briefly a member of the surrealist movement, outlined his theories in The Theatre and Its Double.

B. An unreliable narrator is a narrator whose credibility is compromised. They can be found in fiction and film and range from children to mature characters. **The term was coined in 1961 by Wayne C. Booth in The Rhetoric of Fiction.**

Question 68

Which of the following is applicable to "New Criticism"?

A. It draws considerably from the works of I. A. Richards and the critical essays of T.S Eliot.
B. Some of its concepts are pre-empted by F.R. Leavis.
C. It distinguishes between literary and scientific usage of language.
D. It encourages an extensive exploration of the contextual and autobiographical background of literary production.
E. It vouches for a historical analysis of a text.

Choose the correct answer from the options given below:

1. **A, B and C only**
2. B, E and D only
3. A, C and D only
4. B and D only

Correct Explanations:

A. **"New Criticism" draws considerably from the works of I.A. Richards and the critical essays of T.S. Eliot.** These two figures were key influences on the movement, and their ideas about language, meaning, and interpretation helped to shape the core principles of "New Criticism."

B. **Some of the concepts of "New Criticism" are pre-empted by F.R. Leavis.** Leavis was a prominent literary critic who wrote extensively about the importance of close reading and the study of literary form. His ideas about the centrality of language and form in literary analysis were influential in the development of "New Criticism."

C. **"New Criticism" distinguishes between literary and scientific usage of language.** One of the central tenets of the movement is that literary language is a unique and complex form of discourse that cannot be reduced to simple statements of fact or scientific observation. "New Critics" believed that literature should be studied on its own terms, and that the meaning of a text should be derived from its internal structure and language rather than from external factors such as historical context or authorial intent.

Other Explanations:
These two statements are not applicable to "New Criticism" because the movement emphasizes close reading and analysis of the text itself, rather than the context or background of the author or the historical period in which the work was written.

D. "New Criticism" does not encourage an extensive exploration of the contextual and autobiographical background of literary production. **Instead, it focuses on the formal and linguistic aspects of the text, such as the use of imagery, metaphor, and symbolism.** "New Critics" believed that the meaning of a text should be derived from the text itself, and that external factors such as the author's biography or the historical context in which the work was written were not relevant to literary analysis.

E. Similarly, "New Criticism" does not vouch for a historical analysis of a text. While historical context may be considered as one factor in the interpretation of a text, "New Critics" believed that the text itself was the primary source of meaning, and that the meaning of a work was not necessarily tied to its historical or cultural context. "New Criticism" rejected the idea that a work of literature could be reduced to its historical context or seen as a reflection of the culture or society in which it was produced.

Question 69

Given below are two statements.

Statement I: The term "Negative Capability" was coined by John Keats,
Statement II: While analysing the term "Dissociation of sensibility", T. S. Eliot proclaims that Hamlet is an artistic failure.

In light of the above statements, choose the correct answer from the options given below:

1. Both Statement II and I are true
2. Both Statements I and Statement II are false
3. **Statement I is true, but Statement II is false**
4. Statement I is false, but Statement II is true

Correct Explanations:
Statement I: Negative capability is a phrase first used by Romantic poet John Keats in 1817 to explain the capacity of the greatest writers to pursue a vision of artistic beauty even when it leads them into intellectual confusion and uncertainty, as opposed to a preference for philosophical certainty over artistic beauty.

Statement II: Dissociation of sensibility is a literary term first used by T. S. Eliot in his essay "The Metaphysical Poets". It refers to the way in which intellectual thought was separated from the experience of feeling in seventeenth century poetry.

Statement III: Hamlet and His Problems is an essay written by T.S. Eliot in 1919 that offers a critical reading of Hamlet. The essay first appeared in Eliot's The Sacred Wood: Essays on Poetry and Criticism in 1920. T.S. Eliot has called it as an artistic failure because of the fact that there is delay on the part of Hamlet in executing the revenge. There are many critics who interpret Hamlet in terms of revenge motif where the prince makes an unnecessary delay. **Eliot's critique gained attention partly due to his claim that Hamlet is "most certainly an artistic failure." Eliot also popularised the concept of the objective correlative—a mechanism used to evoke emotion in an audience—in the essay.**

Question 70

Match List I with List II

LIST I	LIST II
A. Bertrand Russell	I. The Verbal Icon
B. Thomas Stearns Eliot	II. The Well Wrought Urn
C. W.K. Wimsatt	III. History of Western Philosophy
D. Cleanth Brooks	IV. The Sacred Wood

Choose the correct answer from the options given below:

1. A-III, B-IV, C-I, D-II
2. A-III, B-I, C-IV, D-II
3. A-III, B-II, C-I, D-IV
4. A-III, B-I, C-II, D-IV

Explanations:

Ans: A-III, B-IV, C-I, D-II

A. Bertrand Russell's "History of Western Philosophy" is a comprehensive survey of the major philosophical thinkers and movements in Western philosophy from the pre-Socratic philosophers to the mid-twentieth century.

B. T.S. Eliot's "The Sacred Wood" is a collection of essays on literary criticism and aesthetics. In the book, Eliot discusses the nature of poetry, the relationship between tradition and individual talent, and the role of the critic in evaluating literary works.

C. W.K. Wimsatt's "The Verbal Icon" is an influential essay in literary theory that explores the concept of literary language and its relationship to meaning. Wimsatt argues that literary language is different from everyday language, and that its meaning is shaped by its form.

D. Cleanth Brooks' "The Well Wrought Urn" is a collection of essays on poetry that explores the relationship between form and meaning. Brooks argues that the form of a poem is integral to its meaning, and that a poem's meaning is shaped by its use of language and form.

Question 71

Match List I with List II

LIST I	LIST II
A. "Negative Capability"	I. Matthew Arnold
B. "Sweetness and light"	II. Samuel Taylor Coleridge
C. "Esemplastic"	III. T.S. Eliot
D. "Dissociation of Sensibility"	IV. John Keats

Choose the correct answer from the options given below:

1. A-II, B-IV, C-I, D-III
2. A-II, B-I, C-IV, D-III
3. A-IV, B-III, C-II, D-I
4. A-IV, B-I, C-II, D-III

Explanations:

Ans: A-IV, B-I, C-II, D-III

A. **"Negative Capability" - John Keats: Negative Capability is a term coined by John Keats in a letter to his brothers in 1817**, where he described it as the ability to tolerate uncertainty and the mysterious without resorting to oversimplification, explanation or absolute knowledge.

B. **"Sweetness and light" - Matthew Arnold: "Sweetness and light" is a phrase used by Matthew Arnold** to describe the goal of cultural criticism, which is to help people to see the world more clearly, to appreciate beauty, and to lead better lives.

C. **"Esemplastic" - Samuel Taylor Coleridge: Esemplastic is a term coined by Samuel Taylor Coleridge** to describe the power of imagination to unify or combine different elements into a single, integrated whole.

D. **"Dissociation of Sensibility" - T.S. Eliot: "Dissociation of Sensibility" is a term coined by T.S. Eliot in his essay "The Metaphysical Poets"** to describe a separation of thought and feeling in 17th century poetry.

Question 72

Choose the correct chronological sequence in which the following texts were written.

    A.   Lycidas
    B.   Hero and Leander
    C.   Masque of Comus
    D.   Paradise Lost
    E.   The Waste Land

Choose the correct option from the following

    1.   A, B, D, E, C
    2.   B, C, A, D, E
    3.   B, A, E, C, D
    4.   B, E, D, C, A

Explanations:
Ans: B, C, A, D, E

- ➢ *Hero and Leander,* a narrative poem by Christopher Marlowe in **1593**.
- ➢ *Masque of Comus,* a masque by John Milton in **1634.**
- ➢ *Lycidas,* a pastoral elegy **by** John Milton in **1637.**
- ➢ *Paradise Lost,* an epic poem by John Milton **in 1667.**
- ➢ *The Waste Land*, a modernist poem by T.S. Eliot **in 1922.**

Match List I with List II

List I	List II
A. Response to Stephen Gosson	I. Aristotle
B. The Individual Talent	II. Matthew Arnold
C. Catharsis	III. T.S. Eliot
D. Sweetness and Light	IV. Philip Sidney

Choose the correct answer from the options given below:

1. A- IV. B- II, C- III. D-I
2. A - IV, B - III. C - I. D -II
3. A - IV. B - III, C - II, D - I
4. A- IV. B - I, C - II, D - III

Explanations

Answer: 2. A - IV, B - III, C - I, D -II

I. Aristotle - Catharsis: In his work "Poetics,"
II. Matthew Arnold - Sweetness and Light: Matthew Arnold
III. T.S. Eliot - The Individual Talent: T.S. Eliot
IV. Philip Sidney - Response to Stephen Gosson in "An Apology for Poetry.

The author of The Golden Bough, a text that influenced Eliot's poetry and criticism substantially.

1. John Ruskin
2. James George Frazer
3. Thomas Carlyle

4. David Wilson

Explanations
Answer: 2. James George Frazer

The Golden Bough **is a comprehensive study of comparative religion by Sir James Frazer.** Originally published in 1890, it was later expanded into a twelve-volume work titled *A Study in Magic and Religion* (1911-1915).

T.S. Eliot, in his literary works, draws on a diverse range of sources, including Scriptural writings such as the *Bible* **and** *the Book of Common Prayer,* **as well as cultural and anthropological studies like Sir James Frazer's** *The Golden Bough* **and Jessie Weston's** *From Ritual to Romance.* These sources contribute to Eliot's exploration of themes and motifs, such as the Wasteland motif in Celtic mythology, enriching his works with a deep intertextual and cultural resonance.

Question 75

"The Love Song of J. Alfred Prufrock" names the following figures:

    A. Ezra Pound
    B. Michelangelo
    C. Valerie Eliot
    D. Hamlet
    E. Walt Whitman

Choose the correct answer from the options given below:

    1. A, C, and E
    2. B, and D
    3. B, D, and E
    4. D, and E

Explanations
Answer: 2. B, and D

"The Love Song of J. Alfred Prufrock," also known as "Prufrock," is the debut poem of T. S. Eliot (1888–1965), an American-born British poet. Written in February 1910 and published in June 1915 in Poetry: A Magazine of Verse, it was later included in the pamphlet "Prufrock and Other Observations" in 1917. Initially considered outlandish, the poem now marks a significant shift from late 19th-century Romantic verse to Modernism.

Eliot's poem draws influence from Dante Alighieri and incorporates references to the Bible, as well as works —including William **Shakespeare's plays Henry IV Part II, Twelfth Night, and Hamlet, the poetry of seventeenth-century metaphysical poet Andrew Marvell, and the nineteenth-century French Symbolists. This repeated mention of Michelangelo by the women in "The Love Song of J. Alfred Prufrock" serves as more than just a representation of the idle chatter of the attendees of the tea party.** Using the stream of consciousness technique, Eliot presents the experience of Prufrock, an urban man struggling with isolation and indecision. The poem is described as a "drama of literary anguish," portraying the frustrations and disillusionment of the modern individual and their unfulfilled desires.

"In the room the women come and go
Talking of Michelangelo.

—-----------

—-----------

No! I am not Prince Hamlet, nor was meant to be;
Am an attendant lord, one that will do
To swell a progress, start a scene or two,
Advise the prince; no doubt, an easy tool,
Deferential, glad to be of use,
Politic, cautious, and meticulous;
Full of high sentence, but a bit obtuse;
At times, indeed, almost ridiculous—
Almost, at times, the Fool."

Question 76

Arrange the following in accordance with their dates of first publication:

> A. Edward Said, Orientalism: Western Conceptions of the Orient
> B. Fredric Jameson, The Political Unconscious: Narrative as a Socially Symbolic Act
> C. TS Eliot, Notes towards the Definition of Culture
> D. Raymond Williams, Keywords

E. Ian Watt, The Rise of the Novel

Choose the correct answer from the following options:

1. C, E, D, A, B
2. D, B, E, A, C
3. B. D. A, E. C
4. A, E, B. D, C

Explanations:
Answer: **1.** C, E, D, A, B

C. T.S. Eliot, *Notes towards the Definition of Culture* (1948)
E. Ian Watt, *The Rise of the Novel* (1957)
D. Raymond Williams, *Keywords* (1976)
A. Edward Said, *Orientalism: Western Conceptions of the Orient* (1978)
B. Fredric Jameson, *The Political Unconscious: Narrative as a Socially Symbolic Act* (1981)

Question 77

Arrange the chronological sequence in which the following works of T. S. Eliot were first published:

A. The Sacred Wood
B. Notes towards the Definition of Culture
C. The Metaphysical Poets
D. The Function of Criticism
E. The Use of Poetry and the Use of Criticism

Choose the correct answer from the options given below:

1. C, D, A, E, B
2. D, C, A, B, E
3. A. C, D, E, B
4. B, A, C, D, E

Explanations:
Answer: 3. A. C, D, E, B

A. "The Sacred Wood first published in **1920**

C. "The Metaphysical Poets first published in **1921.**

D. "The Function of Criticism" first published in **1923.**

E. "The Use of Poetry and the Use of Criticism" first published in **1933**

B. "Notes towards the Definition of Culture" first published in **1948.**

Arrange the chronological sequence in which the following works were published:

A. Culture and Society

B. Culture and Anarchy

C. To Hell with Culture

D. Studies in Dying Culture

E. Notes towards the Definition of Culture

Choose the correct answer from the options given below:

1. (E), (B), (A), (D),(C)
2. (C),(E),(D), (B),(A)
3. (A),(D),(E), (B), (C)
4. (B),(A),(D), (C),(E)

Explanations:

Answer: 3. (A),(D),(E), (B), (C)

- *Culture and Anarchy: An Essay in Political and Social Criticism* **(1867-1868)** by Matthew Arnold.
- *Notes Towards the Definition of Culture (1948)* by T.S. Eliot.
- *To Hell With Culture* by Sir Herbert Read (**1941**)
- *Culture and Society (1958)* by Raymond Williams
- *Further Studies in a Dying Culture* by Christopher Caudwell (Publication Date Unknown)

Which of the following assumptions are true in the context of New Criticism?

A. The new movement in literature popularised closed reading of the text.
B. The leading critics of New Criticism are Allen Tate, Robert Penn Warren, R.P. Blackmur and Kenneth Burke.
C. The critical approach is extensively used in the study of novels and plays.
D. This critical approach tends to discredit historical, social and political contexts of a work of literature.
E. J.C. Ransom published a book New Criticism wherein he appreciates I.A. Richards, William Empson and T.S. Eliot.

Choose the correct answer from the options given below:

1. (A), (B) and (C) Only
2. (B), (C) and (D) Only
3. (C), (D) and (E) Only
4. (A), (B) and (D) Only

Explanations:

Answer: 4. (A), (B) and (D) Only

New Criticism

- New Criticism focused on art's intrinsic value exclusively.
- Emphasized text's autonomy, ignoring author's or historical context.
- **Introduced refined close analytic reading techniques for texts.**
- Early influences include I.A. Richards and William Empson.
- T.S. Eliot contributed with essays on literary tradition.
- **John Crowe Ransom's work formally identified New Criticism principles.**
- Associated figures: **Cleanth Brooks, R.P. Blackmur, Warren, Wimsatt.**
- Diverse pronouncements, not a uniform school of thought.
- Eclipsed by other critical modes in Anglo-American criticism by 1970s.
- Poetry seen as unique discourse for conveying feeling, thought.
- Distinguished from scientific or philosophical language, yet equally valid.
- Defined and formalized poetic thought, language qualities.
- Close reading emphasized words' connotative, associative values.

- ➤ **Focused on figurative language's multiple functions in poetry.**
- ➤ Poetic form and content deemed inseparable by critics.
- ➤ Reading particular words, including tensions, is poem's meaning.
- ➤ Rephrasing poem's language considered to alter its content.
- ➤ **Coined phrase "the heresy of paraphrase" by Cleanth Brooks.**
- ➤ **The Well Wrought Urn illustrated close reading importance.**
- ➤ Asserted that art communicates unexpressable in other language forms.
- ➤ Believed in defining formal qualities of poetic language.
- ➤ Utilized close reading for connotative value in words.
- ➤ Analyzed figurative language: symbol, metaphor, image in works.
- ➤ Viewed poetic experience as inseparable from poem's form.
- ➤ Promoted understanding poetry through unresolved tensions within.

Question 80

Which one of these is not a literary journal/ magazine?

1. The Egoist
2. The Criterion
3. The English Review
4. The Hundred and One Dalmatians

Explanations:

Answer: The Hundred and One Dalmatians

- ➤ *The Hundred and One Dalmatians*: **A children's novel** by Dodie Smith.
- ➤ *The Egoist* by **George Meredith,** published in three volumes in 1879.
- ➤ **The Egoist: Magazine:** Operating from 1914 to 1919, "The Egoist".
- ➤ **The Criterion** founded by T.S. Eliot, from October 1922 to January 1939.
- ➤ **The English Review,** initiated by Ford Madox Hueffer in 1908.

Question 81

Match List I with List II

List I (Work)	List II (Character)
A. Charles Dickens' Martin Chuzzlewit	I. Abraham Durbeyfield -
B. G.B. Shaw's The Doctor's Dilemma	II. Harry

C. Thomas Hardy's Tess of d' Urbervilles	III. Sir Ralph Bloomfield Bonnington
D. T.S. Eliot's The Family Reunion	IV. Mrs Gamp

Choose the correct answer from the options given below:

1. A - IV, B - III, C - II, D - I
2. A - III, B -II, C -IV, D - I
3. A - III, B - II, C - I, D - IV
4. A - IV, B -III, C - I, D- II

Explanations:

Answer: 4. A - IV, B -III, C - 1, D- II

> **Sarah Gamp** *from Martin Chuzzlewit* **by Charles Dickens.**
> **Sir Ralph Bloomfield Bonington** *from The Doctor's Dilemma* **by Shaw**.
> *Tess of the d'Urbervilles* by Thomas Hardy, first serialized in 1891.
> **Harry from *The Family Reunion,*** a play by T. S. Eliot..

Question 82

Arrange the following critical texts chronologically on the basis of their publication:

A. The Historical Novel (George Lukacs)
B. The New Criticism (T.S. Eliot) (Wrong option)
C. The Business of Criticism (Helen Gardner)
D. The Political Unconscious (Frederic Jameson)
E. Essays on Ideology (Louis Althusser)

Choose the correct answer from the options given below:

1. B,E,D,A,C
2. B,C,A,D,E
3. B,C,D,A,E
4 B,E,A,D,C

Explanations:

Answer: 2. B,C,A,D,E Corrected (**BACED**)

- ➢ B. John Crowe Ransom's <u>1941 book The New Criticism.</u>
- ➢ A. György Lukács' *The Historical Novel (1955)*
- ➢ C. *The Business of Criticism (1959)* by Dame Helen Gardner
- ➢ E. Louis Althusser's <u>essay, "Ideology and Ideological State Apparatuses" (1969</u>
- ➢ D. Fredric Jameson's <u>1981 book, *The Political Unconscious: Narrative as a Socially Symbolic Act.*</u>

Question 83

Chronologically arrange the following works on literary criticism in order of their publication:

A. An Apologie for Poetrie
B. The Art of Rhetorique
C. Preface to Lyrical Ballads
D. An Essays in Criticism
E. The Metaphysical Poets

Choose the correct answer from the options given below:

1. E,A,B,C,D
2. B,A,C,D,E
3. C,D,B,A, E
4. ACE D.B

Explanations:
Answer: 2. B,A,C,D,E **Corrected (B,A,D,C,E)**

- ➢ Thomas Wilson (1524–1581) known for his contributions to <u>English literature, his works "The Art of Logique" (1551) and "The Arte of Rhetorique" (1553)..</u>
- ➢ Sir Philip Sidney wrote *An Apologie for Poetrie* written in 1581 but published in 1595.
- ➢ *An Essay on Criticism (1711)* by Alexander Pope (1688–1744).
- ➢ *The Preface to Lyrical Ballads (1800)* by William Wordsworth.
- ➢ *The Metaphysical Poets (1921)* by Eliot first published in the Times Literary Supplement..

Aldous Huxley (1894-1963)

Life and Literary Career

- **Aldous Huxley**: English novelist known for **wit** and satire.
- Best known for **Brave New World (1932)** dystopia.
- Born into the **prominent Huxley family** in England.
- Graduated from **Balliol College, Oxford**, in English literature.
- Early works include **short stories, poetry, and travel writing**.
- Edited **Oxford Poetry** and wrote **screenplays**.
- Lived in **Los Angeles, USA**, from 1937 until death.
- Nominated for the **Nobel Prize in Literature** nine times.
- Elected **Companion of Literature**, Royal Society of Literature.
- First novels, **Crome Yellow** and **Antic Hay**, satirical.
- Works like **Those Barren Leaves** mocked intellectual pretensions.
- **Point Counter Point** continued satirical themes on society.
- **Brave New World** critiqued **politics** and **technology** trends.
- Vision of a **scientifically controlled caste system** depicted.
- **Eyeless in Gaza** explored **emptiness** and **Hindu mysticism**.
- **Hindu philosophy** influenced later works like **The Perennial Philosophy**.
- In **After Many a Summer**, critiqued **American culture**.
- **The Devils of Loudun**: Psychological study of **demonic possession**.
- **The Doors of Perception** described **mescaline experiences**.
- Last novel, **Island (1962)**, envisioned a **utopian society**.
- Recognized as one of the **foremost intellectuals** of his time.
- Blended satire, **philosophy**, and **spirituality** in diverse works.

Novels:

- *Crome Yellow (1921)*
- *Antic Hay (1923)*
- *Those Barren Leaves (1925)*
- *Point Counter Point (1928)*
- *Brave New World (1932)*
- *Eyeless in Gaza (1936)*
- *After Many a Summer (1939)*
- *Time Must Have a Stop (1944)*
- *Ape and Essence (1948)*
- *The Genius and the Goddess (1955)*
- *Island (1962)*

Crome Yellow (1921)

- ➤ **Characters**: Denis Stone, Anne, Mr. Barbecue-Smith, and others.
- ➤ **Setting**: Guests visit Crome Yellow estate, debating art, life.
- ➤ **Plot Start**: Denis loves Anne but struggles to express feelings.
- ➤ **Key Theme**: Satire on intellectuals' shallow philosophies and pretensions.
- ➤ **Conflict**: Denis's jealousy grows as Anne flirts with others.
- ➤ **Important Line**: "Words are the only things that last forever."
- ➤ **Event**: Mr. Barbecue-Smith writes using "automatic inspiration" humorously mocked.
- ➤ **Revelation**: Anne reveals her romantic interest lies elsewhere.
- ➤ **Resolution**: Denis departs, disillusioned but wiser about human nature.
- ➤ **Ending Note**: Satirical take on 1920s intellectual and artistic society.

Point Counter Point (1928)

- ➤ **It is Huxley's longest novel.**
- ➤ **Characters**: Philip, Elinor, Spandrell, Rampion, and Walter pivotal figures.
- ➤ **Theme**: Explores contrasting philosophies, science, art, and morality.
- ➤ **Philip**: Struggles with emotional detachment and intellectualism.
- ➤ **Elinor**: Represents loyalty, struggles with Philip's indifference.
- ➤ **Spandrell**: Nihilistic, plots a murder to find life's meaning.
- ➤ **Rampion**: Critiques modern society, embodies creative, natural living.
- ➤ **Walter**: Seeks sensual pleasure but suffers from moral emptiness.
- ➤ **Important Event**: Spandrell's orchestration of a murder reveals nihilism.
- ➤ **Important Line**: "Music of life lacks harmony or counterpoint."
- ➤ **Ending**: Novel concludes ambiguously, reflecting unresolved human conflict.

Brave New World (1932)

- ➤ **Brave New World** is a **dystopian novel** by **Aldous Huxley**.
- ➤ Written in **1931**, published in **1932**.
- ➤ Set in a **futuristic World State**, hierarchically engineered.
- ➤ Explores **reproductive technology**, **psychological manipulation**, **conditioning**.
- ➤ Society's structure challenged by the **story's protagonist**.

- ➤ Huxley revisited themes in **Brave New World Revisited (1958)**.
- ➤ **Island (1962)** serves as a **utopian counterpart**.
- ➤ Compared with **George Orwell's 1984 (1949)** inversion.
- ➤ Ranked **5th best 20th-century novel** by **Modern Library**.

Summary:

- ➤ **Set in 2540 CE**, or **AF 632** ("after Ford").
- ➤ **Henry Ford's assembly line** is revered as **god-like**.
- ➤ **World State** society emphasizes **science and efficiency**.
- ➤ **Emotions and individuality** are conditioned out of **children**.
- ➤ **"Every one belongs to everyone else"** governs relationships.
- ➤ Children created at **Central London Hatchery and Conditioning Centre**.
- ➤ **Cloning increases population** in the futuristic **World State**.
- ➤ Citizens sorted into **classes** as **embryos**.
- ➤ **Chemicals condition embryos** into predetermined **classes**.
- ➤ **Alphas bred as leaders, Epsilons as laborers**.
- ➤ **Class system:** Alpha, Beta, Gamma, Delta, **Epsilon**.
- ➤ **Bernard Marx**, an Alpha, is the **main character**.
- ➤ Marx and **Lenina Crowne** visit a **"savage reservation"**.
- ➤ Find **Linda** and her son **John (Savage)** there.
- ➤ **John is the Director's son**, a lost family secret.
- ➤ Marx uses John to expose the **Director's procreation**.
- ➤ **Director resigns** after being called **"father"** publicly.
- ➤ **Linda addicted to soma**, dies in **a hospital**.
- ➤ **John protests soma**, causes **chaos in the hospital**.
- ➤ **John hates society**, escapes to **a lighthouse**.
- ➤ **Tourists gawk** at John's **self-flagellation spectacle**.
- ➤ Whips himself, a woman, and crowds intensify spectacle.
- ➤ **Lenina appears**, John tries to whip **her too**.
- ➤ Appalled by soma use, John **hangs himself**.
- ➤ **John's death** reflects rejection of **World State's values**.

WH Auden (1907-1973)

Life and Career

- ➤ **W.H. Auden** born in **York, England**, February **21, 1907**.
- ➤ Moved to **Birmingham** during **childhood**, educated at **Oxford**.
- ➤ Influenced by **Thomas Hardy, Robert Frost**, and others.

- ➢ Inspired by **William Blake**, **Dickinson**, and **Hopkins**.
- ➢ **Old English verse** shaped his poetic style.
- ➢ At **Oxford**, Auden's **poetic talent** became apparent.
- ➢ Formed friendships with **Stephen Spender, Isherwood**.
- ➢ **Privately printed Poems** appeared in **1928**.
- ➢ 1930's **Poems** established Auden's **poetic voice**.
- ➢ Admired for **technical virtuosity**, diverse verse forms.
- ➢ Incorporated **popular culture** and **current events**.
- ➢ Intellectual range included **literature**, **art**, and **theories**.
- ➢ Mimicked writing styles of **Yeats**, **Dickinson**, and others.
- ➢ Poems reflect **journeys**, literal or metaphorical.
- ➢ Travels to **Germany**, **Iceland**, **China**, influenced verse.
- ➢ Served in **Spanish Civil War**, moved to **U.S.**
- ➢ Met **Chester Kallman**, became **American citizen**.
- ➢ Early career advocated **socialism, Freudian psychoanalysis**.
- ➢ Later focused on **Christianity**, modern **Protestant theology**.
- ➢ Auden was **playwright, librettist**, and **essayist**.
- ➢ Influenced poets on **both sides of Atlantic**.
- ➢ Served as **Chancellor**, Academy of **American Poets**.
- ➢ Divided life between **New York** and **Austria**.
- ➢ Died in **Vienna**, September **29, 1973**.
- ➢ Considered **greatest English poet** of twentieth century.
- ➢ **F. R. Leavis**, wrote that Auden's ironic style was *"self-defensive, self-indulgent or merely irresponsible"*;
- ➢ **Harold Bloom**, who wrote *"**Close thy Auden, open thy [Wallace] Stevens**,"*
- ➢ The first full-length study of Auden was Richard Hoggart's ***Auden: An Introductory Essay (1951).***

- ➢ In 1928 he wrote his first dramatic work, ***Paid on Both Sides***, subtitled ***"A Charade"***
- ➢ ***The Orators: An English Study*** (1932; revised editions, 1934, 1966)
- ➢ His verse drama ***The Dance of Death (1933)***.
- ➢ His next play ***The Dog Beneath the Skin (1935)***.
- ➢ ***The Ascent of F6 (1937)***, another play written **with Isherwood**.
- ➢ This **play included** the first version of ***"Funeral Blues" ("Stop all the clocks")***.
- ➢ ***On This Island*** is a book of poems first published under the title

- ***Look, Stranger!*** in 1936.
- ➤ ***Letters from Iceland*** is a travel book written **with Louis MacNeice**, published in 1937.
- ➤ ***Journey to a War (1939)*** a travel book in prose and verse, was written **with Isherwood**.
- ➤ ***Another Time (1940)***, together with poems including:
  - ○ *"Dover"*,
  - ○ *"As He Is"*,
  - ○ *"Musée des Beaux Arts"*
  - ○ All of which were written before he moved to America in 1939),
  - ○ *"In Memory of W. B. Yeats"*
  - ○ *"The Unknown Citizen"*,
  - ○ *"Law Like Love"*,
  - ○ *"September 1, 1939"*,
  - ○ "In Memory of Sigmund Freud" (all written in America).
- ➤ In 1940 Auden wrote a long philosophical poem *"New Year Letter"*.
- ➤ **The Double Man (1941)**
  - ○ *"Canzone"*
  - ○ *"Kairos and Logos"*
- ➤ ***For the Time Being***, 1944
  - ○ *"For the Time Being: A Christmas Oratorio"*
  - ○ *"The Sea and the Mirror: A Commentary on Shakespeare's The Tempest.*
- ➤ ***The Age of Anxiety: A Baroque Eclogue*** (published separately in 1947)
- ➤ *The Enchafèd Flood: The Romantic Iconography of the Sea (1950)*
  - ○ Based on a series of lectures on the image of the sea in romantic literature.
- ➤ Between 1949 and 1954 he worked on a sequence of seven ***Good Friday poems, titled "Horae Canonicae"***
- ➤ ***The Shield of Achilles (1955)***
- ➤ ***Homage to Clio (1960)***
- ➤ ***His prose book The Dyer's Hand (1962)***
- ➤ ***About the House (1965)***
  - ○ ***"Thanksgiving for a Habitat"***
  - ○ Written in various styles that included an imitation of William Carlos Williams.

- ➤ **"Funeral Blues"** first appeared in **The Ascent of F6**.
- ➤ Auden **rewrote** it later as a **cabaret song**.
- ➤ Both versions set to **music by Benjamin Britten**.
- ➤ Published as **"Funeral Blues"** in **1940 Another Time**.
- ➤ **Seamus Perry** notes similarities to **Cole Porter's poems**.
- ➤ Perry calls Auden's work **"ingenious" and "witty"**.
- ➤ Not as **"light"** as its **cabaret origins suggest**.
- ➤ **"True immensity of love learned through absence."**
- ➤ **Key line**: "I thought love would last forever."
- ➤ Final lines: **"Pour away the ocean... no good."**
- ➤ Lack of rhyme in **"woods" and "wood"** intentional.
- ➤ Poem **"momentarily distracted by grief,"** Perry says.
- ➤ **John G. Blair** highlights **imperative mood's attention**.
- ➤ **Heidi Hartwig**: Interpretation depends on **presentation**.
- ➤ **Joseph Warren Beach**: First stanzas reference **mundane things**.
- ➤ Second stanzas reference **balladic elements** like **heavens**.
- ➤ Two halves show **"cosmic disillusion"** of interwar period.
- ➤ Piecing halves together makes poem **"lively,"** Beach notes.
- ➤ Combines **everyday and cosmic themes**, enhancing **appeal**.
- ➤ Poem resonates with readers' **diverse interpretations**.

Stop all the clocks, cut off the telephone,
Prevent the dog from barking with a juicy bone,
Silence the pianos and with muffled drum
Bring out the coffin, let the mourners come.

Let aeroplanes circle moaning overhead
Scribbling on the sky the message 'He is Dead'.
Put crepe bows round the white necks of the public doves,
Let the traffic policemen wear black cotton gloves.

He was my North, my South, my East and West,
My working week and my Sunday rest,
My noon, my midnight, my talk, my song;
I thought that love would last forever: I was wrong.

The stars are not wanted now; put out every one,
Pack up the moon and dismantle the sun,

Pour away the ocean and sweep up the wood;
For nothing now can ever come to any good.

The Ascent of F6 (1936)

- **The Ascent of F6** by **Auden and Isherwood.**
- Published in **1936**, their most **successful play.**
- Major contribution to **English poetic drama (1930s).**
- **Seen as parable** on will, leadership, power.
- Reflects concerns about **Europe's political tensions.**
- Story of **Michael Ransom**, climber on **F6 mountain.**
- Sponsored by **British press** and **government.**
- **Ransom's haste** to compete destroys his expedition.
- Set on **British-Ostnian colony border.**

September 1, 1939 (1939)

- **"September 1, 1939"** by **W.H. Auden**, published **1940.**
- Reflects Auden's **emotional response** to **World War II.**
- Title refers to **Germany's invasion** of **Poland.**
- Became one of Auden's **best-known poems.**
- Auden criticized its **"incurable dishonesty"**, revising it frequently.
- **Final stanza removed** in **1945** and later **repudiated.**
- Omitted from **Collected Shorter Poems (1966).**
- Echoes stanza form of **Yeats' "Easter, 1916".**
- Describes **historical failures** leading to **war outbreak.**
- Explores Germany's history **"from Luther until now".**
- Discusses **internal conflicts** mirroring **external war conflicts.**
- Influenced by **C.G. Jung's Psychology and Religion (1938).**
- Final stanzas declare **"We must love one another or die."**
- Highlights presence of **"the Just"**, exchanging **hope.**
- Ends with hope to **"show an affirming flame."**

Musée des Beaux Arts (1940)

- **"Musée des Beaux Arts"** published in **Another Time (1940).**
- Starts with **"About suffering they were never wrong."**
- Comments on **indifference** to **suffering** in the world.
- Written in a tone of **critical irony.**
- **Anguish** shown as **commonplace**, not dramatic tragedy.
- First stanza observes **tragedy often goes unnoticed.**
- Even **"dreadful martyrdom must run its course."**

- ➢ Torturer's **horse scratches rump**, ignoring suffering.
- ➢ Second stanza central image: **Fall of Icarus** painting.
- ➢ **Flemish Renaissance painting** depicts **indifference to tragedy**.
- ➢ **Figures in foreground oblivious** to Icarus' fall.
- ➢ Farmer plowing, **ship passing ignore Icarus plunging**.
- ➢ Uses **artwork to explore suffering's impact** on humanity.
- ➢ Poem discusses **"suffering" amidst mundane human actions**.
- ➢ Quotes: **"someone eating or opening a window."**
- ➢ Ekphrasis technique describes **Landscape with Fall of Icarus**.
- ➢ Painting once attributed to **Bruegel**, now **early copy**.
- ➢ **White legs disappear into the green sea.**
- ➢ Disaster caused by **flying too close to sun**.
- ➢ Poem balances **general suffering** and **mythical tragedy**.
- ➢ **Long, irregular lines** enhance **vernacular phrasing**.
- ➢ **Dogs go on** with their **"doggy life."**
- ➢ Relies on **two additional Bruegel paintings** for imagery.
- ➢ Bruegel paintings evoke **details matching Auden's language**.
- ➢ No **martyrdom depicted**, suggesting other works referenced.

The Age of Anxiety (1948)

- ➢ **The Age of Anxiety** by **W.H. Auden**, 1947.
- ➢ Described as a **"baroque eclogue"** by critics.
- ➢ Auden's **last long poem**, Pulitzer winner **1948**.
- ➢ Explores **human isolation** in the **modern age**.
- ➢ Reflects lack of **tradition or religious belief**.
- ➢ **Setting**: Nighttime bar in **New York City**.
- ➢ **Four strangers**—three men, one woman—meet and drink.
- ➢ **Carousing ends** in the **woman's apartment**.
- ➢ Two men leave, third **passes out drunk**.
- ➢ Examines **spiritual emptiness, loneliness**, and anxiety.
- ➢ Ends at **dawn** on New York's **streets**.

The Shield of Achilles (1955)

- ➢ **The Shield of Achilles** is a **poem by W.H. Auden**.
- ➢ First **published in 1952**, part of **1955 collection**.
- ➢ **Response to ekphrasis** of Achilles' shield in **Iliad**.
- ➢ Written in **two stanza forms**, short and long lines.
- ➢ **Shorter lines** describe shield-making by **Hephaestus**.
- ➢ **Thetis expects** peace and happiness on the **shield**.

- ➢ **Hephaestus creates** a barren, impersonal **modern world.**
- ➢ First scene: an **anonymous army listens dispassionately.**
- ➢ Second scene: a **crowd passively watches three executions.**
- ➢ Third scene: a **urchin throws stone at bird.**
- ➢ **"Girls are raped, two boys knife a third."**
- ➢ **No world exists where promises are kept.**
- ➢ **Thetis cries in dismay** at the shield's content.
- ➢ **Her son Achilles** "would not live long."
- ➢ **Contrasts Homer's lyrical world** with Auden's modernity.
- ➢ Homer's world combines **imagination, peace amid warfare.**
- ➢ Auden's world depicts **violence, barrenness, and hopelessness.**
- ➢ **Reflects the despair** of a post-war modern world.

Auden Group or Macspaunday

- ➢ The **Auden Group, or the Auden Generation**, is a group of British and Irish writers active in the 1930s that included:
    - o W. H. Auden,
    - o Louis MacNeice,
    - o Cecil Day-Lewis,
    - o Stephen Spender,
    - o Christopher Isherwood,
    - o and sometimes Edward Upward and Rex Warner.
    - o **They were sometimes called simply the Thirties poets.**
- ➢ "MacSpaunday" was a name invented by Roy Campbell in his Talking Bronco (1946), to designate a composite figure made up of the four poets:
    1. Louis MacNeice ("Mac")
    2. Stephen Spender ("sp")
    3. W. H. Auden ("au-n")
    4. Cecil Day-Lewis ("day")

Question 84

Who among the following is not a recipient of the Nobel Prize for Literature?

1. Winston Churchill
2. Madam Curie
3. T.S. Eliot
4. W.H. Auden

5. **W.H. Auden and Madam Curie**

Correct Explanations:
Sir Winston Leonard Spencer Churchill won the Nobel prize in 1953.

The publication of Four Quartets led to T.S. Eliot's recognition as the greatest living English poet and man of letters, and in **1948 he was awarded both the Order of Merit and the Nobel Prize for Literature.**

Other Explanations:
W. H. Auden was an English-born poet and man of letters who achieved early fame in the 1930s as a hero of the left during the Great Depression.

Marie Curie was a Polish and naturalized-French physicist and chemist who conducted pioneering research on radioactivity. **She was the first woman to win a Nobel Prize, the first person and the only woman to win a Nobel Prize twice, and the only person to win a Nobel Prize in two scientific fields.**

Question 85
Given below are two statements :

Statement I: According to W.H. Auden, The Importance of Being Earnest is the purest example in English Literature of a 'Verbal Opera'.
Statement II: Oscar Wilde possessed profound insight into the range of the arts that, in a combined form, make theatre performance possible.

In light of the above statements. Choose the correct answer from the options given below:

1. **Both Statement I and Statement I are true**
2. Both Statement I and Statement II are false
3. Statement I is true but Statement II is false
4. Statement II is false but Statement I is true

Correct Explanations:
The key to decoding the play's meaning lies in its style, which transforms this silliness into a way of life. Wilde's wit floats like a butterfly over the play's absurdities and stings like a bee, exposing the deep triviality of "earnest"

social convention. For example, in the play's opening scene, Algernon and his butler Lane glide effortlessly among taboo topics, touching on music and philosophy, science and life, bachelorhood and marriage, and all points. It is one of the most dazzling scenes of comic dialogue ever written in English, a virtuosic pas de deux. **W.H. Auden called The Importance of Being Earnest "the only pure verbal opera in English," and there can be no doubting its crystalline brilliance.**

Match List I with List II

List I	List II
A. Stephen Spender	l. Cargoes
B. W.H, Auden	II. Consider
C. John Masefield	lll. Adlestrop
D. Edward Thomas	IV. The Pylons

Choose the correct answer from the options given below:

1. A - I. B - II. C - III. D - IV
2. **A - IV, B - II, C - I, D - III**
3. A - II. B - I. C - IV. D - III
4. A - III. B - IV. C - I. D - II

Correct Explanations:
A. **"The Pylons" is a poem by the English poet Stephen Spender, first published in 1935**. The poem describes the modern, industrial landscape of England and the contrast between the natural world and the man-made structures that dominate it.

B. **"Consider" is a poem by the English-American poet W. H. Auden,** first published in 1947. The poem is a meditation on the nature of human suffering and the role of religion in offering hope and consolation in the face of hardship.

C. **"Cargoes" is a poem by the English poet John Masefield,** first published in 1902. The poem is a celebration of the diversity and richness of the world's trade and commerce, with each verse describing a different cargo from a different part of the world.

D. "Adlestrop" is a poem by the English poet Edward Thomas, first published in 1917. The poem describes a moment of stillness and tranquility in the midst of a train journey, as the speaker overhears the sounds and sights of the English countryside from the platform at Adlestrop station. The poem is often cited as an example of Thomas's ability to capture the beauty and fragility of the natural world.

Match List I with List II

List I	List II
A. Lions and Shadows	I. W.H. Auden
B. The Still Centre	II. Louis MacNeice
C. Translation of Agamemnon	III. Stephen Spender
D. The Sea and the Mirror	IV. Christopher Isherwood

Choose the correct answer from the options given

1. (A)-(IV), (B)-(III), (C)-(II), (D)-(I)
2. (A)-(II), (B)-(III), (C)-(I), (D)-(IV)
3. (A)-(III), (B)-(II), (C)-(IV), (D)-(I)
4. (A)- (IV), (B)-(II), (C)-(I), (D)-(III)

Explanations

Answer: 1. (A)-(IV), (B)-(III), (C)-(II), (D)-(I)

At Repton, his boarding school in Derbyshire, **Isherwood** met his lifelong friend Edward Upward, with whom he invented an imaginary English village called Mortmere, as related in his fictional autobiography, **Lions and Shadows (1938).**

The Agamemnon of Aeschylus. Translated by Louis MacNeice

"The Sea and the Mirror: A Commentary on Shakespeare's The Tempest" is a long poem by W.H. Auden, written 1942–44, and first published in 1944. Auden regarded the work as "my Ars Poetica, in the same way I believe The Tempest to have been Shakespeare's."

Arrange the correct chronological sequence of the publication of the following texts:

      A. *September 1, 1939*
      B. *The Collar*
      C. *Beppo*
      D. *Paradise Lost*
      E. *Seeing Things*

Choose the correct answer from the options given below:

      1. B, D. C, A. E
      2. B. A, E, C, D
      3. A, E, B. C, D
      4. C, B. A, D, E

Explanations
Answer: 1. B, D. C, A. E

"The Collar" is a poem written by the Welsh poet George Herbert and was published in **1633**.

Paradise Lost in blank verse by Milton. The initial version was published in **1667**.

Beppo: A Venetian Story is an extensive poem written by Lord Byron in **1817**.

"September 1, 1939" is a poem by W. H. Auden initially published in The New Republic on October 18, **1939**.

Seeing Things is the eighth collection of poetry by Seamus Heaney, the recipient of the 1995 Nobel Prize in Literature. It was published in **1991**.

W. Somerset Maugham (1874-1965)

- **W. Somerset Maugham** born **Jan. 25, 1874**, Paris.
- Known for **clear style, cosmopolitan settings**, human nature.
- **Orphaned at 10**, raised by an **uncle**.
- Educated at **King's School**, later **St. Thomas' medical school**.
- Qualified as a **doctor** in **1897**.
- First novel **Liza of Lambeth (1897)** based on experiences.
- **Success encouraged** him to **abandon medicine**.
- **Traveled in Spain**, Italy; **1908 theatrical triumph**.
- **Four plays ran simultaneously** in **London, 1908**.
- Worked as a **secret agent** during **World War I**.
- Bought a **villa on Cape Ferrat, 1928**.
- Best novels: **Of Human Bondage (1915)**, semi-autobiographical.
- **The Moon and Sixpence (1919)** inspired by **Paul Gauguin**.
- **Cakes and Ale (1930)**, caricatures of **Hardy, Walpole**.
- **The Razor's Edge (1944)** about **war veteran's quest**.
- Plays became dated, but **short stories gained popularity**.
- **Stories depict Europeans** in **alien surroundings**.
- **Philosophy explained** in **The Summing Up (1938)**.
- Work reflects **resigned atheism, cynical skepticism**.

Notable Works

- *Liza of Lambeth* include *Of Human Bondage (1915).*
- *The Moon and Sixpence (1919).*
- *The Painted Veil (1925).*
- *Cakes and Ale (1930).*
- *The Razor's Edge (1944).*
- His short stories were published in collections such as *The Casuarina Tree (1926)* and *The Mixture as Before (1940)*.

Of Human Bondage (1915)

- **Of Human Bondage** published in **1915**, Maugham's **masterwork**.
- A **semiautobiographical novel** exploring **emotional isolation**.
- **Philip Carey**, born with a **club foot**, feels sensitive.
- Becomes a **medical student** in **London**.
- Falls for a **selfish waitress**, causing **all-consuming passion**.

- ➤ Enters a **loving relationship** after finishing **medical school**.
- ➤ Possible **pregnancy forces Philip** to **reexamine life**.
- ➤ **Philip Carey**: Orphaned, sent to strict uncle's vicarage.
- ➤ **Philip's deformity**: Clubfoot shapes his insecurities, social struggles.
- ➤ **Art studies**: Moves to Paris, abandons dreams for medicine.
- ➤ **Mildred**: Obsessed with waitress; she manipulates and betrays.
- ➤ **Romantic suffering**: Mildred ruins Philip financially and emotionally.
- ➤ **Education**: Philip struggles through medical school, faces poverty.
- ➤ **Losses**: Philip loses money, suffers deaths of loved ones.
- ➤ **Sally**: Finds genuine love with kind, steady Sally.
- ➤ **Freedom**: Realizes life's meaning doesn't require grand purpose.
- ➤ **Final lesson**: Embraces ordinary happiness over unattainable ideals.

Cakes and Ale, or, The Skeleton in the Cupboard (1930)

- ➤ **Cakes and Ale** (1930) by **W. Somerset Maugham**.
- ➤ Novel exposes **social snobbery** against **Rosie Driffield**.
- ➤ Rosie's **honesty and sexual freedom** challenge propriety.
- ➤ Narrator **Ashenden** portrays Rosie in **favourable light**.
- ➤ Rosie was a **muse** for many **artists**.
- ➤ Ashenden also **enjoyed Rosie's sexual favours**.
- ➤ Title comes from **Sir Toby Belch's** remark.
- ➤ Quote from Shakespeare's **Twelfth Night**:
  "Dost thou think...no more cakes and ale?"
- ➤ **Cakes and ale** symbolize **life's pleasures**.
- ➤ Referenced in Aesop's fable, **The Town Mouse**.
- ➤ Fable moral: **"Better beans and bacon in peace..."**
- ➤ Maugham critiques **hypocrisy** and celebrates **simple joys**.
- ➤ **Characters**: Driffield, Rosie, Ashenden, and Alroy Kear introduced.
- ➤ **Plot**: Ashenden recounts his memories of Rosie Driffield.
- ➤ **Conflict**: Rosie's free spirit clashes with social conventions.
- ➤ **Flashback**: Ashenden recalls Rosie's affair during her marriage.
- ➤ **Themes**: Hypocrisy of society, art, love, and morality explored.
- ➤ **Kear's Motive**: Alroy plans to glorify Driffield's public image.
- ➤ **Important Line**: "Rosie was the true muse of life."
- ➤ **Irony**: Society venerates Driffield while dismissing Rosie's influence.
- ➤ **Symbolism**: Cakes and ale represent joy and human passion.
- ➤ **Resolution**: Rosie remains unforgettable despite societal rejection.

- ➢ **The Moon and Sixpence** published in **1919**.
- ➢ Loosely based on **French artist Paul Gauguin**.
- ➢ **Charles Strickland**, a **London stockbroker**, abandons everything.
- ➢ Moves to **Paris**, wins a friend's **wife to paint**.
- ➢ **Wife kills herself**, Strickland leaves **unaffected**.
- ➢ Settles in **Tahiti** with a **native woman**.
- ➢ **Characters**: Strickland, Blanche, Dirk, Ata; a painter's journey.
- ➢ **Plot**: Strickland abandons family for art in Tahiti.
- ➢ **Conflict**: Strickland's passion destroys lives, including Blanche's suicide.
- ➢ **Climax**: Strickland paints a masterpiece, blinded by illness.
- ➢ **Message**: "Art demands sacrifice; beauty emerges from pain."

The Razor's Edge (1944)

- ➢ **The Razor's Edge** (1944) by **W. Somerset Maugham**.
- ➢ The **epigraph** is taken from the **Katha Upanishad**.
- ➢ Story of **Larry Darrell**, traumatized **WWI pilot**.
- ➢ **Larry searches** for transcendent **meaning in life**.
- ➢ Told through **friends' eyes**, showing Larry's **changes**.
- ➢ **Larry thrives**, while materialistic characters face **reversals**.
- ➢ **Characters**: Larry Darrell seeks spiritual fulfillment, rejecting materialism.
- ➢ **Plot**: Larry leaves Isabel, travels to find life's meaning.
- ➢ **Conflict**: Isabel desires wealth; Larry chooses simplicity.
- ➢ **Key Event**: Sophie's tragic downfall symbolizes moral struggle.
- ➢ **Resolution**: Larry embraces enlightenment; others remain entangled.

Question 89

Which of the following novels has its epigraph taken from the Katha Upanishad?

1. The Island of Doctor Moreau by H. G. Wells
2. **The Razor's Edge by Somerset Maugham**
3. Point Counter Point by Aldous Huxley
4. A Room with a View by E. M. Forster

Correct Explanations:

The epigraph of The Razor's Edge by Somerset Maugham Wells is taken from the Katha Upanishad, an ancient Sanskrit text that is part of the Hindu scriptures. The epigraph reads: "The sharp edge of a razor is difficult to pass over; thus the wise say the path to Salvation is hard." This quote captures the essence of the novel, which follows the spiritual journey of Larry Darrell, a young American who is searching for meaning and purpose in his life. The novel deals with the themes of enlightenment, self-discovery, and the pursuit of a higher truth, and the epigraph sets the tone for the challenging and difficult path that Larry must undertake to achieve his goals. The quote also reflects the influence of Eastern philosophy and spirituality on Maugham, who spent time in India and was fascinated by its culture and traditions.

Question 90

Match List I with List II

List I	List II
A. "The Lion's Skin"	I. Washington Irving
B. "The Man who liked Dickens"	II. W. Somerset Maugham
C. "Rip Van Winkle"	III. Stephen Crane
D. "The Bride tomes to Yellow Sky"	IV. Evelyn Waugh

Choose the correct answer from the options given below:
1. A - I. B - II. C - IV. D - III
2. A - III, B - IV, C - I, D - I
3. **A - II. B - IV. C - I. D - III**
4. A - IV, B - I, C - III, D - I

Correct Explanations:

A. *"The Lion's Skin"* is actually a short story written by **W. Somerset Maugham**, a British playwright, novelist, and short story writer.
B. *"The Man who liked Dickens"* is a short story written by **Evelyn Waug.**
C. *"Rip Van Winkle"* is a short story written by **Washington Irving.**
D. *"The Bride Comes to Yellow Sky"* is a short story written by **Stephen Crane.**
E. *"The Lion's Skin"* is a short story written by Saki (H.H. Munro)

Question 91

"I recognise that its heroine is a little prig and its hero a pompous ass, but I do not care."

About which novel by Jane Austen does Somerset Maugham make this statement

1. Pride and Prejudice
2. Northanger Abbey
3. Sense and Sensibility
4. **Mansfield Park**

Explanations:
The novel by Jane Austen about which Somerset Maugham makes this statement is "Mansfield Park".

In his statement, Somerset Maugham is expressing his fondness for "Mansfield Park", despite his recognition that its heroine is a little prig (a person who is self-righteous and moralistic) and its hero a pompous ass (a person who is arrogant and conceited).

JB Priestley (1894-1984)

> - **J.B. Priestley**: British novelist, playwright, and essayist.
> - Known for **shrewd characterization** and **Yorkshire background**.
> - Achieved fame with **The Good Companions** (1929).
> - Plays explore **time slips** and **dimensions of time**.
> - Served in **World War I**, studied at **Cambridge**.
> - Early works include **The English Comic Characters** (1925).
> - Wrote **Angel Pavement** (1930), realistic depiction of office workers.
> - Famous novels include **Bright Day** (1946), **Lost Empires** (1965).
> - Plays like **Laburnum Grove** (1933) gained early success.
> - **An Inspector Calls** (1946) used **time distortion** brilliantly.

An Inspector Calls (1945)

> - **J. B. Priestley** wrote *An Inspector Calls* in **1945**.
> - Set in **April 1912**, in **fictional Brumley**, Midlands.
> - Focuses on the **wealthy Birling family**.
> - **Arthur Birling** celebrates daughter **Sheila's engagement**.

- ➢ **Gerald Croft**, Sheila's fiancé, from rival **magnate family**.
- ➢ **Eric Birling** struggles with a **drinking problem**.
- ➢ **Arthur lectures** on **self-reliance** and future success.
- ➢ Evening interrupted by **Inspector Goole's arrival**.
- ➢ **Eva Smith's suicide** investigated by **Goole**.
- ➢ **Arthur admits** firing Eva for **strike involvement**.
- ➢ **Sheila recognizes Eva**, fired her over **jealousy**.
- ➢ **Gerald startled** by Eva's alias, **Daisy Renton**.
- ➢ Gerald gave Eva **money** and a **place to stay**.
- ➢ **Eva became Gerald's mistress**, later they **parted**.
- ➢ Sheila **returns her ring**; Gerald leaves briefly.
- ➢ **Sybil Birling**, charity head, **denied Eva's financial aid**.
- ➢ **Eva pregnant**, turned away by **Sybil's committee**.
- ➢ Sybil blames **"drunken young man"** for Eva's **pregnancy**.
- ➢ **Eric admits fathering Eva's child** after heavy drinking.
- ➢ **Eric stole money** to support Eva, but she refused.
- ➢ **Goole reveals** everyone contributed to Eva's **despair**.
- ➢ **Goole warns** society of **"fire, blood, and anguish"**.
- ➢ Gerald suspects **Inspector Goole is a fraud**.
- ➢ **Arthur confirms** no **Inspector Goole** exists.
- ➢ No **recent suicide** cases reported at the infirmary.
- ➢ **Gerald and elder Birlings celebrate**, feel relieved.
- ➢ **Sheila and Eric feel guilty**, resolve to change.
- ➢ Arthur receives a **call** about a **real suicide**.
- ➢ **Police arriving** to investigate the **Birling family**.
- ➢ **Goole's identity remains unexplained**, confessions remain true.

Evelyn Waugh (1903-1966)

- ➢ **Arthur Evelyn St. John Waugh**, English **writer** of novels.
- ➢ Wrote **biographies, travel books,** and reviews.
- ➢ Novels derived from **firsthand experience**, precisely written.
- ➢ Pre-1939 novels described as **satirical works**.
- ➢ Key novels: **Decline and Fall (1928)** and **Vile Bodies (1930)**.
- ➢ Other satirical works: **Black Mischief (1932)** and **Scoop (1938)**.
- ➢ **The Loved One (1948)** satirized California's **mortician industry**.
- ➢ **Brideshead Revisited (1945)** explored faith and providence.
- ➢ **Converted to Roman Catholicism** in **1930**.
- ➢ **Helena (1950)** depicted mother of **Constantine the Great**.
- ➢ Focused on a moment in **Christian history**.

- ➢ War trilogy: **Men at Arms (1952)** and sequels.
- ➢ Sequels: **Officers and Gentlemen (1955)** and **Unconditional Surrender (1961)**.
- ➢ **"The Man who liked Dickens"** is a short story written by **Evelyn Waugh**
- ➢ Trilogy examined **World War II's eternal struggles**.
- ➢ Themes: **Good vs. Evil** and **civilization vs. barbarism**.
- ➢ Waugh's works balance **satire and theological depth**.
- ➢ His most famous works include:
    1. *Decline and Fall (1928)*
    2. *A Handful of Dust (1934).*
    3. *Brideshead Revisited (1945).*
    4. *The Second World War trilogy Sword of Honour (1952–1961).*

Decline and Fall (1928)

- ➢ **Decline and Fall**, Evelyn Waugh's **first novel**, published **1928**.
- ➢ A **social satire** based on **teaching experiences**.
- ➢ **Protagonist Paul Pennyfeather** passively accepts life's **challenges**.
- ➢ Expelled for **indecent behaviour** from **Scone College**, Oxford.
- ➢ Becomes a **teacher**, later involved with **Margot**, a society woman.
- ➢ **Margot's white slave trade** leads to **Paul's imprisonment**.
- ➢ Margot **engineers his escape**, Paul **returns to Scone College**.
- ➢ Pretends to be **Paul Pennyfeather**, cousin of notorious namesake.

A Handful of Dust (1934)

- ➢ **A Handful of Dust**, satirical novel by **Evelyn Waugh**.
- ➢ Published in **1934**, often considered Waugh's **best**.
- ➢ Explores **amorality** and **death of spiritual values**.
- ➢ Influenced by Waugh's **failed marriage** and **Catholicism**.
- ➢ Highlights parallels between **London society** and **jungle barbarity**.
- ➢ **Tony Last**: A traditionalist, loves his Gothic estate, Hetton.
- ➢ **Brenda Last**: Unfaithful wife, begins affair with John Beaver.
- ➢ **John Beaver**: A social climber, charms Brenda for advantage.
- ➢ **Hetton**: Tony's beloved home symbolizes decaying traditions.
- ➢ **Affair revealed**: Brenda demands divorce and financial settlement.
- ➢ **Tragedy strikes**: Son John Andrew dies in horse accident.
- ➢ **Tony escapes**: Joins expedition to South America after loss.
- ➢ **Jungle ordeal**: Tony held captive by crazed Mr. Todd.

- ➢ **Famous line**: "Better to exist in squalor than Hetton."
- ➢ **Bleak ending**: Tony trapped reading Dickens, Brenda remarries.

Brideshead Revisited (1945)

- ➢ **Brideshead Revisited** by **Evelyn Waugh**, published **1945**.
- ➢ Set from the **1920s to early 1940s**.
- ➢ Follows **Charles Ryder's life**, romances, and friendships.
- ➢ Explores Ryder's ties with **wealthy Flyte family**.
- ➢ Flytes live in **Brideshead Castle**, a palatial mansion.
- ➢ Ryder's relationships include **Sebastian** and **Julia Flyte**.
- ➢ Themes of **English aristocracy nostalgia** and **Catholicism**.
- ➢ **Waugh** aimed to show **"the operation of divine grace."**
- ➢ Story depicts the **Roman Catholic Marchmain family**.
- ➢ Family includes **Lord Marchmain**, **Sebastian**, and **Julia**.
- ➢ Members show **indifference** or **rejection of faith initially**.
- ➢ By the end, signs of **faith acceptance emerge**.

Graham Green (1904-1991)

Life and Career

- ➢ **Greene born** October 2, 1904, in **Berkhamsted**, England.
- ➢ Avid **reader**, enjoyed **Rider Haggard's works**.
- ➢ **Father**: Headmaster at **prestigious Berkhamsted School**.
- ➢ Hated **boarding school**, ran away to **London**.
- ➢ Underwent **six months psychoanalysis**, fascinated by **dreams**.
- ➢ Studied **modern history** at **Oxford College**.
- ➢ Published first book, **Babbling April**, in **1925**.
- ➢ Worked as **journalist**, converted to **Roman Catholicism** in 1926.
- ➢ Married **Vivien Dayrell-Browning** in **1927**, had two children.
- ➢ First affair in **1946** with **Catherine Walston**.
- ➢ Separated from **Vivien** in **1948**, never divorced.
- ➢ First novel, **The Man Within** (1929), earned **critical praise**.
- ➢ Next two books were **commercial failures**.
- ➢ Became **book reviewer** at The Spectator.
- ➢ Wrote **Stamboul Train** (1932), a **popular spy novel**.
- ➢ Traveled to **Liberia**, inspiring **famous travelogues**.
- ➢ Returned to **Spectator** in 1936 as **film critic**.
- ➢ Published **Brighton Rock** (1938), a **celebrated work**.

- ➤ **Mexico trip** inspired **The Power and the Glory.**
- ➤ Works include **"Catholic Trilogy"**: *Power, Heart, Affair.*
- ➤ Too **old to enlist**, joined **Secret Service.**
- ➤ War experience inspired **The Heart of the Matter.**
- ➤ Wrote **Our Man in Havana** (1960), inspired by **service.**
- ➤ Became **director** at **Eyre and Spottiswoode** post-war.
- ➤ Famous screenplay, **The Third Man**, written in **1949.**
- ➤ Traveled to **Malaya, Vietnam,** inspired **The Quiet American.**
- ➤ Wrote **novels, short stories, plays, travel pieces.**
- ➤ Settled in **Switzerland**, died of **pneumonia** in 1991.
- ➤ Greene lived to **86 years**, buried in **Corseaux Cemetery.**
- ➤ Remembered for **cinematic style** and **profound works.**

Works of Graham Green:

- ➤ *The Man Within (début—1929)*
    - o It tells the story of **Francis Andrews**, a reluctant smuggler.
    - o **Title taken from Browne's Religio Medici:**
        - ▪ *'There's another man within me that's angry with me.'*
- ➤ *Stamboul Train (1932) (also published as Orient Express in the U.S.)*
- ➤ *It's a Battlefield (1934)*
- ➤ *England Made Me (also published as The Shipwrecked) (1935)*
        - ▪ Tthe travails of **ne'er-do-well** Anthony Farrant
- ➤ *A Gun for Sale (1936)*
- ➤ *Journey Without Maps (1936)*
- ➤ *Brighton Rock (1938)*
    - o **Characters**: Pinkie, a violent gang leader; Rose, his naïve lover.
    - o **Plot**: Pinkie murders Hale, a journalist, to secure power.
    - o **Conflict**: Ida investigates Hale's death, challenging Pinkie's control.
    - o **Key Event**: Pinkie manipulates Rose, marries her for silence.
    - o **Resolution**: Pinkie's death leaves Rose reflecting on sin.
- ➤ *The Lawless Roads (1939) (also published as Another Mexico in the U.S.)*
- ➤ *The Confidential Agent (1939)*
    - o A thriller novel. Fuelled by Benzedrine, Greene wrote it in six weeks.
    - o **D.**, a foreign agent, arrives in England undercover.
    - o Meets **Rose**, faces betrayal, murder, and emotional conflict.

- o Coal deal determines war's fate; danger intensifies.
  - o **D.** learns trust amidst deception; Rose helps him.
  - o "In chaos, humanity survives through courage and loyalty."
- ➢ ***The Power and the Glory (1940)***
- o The **title is an allusion** to the doxology often recited at the end of the **Lord's Prayer**:
  - o ***"For thine is the kingdom, the power, and the glory, forever and ever, amen."***
- o It was initially published in the United States under the title ***The Labyrinthine Ways***.
- o **Characters**: The priest (Whisky Priest) and Lieutenant.
- o **Setting**: Anti-Catholic Mexican state enforces religious suppression.
- o **Conflict**: Whisky Priest struggles with faith & moral guilt.
- o **Important Event**: Priest offers mass secretly despite persecution risks.
- o **Lieutenant's Hunt**: Determined to capture the fugitive priest.
- o **Symbolism**: The priest represents flawed yet persistent spirituality.
- o **Climactic Betrayal**: Priest caught while aiding a dying man.
- o **Execution**: Priest faces death with courage, embracing redemption.
- o **Important Line**: "God might love a coward more than most."
- o **Theme**: Grace exists despite human flaws and persecution.
- ➢ *The Ministry of Fear (1943)*
- ➢ ***The Heart of the Matter (1948)***
  - o The book details a life-changing moral **crisis for Henry Scobie.**
  - o **Characters**: Scobie, Louise, Helen, and Wilson drive the plot.
  - o **Conflict**: Scobie's love for Helen tests his faith.
  - o **Event**: Scobie falsifies actions, guilt consumes his conscience.
  - o **Climax**: "To love is to destroy one's self."
  - o **Resolution**: Scobie's suicide reveals his tortured moral struggle.
- ➢ *The Third Man (1949) (novella written as a preliminary to Greene's screenplay for the film The Third Man)*
- ➢ ***The End of the Affair (1951)***
- o **It is the fourth and final of Greene's "Catholic novels" tetralogy**, following *Brighton Rock (1938), The Power and the Glory (1940), and The Heart of the Matter (1948)*.
- o **Set in London** during and just after the **Second World War.**
- o **Characters**: Bendrix, Sarah, Henry, and their intertwined relationships.

- o **Plot**: Bendrix recalls his passionate affair with Sarah.
- o **Conflict**: Sarah ends the affair, citing divine intervention.
- o **Resolution**: Bendrix confronts jealousy, faith, and Sarah's death.
- o **Important Line**: "Hatred seems to survive longer than love."
- ➢ *Twenty-One Stories (1954) (short stories)*
- ➢ *Loser Takes All (1955)*
- ➢ ***The Quiet American (1955)***
    - o The novel concerns the relationship between the **American Alden Pyle, a quiet, naive CIA operative**, and the story's narrator, **Thomas Fowler, a world-weary British journalist.**
- ➢ *The Potting Shed (1956)*
- ➢ ***Our Man in Havana (1958)***
    - o **Set in Cuba**, before the **communist revolution**.
    - o A **comical spy story** with **British intelligence**.
    - o Follows a **vacuum-cleaner salesman's misadventures**.
    - o **Characters**: Wormold, a vacuum cleaner salesman, becomes a spy.
    - o **Plot**: Wormold fabricates intelligence, selling fake reports to MI6.
    - o **Conflict**: Drawings of vacuum parts pose as weapons.
    - o **Climax**: Wormold's lies endanger lives, including his own.
    - o **Resolution**: "A good liar," Wormold escapes unscathed.
- ➢ *A Burnt-Out Case (1960)*
- ➢ *In Search of a Character: Two African Journals (1961)*
- ➢ *The Comedians (1966)*
- ➢ *Travels with My Aunt (1969)*
- ➢ ***A Sort of Life (1971)***
    - o The first volume of autobiography.
- ➢ *The Honorary Consul (1973)*
- ➢ *The Human Factor (1978)*
- ➢ *Ways of Escape (1980)*
- ➢ *Doctor Fischer of Geneva (1980)*
- ➢ *Monsignor Quixote (1982)*
- ➢ *Getting To Know The General: The Story of an Involvement (1984)*
- ➢ *The Tenth Man (1985)*
- ➢ *The Last Word (1990) (short stories)*

Story to Remember all the works in chronological order:

In a **quiet countryside**, a young man, **The Man Within** (1929), boarded the mysterious **Stamboul Train** (1932). He overheard a stranger saying, **"It's a Battlefield"** (1934). This motivated him to leave behind his past in **England Made Me** (1935), becoming **The Shipwrecked**.

To survive, he planned **A Gun for Sale** (1936), which led to a dangerous **Journey Without Maps** (1936). In the gritty streets of **Brighton Rock** (1938), he discovered the **Lawless Roads** (1939) while escaping **Another Mexico**. He disguised himself as **The Confidential Agent** (1939), tasked with exposing **The Power and the Glory** (1940).

In the dark alleys, he felt **The Ministry of Fear** (1943) growing. But he held on to **The Heart of the Matter** (1948) to complete his mission. Then came a surprising twist: a secret plan tied to **The Third Man** (1949), a strange figure who held **The End of the Affair** (1951).

Soon after, he stumbled upon **Twenty-One Stories** (1954), detailing his exploits. But fate played a cruel game, where the **Loser Takes All** (1955). He later uncovered the shocking truth in **The Quiet American** (1955). Reflecting on life, he found solace in **The Potting Shed** (1956).

While on his final mission in **Our Man in Havana** (1958), he felt like **A Burnt-Out Case** (1960). He kept searching **In Search of a Character** (1961), recording his journey in **Two African Journals**. The discovery of **The Comedians** (1966) offered him comic relief during dark times.

On a lighter note, he went on adventures with **Travels with My Aunt** (1969). Writing **A Sort of Life** (1971) helped him make peace with his past. Later, he worked undercover as **The Honorary Consul** (1973), guided by his instincts, or rather, **The Human Factor** (1978).

Finally, he detailed his **Ways of Escape** (1980) and sought solace in the bizarre tale of **Doctor Fischer of Geneva** (1980). In his last days, he found inspiration in **Monsignor Quixote** (1982) while **Getting to Know the General** (1984). Before his curtain call, he wrote **The Tenth Man** (1985), and his swan song, **The Last Word** (1990), solidified his literary legacy.

Question 92

Which of the following works is set in the backdrop of the religious persecution in Mexico?

1. **The Power and the Glory**
2. For Whom the Bell Tolls
3. In Our Time

4.   All of the above

Correct Explanations:

1.   **The Power and the Glory by Graham Greene is set in the Mexican state of Tabasco during the 1930s,** at a time when the Mexican government was cracking down on the Catholic Church and its priests.
2.   **For Whom the Bell Tolls by Ernest Hemingway is set during the Spanish Civil War in the 1930s, in the mountains of central Spain.**
3.   **In Our Time by Ernest Hemingway is a collection of short stories, many of which are set in various locations in Europe and the United States during and after World War I.**

Match List I with List II

List I	List II
A. Graham Greene	I. Down and Out in Paris and London
B. Daniel Defoe	II. The Grass is Singing
C. George Orwell	III. Journal of the Plague Year
D. Doris Lessing	IV. A Sort of Life

Choose be correct answer from the options given below:

1. (A)-(IV), (B)-(I), (C)-(II), (D)-(III)
2. (A)-(IV), (B)-(III), (C)-(I), (D)-(II)
3. (A)-(II), (B)-(IV), (C)-(I), (D)-(III)
4. (A)-(III), (B)-(IV), (C)-(I), (D)-(II)

Explanations

Answer: 2. (A)-(IV), (B)-(III), (C)-(I), (D)-(II)

Down and Out in Paris and London, published in 1933, is George Orwell's debut full-length work. It is a memoir divided into two parts that explores the theme of poverty in the cities of Paris and London. The book aimed to shed light on the plight of the poor to a middle- and upper-class readership, exposing the harsh reality of poverty in seemingly prosperous cities.

A Journal of the Plague Year, first published in March 1722, is a book by Daniel Defoe. It serves as an account of one individual's experiences during the Great Plague of London in 1665. The book provides observations and memorials of both public and private occurrences during the epidemic, offering insights into the last major outbreak of the bubonic plague in the city.

A Sort of Life, published in 1971, is the first instalment of Graham Greene's autobiography. The book delves into Greene's personal life and experiences, providing an intimate look into his early years.

The Grass Is Singing, Doris Lessing's inaugural novel published in 1950, is set in Southern Rhodesia (now Zimbabwe) during the 1940s.

Lawrence Durrell (1912-1990)

- **Lawrence Durrell** was a **British novelist, poet, dramatist.**
- Eldest brother of naturalist and writer **Gerald Durrell.**
- Born in **India** to **British colonial parents.**
- Sent to **England** for education at **eleven.**
- Disliked **formal education**, began writing **poetry at 15.**
- Published **first book** in **1935, aged 23.**
- Moved to **Corfu** with family in **March 1935.**
- Lived and traveled widely across the **world.**
- Best work: **The Alexandria Quartet** (1957–1960).
- **Justine**, first novel in the series, **best-known.**
- Published **The Avignon Quintet**, starting in **1974.**
- **Monsieur** won the **James Tait Black Memorial Prize.**
- **Constance** was nominated for the **1982 Booker Prize.**
- Worked in **British Foreign Service** to support writing.
- Experiences in **Alexandria** inspired much of his **work.**
- Married **four times**, had daughters with **first two wives.**

Alexendria Quartet

- **The Alexandria Quartet** by **Lawrence Durrell**, published **1957-1960.**
- **First three books** offer perspectives on **WWII-era Alexandria.**
- **Fourth book** is set **six years later.**
- Durrell calls it an exploration of **relativity.**
- Themes include **continuum, subject–object relation, modern love.**

- ➤ **First three books** present events through **multiple viewpoints.**
- ➤ The four novels are:
    1. Justine (1957)
    2. Balthazar (1958)
    3. Mountolive (1958)
    4. Clea (1960).

John Masters (1914-1983)

- ➤ **Lieutenant Colonel John Masters**: British **novelist** and officer.
- ➤ Served with **Chindits** in Burma during **World War II**.
- ➤ Became **GSO1** of **19th Indian Infantry Division**.
- ➤ Known for historical novels, especially **Bhowani Junction**.
- ➤ **Bhowani Junction** adapted into a **successful film**.
- ➤ Wrote **three autobiographies**, positively received by **critics**.

Bhowani Junction (1954)

- ➤ **Bhowani Junction** is a 1954 novel by **John Masters**.
- ➤ Inspired the **1956 film** starring **Ava Gardner**.
- ➤ Set during **British withdrawal** from **India**.
- ➤ Explores **Eurasian (Anglo-Indian) community loyalties**.
- ➤ **Anglo-Indians divided** between **British** and **Indian population**.
- ➤ **Anglo-Indians deeply connected** to the **railway system**.
- ➤ **Characters**: Victoria Jones, Patrick Taylor, Colonel Savage struggle identity.
- ➤ **Setting**: India during Partition; cultural tensions rise.
- ➤ **Plot**: Victoria torn between duty, love, and heritage.
- ➤ **Conflict**: Partition impacts loyalties; British-Indian identity questioned.
- ➤ **Resolution**: Victoria chooses independence, rejecting colonial control.

JG Farrell (1935-1979)

- ➤ **James Gordon Farrell** (1935–1979) was **English-born**, of **Irish descent**.
- ➤ Known for the **Empire Trilogy**: *Troubles, Siege, Singapore Grip*.
- ➤ Trilogy explores **British colonial rule's** political, human consequences.
- ➤ *Troubles* won the **1971 Geoffrey Faber Memorial Prize**.

> *Siege of Krishnapur* won the **1973 Booker Prize**.
> *Troubles* awarded the **Lost Man Booker Prize** in 2010.
> Eligibility rule changes excluded *Troubles* in **1970**.

Empire Trilogy

Troubles (1970): The plot concerns the dilapidation of a once-grand Irish hotel (the Majestic), amid the political upheaval during the Irish War of Independence (1919– 1921).

The Siege of Krishnapur (1973): Inspired by events such as the sieges of Cawnapore (Kanpur) and Lucknow, the book details the siege of a fictional Indian town, Krishnapur, during the Indian Rebellion of 1857 from the perspective of the British residents.

The Singapore Grip (1978): It was published in 1978, a year before his death. In 2015, The Straits Times' Akshita Nanda selected The Singapore Grip as one of ten classic Singapore novels.

Question 94

Which of the following novels have represented anglo-Irish relations in the 20 Century?

A. Elizabeth Bowen - The Last September
B. May Sinclair - The Divine Fire
C. J G Farrell - Troubles
D. J G Farrell - The Siege of Krishnapur
E. Jeffery Farnol - Black Bartlemy's Treasure

Choose the most appropriate answer from the options given below:

1. **A and C only**
2. D, E and B only
3. A, B and C only
4. B, C and A only

Correct Explanation:
The Last September is a 1929 novel by the Anglo-Irish writer Elizabeth Bowen, concerning life in Danielstown, Cork, during the Irish War of

Independence, at a country mansion. John Banville wrote a screenplay based on the novel; the film adaptation was released in 1999.

CHAPTER 3

Dylan Thomas (1914-1953)

Life and Literary Career

- **Dylan Marlais Thomas** born **October 27, 1914**, in Swansea.
- Father taught **English Literature**, loved **Shakespeare** recitations.
- Influenced by **Hopkins, Yeats**, and **Edgar Allan Poe**.
- Left school at **sixteen**, became **junior reporter**.
- Quit job to focus on **poetry full-time**.
- Wrote **half his collected poems** as a teenager.
- Published **18 Poems** in **1934**, aged **twenty**.
- Won the **Poet's Corner prize**, moved to **London**.
- Poetry had **lyricism** and emotion, akin to **Romanticism**.
- Avoided **social** and **intellectual themes** like contemporaries.
- Described technique as **"conflicting images"** breeding new ones.
- Met Caitlin Macnamara, married her in **1937**.
- Moved to **London** in **1940** with **Caitlin**.
- Served as **anti-aircraft gunner**, rejected for active duty.
- Left **London** in **1944**, settled in **Laugharne**.
- Lived at **Boat House**, wrote **later poems**.
- Worked for **BBC**, scripted over **100 broadcasts**.
- Experimented with **Under Milk Wood** characters in **radio show**.
- Awarded **Society of Authors Scholarship** in **1947**.
- Wrote **In Country Sleep**, including **"Do not go gentle"**.
- Returned to **Oxfordshire**, scripted films for **Gainsborough Films**.
- Filmscripts later published as **Dylan Thomas: The Filmscripts**.
- First visited **America** in **1950**, aged **thirty-five**.
- Popularized **poetry readings** during **US tours**.
- Known for **theatrical, roaring disputes** in public.
- Toured **America** four times; last at **City College NY**.
- Collapsed after drinking at **White Horse Tavern**.
- Died at **St. Vincent's Hospital**, aged **thirty-nine**.

- ➤ Buried in **Laugharne**, remembered for life and work.
- ➤ Poems combined **intensity** with lyrical **authority**.
- ➤ Famous later poem themes: **erotic, elegiac personality**.
- ➤ "Quite Early One Morning" inspired **Under Milk Wood**.
- ➤ Celebrated as **archetypal Romantic poet** of imagination.
- ➤ Plaque unveiled in **Poet's Corner, Westminster Abbey**.
- ➤ Remains legendary for **work and boisterous life**.

Notable Works:

- ➤ *18 Poems (1934)*
- ➤ *And death shall have no dominion (1936)*
- ➤ *Portrait of the Artist as a Young Dog (1940)*
- ➤ *New Towns for Old (1942) (Documentary)*
- ➤ *Deaths and Entrances (946)*
- ➤ *Fern Hill (1946)*
- ➤ *Do not go gentle into that good night (1951)*
- ➤ *Under Milk Wood (1954) (Radio play)*
- ➤ *The Doctor and the Devils and Other Scripts (1953)*
- ➤ *A Child's Christmas in Wales (1955)*

And death shall have no dominion (1936)

- ➤ **"And death shall have no dominion"** by Dylan Thomas.
- ➤ Title inspired by **St. Paul's epistle to Romans**.
- ➤ Published in **May 1933** in **New England Weekly**.
- ➤ Poem lacks **unifying rhyme scheme**, uses **refrain**.
- ➤ **Lyrical language** pays homage to **Romanticism**.
- ➤ Explores **death's control** but its **limited power**.
- ➤ **Mankind** can unite and **resist evils of death**.
- ➤ **Death unifies**, bringing together those once apart.

And death shall have no dominion.
Dead men naked they shall be one
With the man in the wind and the west moon;
When their bones are picked clean and the clean bones gone,
They shall have stars at elbow and foot;
Though they go mad they shall be sane,
Though they sink through the sea they shall rise again;
Though lovers be lost love shall not;
And death shall have no dominion.

And death shall have no dominion.
Under the windings of the sea
They lying long shall not die windily;
Twisting on racks when sinews give way,
Strapped to a wheel, yet they shall not break;
Faith in their hands shall snap in two,
And the unicorn evils run them through;
Split all ends up they shan't crack;
And death shall have no dominion.

And death shall have no dominion.
No more may gulls cry at their ears
Or waves break loud on the seashores;
Where blew a flower may a flower no more
Lift its head to the blows of the rain;
Though they be mad and dead as nails,
Heads of the characters hammer through daisies;
Break in the sun till the sun breaks down,
And death shall have no dominion.

Fern Hill (1946)

- ➤ **"Fern Hill"** by **Dylan Thomas**, celebrates **childhood joy**.
- ➤ Published in **1946** in **Deaths and Entrances**.
- ➤ Narrated by a **mature poet**, reflecting on **childhood**.
- ➤ Explores **nature, nascent sexuality**, and **mortality**.
- ➤ Balances **celebration and elegy**, avoiding **sentimentality**.
- ➤ Includes the **well-known lines**, a lasting **legacy**.
  "Oh as I was young and easy in the mercy of his means,
  Time held me green and dying
  Though I sang in my chains like the sea."

Do not go gentle into that good night (1951)

- ➤ **"Do Not Go Gentle"** is a **villanelle** by **Dylan Thomas**.
- ➤ Written in **1947**, published in **Botteghe Oscure (1951)**.
- ➤ Later published in **In Country Sleep (1952)**.
- ➤ Believed written for Thomas's **dying father**.
- ➤ Title is the **poem's first line**.
- ➤ Refrains: **"Do not go gentle"** and **"Rage, rage"**.

- ➢ **Copyrighted**, but **text is available online.**
- ➢ Speaker urges father to **resist death actively.**
- ➢ Lists men described as **"wise, good, wild, grave".**
- ➢ Final stanza: speaker **implores father on "sad height".**
- ➢ **"Curse, bless, me now"** with **fierce tears.**
- ➢ **Seamus Heaney**: poem is about **threshold of death.**
- ➢ **Heaney**: villanelle structure conveys **union of opposites.**
- ➢ **Westphal**: "sad height" is a **metaphorical plateau.**
- ➢ Not a literal **bier**, father died later.
- ➢ Represents **aloneness and loneliness before death.**
- ➢ **Heaney**: balance between **grief and necessity** pervades.
- ➢ **Davies** links imagery to **King Lear on heath.**
- ➢ Also evokes **Gloucester at Dover Cliff.**
- ➢ Critics interpret poem as **resistance to death.**

Do not go gentle into that good night,
Old age should burn and rave at close of day;
Rage, rage against the dying of the light.

Though wise men at their end know dark is right,
Because their words had forked no lightning they
Do not go gentle into that good night.

Good men, the last wave by, crying how bright
Their frail deeds might have danced in a green bay,
Rage, rage against the dying of the light.

Wild men who caught and sang the sun in flight,
And learn, too late, they grieved it on its way,
Do not go gentle into that good night.

Grave men, near death, who see with blinding sight
Blind eyes could blaze like meteors and be gay,
Rage, rage against the dying of the light.

And you, my father, there on the sad height,
Curse, bless, me now with your fierce tears, I pray.
Do not go gentle into that good night.
Rage, rage against the dying of the light.

Under Milk Wood (1954)

- **Under Milk Wood**: Play by **Dylan Thomas**, performed **1953**.
- Originally a **radio play**, sometimes staged as **drama**.
- **Rich language**, **comic invention**, evokes Welsh town life.
- Opens at **night**, townspeople shown **dreaming**.
- **Captain Cat** dreams of **drowned shipmates** longing for life.
- **Mog Edwards** and **Myfanwy Price** dream of **each other**.
- **Reverend Jenkins** gives a morning sermon on **village love**.
- **Mrs. Cherry Owen** laughs at her husband's **drunken antics**.
- **Butcher Beynon** teases his wife during **breakfast**.
- **Willy Nilly** steams open Mog's love letter to **Myfanwy**.
- **Mrs. Dai Bread Two** deceives with a **bogus fortune**.
- **Polly Garter** sings about **her past lovers**.
- **Mr. Pugh** imagines **poisoning Mrs. Pugh** during dinner.
- **Lord Cut-Glass** displays insanity in a **kitchen of clocks**.
- **Captain Cat** dreams of **Rosie Probert**, weeping in sorrow.
- **Mae Rose Cottage** wishes for love, vows to **sin**.
- **Reverend Jenkins** writes the **White Book of Llareggub**.
- Town prepares for **evening**, Cherry heads to **Sailors Arms**.
- **Mr. Waldo** sings drunkenly, meets Polly in the **forest**.
- Night falls; citizens return to their **dreams** again.

Question 95

Match List I with List II

List I	List II
A. Sean O'Casey	I. I'm Talking About Jerusalem
B. Dylan Thomas	II. The Winslow Boy
C. Terence Rattigan	III. Juno and the Paycock
D. Arnold Wesker	IV. In the Shadow of the Glen
E. J.M. Synge	V. Under Milk Wood

Choose the correct answer from the options given below:

1. A-II, B-I, C-III, D-V, E-IV
2. A-V, B-IV, C-II, D-I, E-III
3. **A-III, B-V, C-II, D-I, E-IV**
4. A-IV, B-II, C-III, D-V, E-I

Correct Explanations:
I. "I'm Talking About Jerusalem" is a play by Sir Arnold Wesker.
II. "The Winslow Boy" is a play by Terence Rattigan.
III. "Juno and the Paycock" is a play by Sean O'Casey.
IV. "In the Shadow of the Glen" is a play by J.M. Synge.
V. "Under Milk Wood" is a radio drama by Dylan Thomas.

The Movement

- **The Movement** coined by **J.D. Scott** in **1954**.
- Writers included **Larkin**, **Amis**, **Davie**, and others.
- **Essentially English**, excluding poets from other UK regions.
- Members saw themselves as an **actual movement**.
- Emphasized **simple, sensuous content** and **dignified form**.
- Sparked divisions in **British poetry** styles.
- Poems expressed **nostalgia for older England**.
- Focused on **rural imagery** of decaying villages.
- Captured England's **shift to urban ghettoization**.
- Marked a **traditional and conservative poetic revival**.
    - D. J. Enright
    - Kingsley Amis
    - Donald Davie,
    - Thom Gunn,
    - John Holloway,
    - Elizabeth Jennings,
    - Philip Larkin
    - John Wain.

Code: "*The Movement is Right for Amis and Davie, but they point the Gunn at Jennings and Larkin, though the Gunn was Hollow and Wain.*"

Right → D. J. Enright
Amis → Kingsley Amis
Davie → Donald Davie
Gunn → Thom Gunn
Jennings → Elizabeth Jennings
Larkin → Philip Larkin
Hollow → John Holloway
Wain → John Wain

Who among the following was not associated with the Movement Poetry?

    (1) Charles Kingsley
    (2) Donald Davie
    (3) Elizabeth Jennings
    (4) John Wain

Explanations:
Answer: (1) Charles Kingsley

Charles Kingsley was not the part of the movement but **Kingsley Amis.**

Arrange the following groups of poets in their chronological sequence in relation to English literary history:

    A.   The Imagist poets
    B.   The Cavalier poets
    C.   The Movement poets
    D.   The Lake poets

Choose the correct answer from the options given below:

    1.   B, D, C, A
    2.   D, A, B, C
    3.   D, B, A, C
    4.   B, D, A, C

Correct Explanations:
The cavalier poets were a school of English poets of the 17th century.

The Lake Poets were a group of English poets who all lived in the Lake District of England, United Kingdom, in the first half of the nineteenth century.

Imagism was a movement in early-20th-century Anglo-American poetry that favored precision of imagery and clear, sharp language.

The Movement was a term coined in 1954 by J. D. Scott.

Who among the following coined the term The Movement?

1.   FEW. Bateson
2.   F.R. Leavis
3.   **J.D. Scott**
4.   I.A. Richards

Correct Explanations:
The Movement was a term coined in 1954 by J. D. Scott, literary editor of The Spectator, to describe a group of writers **including Philip Larkin, Kingsley Amis, Donald Davie, D. J. Enright, John Wain, Elizabeth Jennings, Thom Gunn and Robert Conquest.** The Movement was quintessentially English in character; poets from other parts of the United Kingdom were not involved.

The Movement poets included:

A. Donald Davie
B. Hilda Dolittle
C. Michael Longley
D. Philip Larkin
E. Derek Walcott

Choose the correct answer from the options given below:

1. A and E
2. A and D
3. B and E
4. C and D

Explanations
Answer: 2. A and D

The Movement was a term coined in 1954 by J. D. Scott, literary editor of The Spectator, to describe a group of writers including **Philip Larkin, Kingsley Amis, Donald Davie, D. J. Enright, John Wain, Elizabeth Jennings, Thom Gunn and Robert Conquest**. The Movement was quintessentially English in character; poets from other parts of the United Kingdom were not involved.

Philip Larkin (1922-1985)

- **Philip Larkin** was a **poet, novelist, librarian.**
- Published **first poetry book**, *The North Ship*, **1945**.
- Novels: *Jill* (1946) and *A Girl in Winter* (1947).
- Rose to fame with *The Less Deceived* (1955).
- Collections include *The Whitsun Weddings* (1964) and *High Windows* (1974).
- Jazz critic for **The Daily Telegraph, 1961–1971**.
- Articles compiled in *All What Jazz* (1985).
- Edited *The Oxford Book of Twentieth-Century English Verse* (1973).
- Received **Queen's Gold Medal for Poetry.**
- Declined **Poet Laureate** role after **John Betjeman's death.**
- Renowned for **modernist themes** and **cultural critiques.**

Notable Work:

- *The North Ship (1945)*
- *Jill (1946)*
- *A Girl in Winter (1947)*
- *The Less Deceived (1955).*
- *"Church Going" (1955)*
- *The Whitsun Weddings (1964)*
- *"MCMXIV" (1964)*
- *High Windows (1974)*

The North Ship (1945)

- **The North Ship**, Philip Larkin's **debut collection** (1945).
- Published by **Reginald A. Caton's Fortune Press.**
- Caton **didn't pay writers**, required copy purchases.
- Similar practice used by **Dylan Thomas** (1934).
- Poem narrates the journey of **three ships.**
- **Third ship symbolizes aspiration**, overcoming **obstacles.**

➢ Written in **first person narrative** as personal experience.
➢ **"I saw three ships go sailing by..."**
➢ First ship: **"rigged for a long journey"** (quatrain 1).
➢ **First ship destroyed**, storm led to **"rich country"**.
➢ **Second ship destroyed** by wind, **"like a beast"**.
➢ **Beast imagery suggests strength** of destructive winds.
➢ Third ship journeyed **north**, avoided **ruin**.
➢ **Decks shining brightly**, covered with **frost**.
➢ First two ships returned after **calm resumed**.
➢ **Third ship never returned**, journeyed **unstoppably**.
➢ Repetition: **"rigged for a long journey"** emphasizes willpower.
➢ Highlights the **inner will** to overcome obstacles.
• Message: **Persistence leads to our goals/destinations**.

The North Ship
I saw three ships go sailing by,

Over the sea, the lifting sea,
And the wind rose in the morning sky,
And one was rigged for a long journey.

The first ship turned towards the west,
Over the sea, the running sea,
And by the wind was all possessed
And carried to a rich country.

The second ship turned towards the east,
Over the sea, the quaking sea,
And the wind hunted it like a beast
To anchor in captivity.

The third ship drove towards the north,
Over the sea, the darkening sea,
But no breath of wind came forth,
And the decks shone frostily.

The northern sky rose high and black
Over the proud unfruitful sea,
East and west the ships came back
Happily or unhappily:

But the third went wide and far
Into an unforgiving sea
Under a fire-spilling star,
And it was rigged for a long journey.

The Less Deceived (1955)

- **The Less Deceived**, published in **1955**, Larkin's first **mature collection**.
- Preceded by **North Ship (1945)** and **XX Poems**.
- **XX Poems**, a **privately printed pamphlet**, mailed to critics.
- **Larkin unaware** of increased **postal rates**.
- Most **recipients refused** to pay additional delivery charges.
- Only **100 copies printed** of **XX Poems**.

Church Going (1955)

- **"Church Going"** is a **masterpiece** by **Philip Larkin**.
- **First draft dated** 24 **April 1954**.
- Took **21 pages of drafts**, finished in **July 1954**.
- Published in **The Less Deceived** collection.
- Highlights **Larkin's love for ecclesiastical architecture**.
- Contrasts **serious mood with cynicism about Christianity**.
- Notable for reference to **"cycle-clips"** and Larkin's image.

The Whitsun Weddings (1964)

- **The Whitsun Weddings**: 32 poems by **Philip Larkin**.
- Published by **Faber** on **28 February 1964**.
- **Sold 4,000 copies** within two months.
- **U.S. edition** appeared **seven months later**.
- "The Whitsun Weddings" is **Larkin's best-known poem**.
- **Written, rewritten**, published in **1964 collection**.
- One of three **Larkin train journey poems**.
- **Eight stanzas**, ten lines each, **longest poem**.
- **Rhyme scheme**: a,b,a,b,c,d,e,c,d,e (like **Keats**).
- Describes **train journey** from **Hull's Paragon station**.
- Set on a **hot Whit Saturday afternoon**.
- **Actual journey debated**, per scholar **John Osborne**.
- Narrator describes **scenery, smells**, countryside views.
- Train windows open due to **heat; wedding bustle**.

- ➤ **Wedding parties**: fathers, uncles, **children, relatives.**
- ➤ Reflects on **newlyweds' permanence** and life changes.
- ➤ Significance seems **disappointing** yet hints at **fertility.**
- ➤ **Rain imagery**: fertility symbol in **final lines.**
- ➤ **Lines 78-80**: "A sense of falling... becoming rain."
- ➤ **Larkin recorded** his own reading of the **poem.**

"MCMXIV" (1964)

- ➤ **"MCMXIV"** by **Philip Larkin**, published in **1964.**
- ➤ Appeared in **The Whitsun Weddings** poetry collection.
- ➤ Poem is a **single sentence, four stanzas** long.
- ➤ Begins with **volunteers enlisting**, describing a **photograph.**
- ➤ Reflects on **England's changes** post-**World War I.**
- ➤ Ends with the line, **"Never such innocence again."**

Those long uneven lines
Standing as patiently
As if they were stretched outside
The Oval or Villa Park,
The crowns of hats, the sun
On moustached archaic faces
Grinning as if it were all
An August Bank Holiday lark;
And the shut shops, the bleached
Established names on the sunblinds,
The farthings and sovereigns,
And dark-clothed children at play
Called after kings and queens,
The tin advertisements
For cocoa and twist, and the pubs
Wide open all day;
And the countryside not caring
The place-names all hazed over
With flowering grasses, and fields
Shadowing Domesday lines
Under wheats' restless silence;
The differently-dressed servants
With tiny rooms in huge houses,
The dust behind limousines;

Never such innocence,
Never before or since,
As changed itself to past
Without a word—the men
Leaving the gardens tidy,
The thousands of marriages
Lasting a little while longer:
Never such innocence again.

Which of the following poems by Philip Larkin deals with the trauma of a rape victim who says, "Even so distant, I can taste the grief"?

1. "Deceptions"
2. "Faith Healing"
3. "Sad Steps"
4. "Wild Oats"

Explanations:

Answer: 1. "Deceptions"

'Deceptions' **by Philip Larkin tells of the aftermath of a young woman's rape and the way both rapist and victim were changed.** The poem begins with Larkin utilizing a passage from Henry Mayhew's work, London Labour and the London Poor. The selection comes from a young woman who was raped. She tells of her distress after the attack was over. This creates a setting for the poem and informs a reader before the text even begins that the events depicted will be graphic, or at least emotionally straining.

Faith Healing: 'Faith Healing' by Philip Larkin describes a procession of women who pray with a faith healer and are then subjected to a new torrent of emotions. The poem begins with the speaker describing the women making their way to the priest. Each is only allowed twenty seconds of contact before they are moved out of line. This does not seem to matter to the women who are emotionally overturned by the experience. Some wander off, others standstill, unable to comprehend what happened. They contemplate God, love, and the life they have lived up until this point.

Sad Steps: 'Sad Steps' was completed by Philip Larkin in April 1968, and was published in his final volume of poetry, High Windows (1974). Larkin was in his mid-forties when he wrote 'Sad Steps', and the poem analyses and explores the poet's awareness of middle age, and the loss of his youth.

Wild Oats: 'Wild Oats' by Philip Larkin is a short poem that tells of Larkin's own emotional struggle to maintain a relationship with his fiancé while in love with another woman. The poem begins with the speaker stating he met two women "twenty years ago." These women were opposite in looks and opposite in how they impacted him.

Question 101

Which of the following poems by Philip Larkin ends with the line "Never such innocence again'?

1. "An Arundel Tomb"
2. "This Be the Verse"
3. "MCMXIV"
4. "Aubade"

Explanations:
Answer: 3. 'MCMXIV"

The final line of the poem is actually: "Never such innocence again." This line reflects on the innocence and idealism of the people before the outbreak of World War I and suggests that such a state of innocence can never be regained or repeated.

Extra Perk:

Here are the opening and closing lines of each poem:

"An Arundel Tomb" by Philip Larkin:
Opening line: "Side by side, their faces blurred,"
Closing line: "What will survive of us is love."

"This Be the Verse" by Philip Larkin:
Opening line: "They fuck you up, your mum and dad."
Closing line: "Man hands on misery to man."

"MCMXIV" by Philip Larkin:
Opening line: "Those long uneven lines"
Closing line: "Never such innocence again."

"Aubade" by Philip Larkin:
Opening line: "I work all day, and get half-drunk at night."
Closing line: "Postmen like doctors go from house to house."

Match List I with List II:

List I	List II
(A) Donald Davie	(I) Against Romanticism
(B) Philip Larkin	(II) Hurry on Down
(C) Kingsley Amis	(III) The Shires
(D) John Wain	(IV) The North Ship

Choose the correct answer from the options given below:

1. **(A)-(III). (B)-(IV). (C)-(I). (D)-(II)**
2. (A)-(IV), (B)-(I). (C)-(II). (D)-(III)
3. (A)-(I). (B)-(III), (C)-(IV). (D)-(II)
4. (A)-(II), (B)-(I), (C)-(III), (D)-(IV)

Correct Explanations:
The Shires (Oxford University Press, 1974) is a collection of poems by Donald Davie.

The North Ship is the debut collection of poems by Philip Larkin (1922–1985), published in 1945 by Reginald A. Caton's Fortune Press. The last of these, "The North Ship" is a set of five poems tracking a ship's northward progress. Of the 30 single poems, only seven have titles. In the 1966 reissue an extra poem, "Waiting for breakfast, while she brushed her hair" was added at the end.

'Against Romanticism,' is a poem by Kingsley Amis.

Hurry On Down (1953) was Wain's first and, to some critics, best novel.

Read the following poem, and answer the questions that follow (96- 100) :

Mr Bleaney

'This was Mr Bleaney's room. He stayed
The whole time he was at the Bodies. till
They moved him.' Flowered curtains. thin and frayed.

Fall to within five inches of the sill,

Whose window shows a strip of building land.
Tussocky. littered. 'Mr Bleaney took
My bit of garden properly in hand.
Bed. upright chair, sixty-watt bulb, no hook

Behind the door, no room for books or bags —
Tll take it." So it happens that I lie
Where Mr Bleaney lay. and stub my fags
On the same saucer-souvenir. and try

Stuffing my ears with cotton-wool. to drown
The jabbering set he egged her on to buy.
I know his habits — what time he came down,
His preference for sauce to gravy. why

He kept on plugging at the four aways —
Likewise their vearly frame: the Frinton folk
Who put him up for summer holidays.
And Christmas at his sister's house in Stoke.

But if he stood and watched the frigid wind
Tousling the clouds. lay on the fusty bed
Telling himself that this was home. and grinned.
And shivered, without shaking off the dread

That how we live measures our own nature.
And at his age having no more to show
Than one hired box should make him pretty sure
He warranted no better, I don't know.

Philip Larkin

Question 103

According to the speaker Mr, Bleany was

1. a humorous person
2. a social and fun-loving person

3. **a sad and dull person**
4. a hard working person

Question 104

The poem "Mr. Bleaney" deals with the portrayal of his:

1. Richness
2. **Luxuriousness**
3. Extravagance
4. ordinariness

Question 105

In the third line "They" refers to:

1. Workers
2. Owners
3. Master
4. Manufacturers
5. **DROP**

Question 106

Mr. Bleaney was the ——————— of the house.

1. Owner
2. Possessor
3. Master
4. **Tenant**

Question 107

The poem, "Mr. Bleaney". is written in a ———————— form.

1. Satirical
2. Lyrical
3. **Dramatic**
4. Philosophical

Read the following poem and answer the question:

Talking in Bed
Talking in bed ought to be easiest,
Lying together there goes back so far,
An emblem of two people being honest.
Yet more and more time passes silently.
Outside, the wind's incomplete unrest
Builds and disperses clouds about the sky,
And dark towns heap up on the horizon.
None of this cares for us.
Nothing shows why
At this unique distance from isolation
It becomes still more difficult to find
Words at once true and kind,
Or not untrue and not unkind

Philip Larkin

Question 108

Which of the following statements is true?

1. The poet says that talking in bed is very easy.
2. The poet says that talking in bed is not very easy.
3. The poet says that talking in bed should be easy but it is not.
4. The poet says that talking in bed can never be easy.

Explanations.

Ans: The poet says that talking in bed should be easy but it is not.

Question 109

The poet says that when two people are lying together, they look like

1. Two Pure Human Beings.
2. Two Hypocrites.
3. Two Innocent Fellows.
4. None Of These

Explanations:

Ans: Two Pure Human Beings.

The poet says that while lying in bed he and his companion pass time

1. By Talking Between Themselves.
2. By Observing The Trees Outside The Window.
3. Silently.
4. By Playing Cards.

Explanations:

Ans: Silently.

The poet and his companion are

1. In A Hotel In The Middle Of A Town.
2. In A Room Of A Hotel On The Margin Of The Town.
3. In The Corridor Of A Hotel Far Away From The Towns.
4. In A Place Away From The Towns.

Explanations:

Ans: In A Place Away From The Towns.

The poet says that while lying in bed with one's companion, it is difficult to find words which are

1. At Once Honest And Caring
2. At Once True And Unkind
3. At Once Pure And Impure
4. At Once Honest And Touching

Explanations:

Ans: At Once Honest And Caring

Choose the correct chronological sequence in which the following texts were published.

A. The Tower
B. The Hind and the Panther
C. The Wild Swans at Coole
D. Mac Flecknoe
E. The Whitsun Weddings

Choose the correct answer from the options given below:

1. ABDEC
2. BCAED
3. BACDE
4. **DBCAE**

Explanations:

The correct chronological sequence of publication for the listed texts is as follows:

1. *Mac Flecknoe by John Dryden (1682)*
2. *The Hind and the Panther by John Dryden (1687)*
3. *The Tower by W. B. Yeats (1928)*
4. *The Wild Swans at Coole by W. B. Yeats (1919)*
5. *The Whitsun Weddings by Philip Larkin (1964)*

Question 114

Which famous English poet, at an early age announcing his admiration for D. H. Lawrence, excitedly wrote to his friend, "I have been reading Sons and Lovers and feel ready to die. If Lawrence had been killed after writing that book he'd still be England's greatest novelist"?

1. Virginia Woolf
2. WH Auden
3. Dylan Thomas
4. Philip Larkin

Explanations:

Answer: 4. Philip Larkin

On 20 March 1942, at the age of nineteen, Philip Larkin expressed his excitement to his friend Jim Sutton about his admiration for D. H. Lawrence. In his letter, Larkin proclaimed his admiration for Lawrence's novel "Sons and Lovers," stating that if Lawrence had died after writing that book, he would still be considered England's greatest novelist.

A few years later, Larkin's own aspirations as a fiction writer began to materialise with the publication of his novels "Jill" in 1946 and "A Girl in Winter" in 1947. These works showcased Larkin's awareness of the diverse range of Modernist experimentation found in the writings of Lawrence, as well as contemporaries such as Virginia Woolf and Katherine Mansfield. The Modernist fiction of the early decades of the twentieth century inspired Larkin to move beyond realistic portrayal and venture into a symbolist approach, exploring intangible subjects such as obscure dreams and desires.

Question 115

Which poetry anthologies have NOT been written by Philip Larkin?

    A. The North Ship
    B. The Less Deceived
    C. The Whitsun Weddings
    D. Death of a Naturalist
    E. Responsibilities

Choose the correct answer from the options given below:

    1. A and B
    2. B and c
    3. C and A
    4. D and E

Explanations:
Answer: 4. D and E

A. "The North Ship": "The North Ship" is a collection of poems by Philip Larkin, published in 1945.

B. "The Less Deceived": "The Less Deceived" is a poetry collection by Philip Larkin, published in 1955.

C. "The Whitsun Weddings": "The Whitsun Weddings" is a poetry collection by **Philip Larkin,** published in 1964.

D. "Death of a Naturalist": "Death of a Naturalist" is a poetry collection by **Seamus Heaney,** published in 1966.

E. "Responsibilities": "Responsibilities" is a poetry collection by John **Ashbery**, published in 1967.

Elizabeth Jennings (1926-2001)

- **Elizabeth Jennings** was an **English poet.**
- Her works addressed **intensely personal matters.**
- Verse reflected **Roman Catholicism** and **love of Italy**.
- *Poems, appeared in 1953,*
- *A Way of Looking (1955)*
- *Song for a Birth or a Death (1961)*
- *Recoveries (1964)*
- *The Mind Has Mountains (1966).*
- *The Animals' Arrival (1969),*
- *Lucidities (1970),*
- *Relationships (1972),*
- *Extending the Territory (1985),*
- *Familiar Spirits (1994).*
- *The Sonnets of Michelangelo (1961).*

Thom Gunn (1929-2004)

- **Thom Gunn** (1929–2004) was an **English poet.**
- Praised in **England** for early **Movement verses.**
- Adopted **looser, free-verse style** in **America.**
- Explored moving to **San Francisco from England.**
- Received numerous **literary honors** for his poetry.
- Poems possess **"restrained elegance of philosophy."**
- Notable Works:
    - *Fighting Terms (1954; rev. ed. 1962)*
    - *The Sense of Movement (1957)*
    - *My Sad Captains (1961)*
    - *Selected Poems (1962)*
    - *Positives (1966)*

- o   *Moly (1971)*
- o   *Jack Straw's Castle (1976)*
- o   *Selected Poems 1950–1975 (1979)*
- o   *The Passages of Joy (1982)*
- o   *The Occasion of Poetry (1982)*
- o   *The Man with Night Sweats (1992)*
- o   *Shelf Life (1993)*
- o   *Boss Cupid (2000)*

On the Move

- ➢ **Introduction**: The poem begins with a description of motorcyclists.
- ➢ **Theme**: Explores restlessness and the search for purpose.
- ➢ **Symbolism**: Motorcycles represent freedom, energy, and existential movement.
- ➢ **Philosophical Reflection**: Highlights human impulse for motion and identity.
- ➢ **Important Line**: "Man must move, man must progress."
- ➢ **Behavioral Study**: Motorcyclists act with instinct, defying societal norms.
- ➢ **Mood**: Combines energy, melancholy, and the inevitability of change.
- ➢ **Contrast**: Nature's stillness opposes human restlessness and drive.
- ➢ **Climax**: Movement is shown as purpose despite uncertainty.
- ➢ **Conclusion**: Life's journey is defined by action and impermanence.

Ted Hughes (1930-1998)

Life and Career

- ➢ **Ted Hughes**, English poet, emphasized **cunning** and **savagery**.
- ➢ Verses featured **animal life**, often **harsh lines**.
- ➢ Studied **folklore** and **anthropology** at **Cambridge**.
- ➢ Married **Sylvia Plath** in **1956**.
- ➢ Moved to the **United States** in **1957**.
- ➢ Published **The Hawk in the Rain** that year.
- ➢ Followed by **Lupercal (1960)** and **Selected Poems (1962)**.
- ➢ Collaborated with **Thom Gunn**, marking **new English verse**.
- ➢ **Plath's suicide** in 1963 paused his **poetry**.
- ➢ Resumed with **Wodwo (1967)** and **Crow (1970)**.
- ➢ Later works include **Wolfwatching (1989)** and **New Selected**

Poems (1995).

- ➢ Wrote **Birthday Letters (1998)** about **Plath**.
- ➢ Edited **Plath's works**, faced **censorship accusations**.
- ➢ **Destroyed journals** she wrote before her **suicide**.
- ➢ Wrote children's book **The Iron Man (1968)**.
- ➢ Collaborated on **Remains of Elmet (1979)**.
- ➢ Translated **The Story of Vasco** into **libretto**.
- ➢ **Opera premiered** in **1974**, revised play **in 2009**.
- ➢ Adapted **Seneca's Oedipus (1968)** and **nonfiction works**.
- ➢ Co-edited **The Rattle Bag (1982)** with **Seamus Heaney**.
- ➢ **Correspondence** released in **2007** as **Letters of Ted Hughes**.
- ➢ **A Ted Hughes Bestiary (2014)** focused on **animals**.
- ➢ Appointed **Britain's Poet Laureate** in **1984**.
- ➢ Known for **translations**, adaptations, and **children's literature**.
- ➢ Prolific editor of **poetry collections** and **anthologies**.
- ➢ **Legacy includes innovation** and **poetic explorations**.

Notable Work:

- ➢ *1957 The Hawk in the Rain*
- ➢ *1960 Lupercal*
- ➢ *1967 Wodwo*
- ➢ *1970 Crow: From the Life and the Songs of the Crow*
- ➢ *1972 Selected Poems 1957–1967*
- ➢ *1975 Cave Birds*
- ➢ *1977 Gaudete*
- ➢ *1979 Remains of Elmet (with photographs by Fay Godwin)*
- ➢ *1979 Moortown*
- ➢ *1983 River*
- ➢ *1986 Flowers and Insects*
- ➢ *1989 Wolfwatching*
- ➢ *1992 Rain-charm for the Duchy*
- ➢ *1994 New Selected Poems 1957–1994*
- ➢ *1997 Tales from Ovid*
- ➢ *1998 Birthday Letters*

Here's a list of famous poems by Ted Hughes:

- ➢ *The Thought-Fox*
- ➢ *Pike*

- *Hawk Roosting*
- *Crow's Fall*
- *The Jaguar*
- *Wind*
- *View of a Pig*
- *Snowdrop*
- *Full Moon and Little Frieda*
- *February 17th*
- *Examination at the Womb-Door*
- *Lovesong*
- *Thrushes*
- *Wodwo*
- *Lupercal*
- *Daffodils*

The Hawk in the Rain (1957)

- **The Hawk in the Rain** contains **40 poems**.
- Published by **Faber and Faber** in **1957**.
- Hughes's **first book of poetry** won **Galbraith Prize**.
- Poems imagine **real and symbolic lives of animals**.
- Themes include **erotic relationships** and **WWI stories**.
- **Hughes's father** survived **Gallipoli** during WWI.
- **Dedicated to Sylvia Plath**, Hughes's **first wife**.
- **Theme**: Focuses on human fragility against nature's power.
- **Hawk Symbolism**: Represents strength, freedom, and primal energy.
- **Contrast**: Man struggles; hawk soars with effortless control.
- **Imagery**: Vivid descriptions of rain, mud, and stormy skies.
- **Tone**: Reflects awe and fear of nature's dominance.
- **Human Struggle**: Man is weighed down by mud and gravity.
- **Hawk's Superiority**: Unaffected by elements, a symbol of resilience.
- **Conflict**: Highlights human vulnerability versus nature's indifference.
- **Style**: Intense, sharp, and focused on elemental imagery.
- **Legacy**: Establishes Hughes' poetic focus on nature's raw power.

The Hawk in the Rain

I drown in the drumming ploughland, I drag up
Heel after heel from the swallowing of the earth's mouth,
From clay that clutches my each step to the ankle

With the habit of the dogged grave, but the hawk

Effortlessly at height hangs his still eye.
His wings hold all creation in a weightless quiet,
Steady as a hallucination in the streaming air.
While banging wind kills these stubborn hedges,

Thumbs my eyes, throws my breath, tackles my heart,
And rain hacks my head to the bone, the hawk hangs
The diamond point of will that polestars
The sea drowner's endurance: and I,

Bloodily grabbed dazed last-moment-counting
Morsel in the earth's mouth, strain towards the master-
Fulcrum of violence where the hawk hangs still,
That maybe in his own time meets the weather

Coming from the wrong way, suffers the air, hurled upside down,
Fall from his eye, the ponderous shires crash on him,
The horizon traps him; the round angelic eye
Smashed, mix his heart's blood with the mire of the land.

The Thought-Fox

- ➤ **Ted Hughes**, author of **'The Thought-Fox,'** born in **Yorkshire**.
- ➤ Son of a **countryman** and **Lancashire Fusiliers veteran**.
- ➤ Deep **interest in animals**, worked at a **zoo**.
- ➤ Animals frequently appear in **Hughes' poetry**.
- ➤ Poetry rooted in **mystical language, old-fashioned models**.
- ➤ Criticized for **traditional style**, unlike **Movement poetry**.
- ➤ **Movement poetry** used a **down-to-earth, humanistic style**.
- ➤ Hughes explored **mysticism** and the **unknown** in writing.
- ➤ Hughes said, **"Now I came a bit later."**
- ➤ **"I hadn't had enough... I was all for opening negotiations."**
- ➤ Hughes referenced **post-war trauma, death camps**, and bombs.
- ➤ He emphasized poets' desire for **peaceful domestic life**.
- ➤ **'The Thought-Fox'** symbolizes a muse, fleeting and elusive.
- ➤ The **fox** disturbs the poet in a **quiet night**.
- ➤ Poem reflects **writing process** and inspiration's **ephemeral nature**.
- ➤ Hughes' work contrasts with the **post-war poetic mood**.

The Thought-Fox

I imagine this midnight moment's forest:
Something else is alive
Beside the clock's loneliness
And this blank page where my fingers move.

Through the window I see no star:
Something more near
Though deeper within darkness
Is entering the loneliness:

Cold, delicately as the dark snow
A fox's nose touches twig, leaf;
Two eyes serve a movement, that now
And again now, and now, and now

Sets neat prints into the snow
Between trees, and warily a lame
Shadow lags by stump and in hollow
Of a body that is bold to come

Across clearings, an eye,
A widening deepening greenness,
Brilliantly, concentratedly,
Coming about its own business

Till, with a sudden sharp hot stink of fox
It enters the dark hole of the head.
The window is starless still; the clock ticks,
The page is printed.

The Thought-Fox

- ➢ **Ted Hughes**, born in **Yorkshire**, son of a **countryman**.
- ➢ Animals **influenced his poetry** and zoo work.
- ➢ Favored **old-fashioned formats**, ridiculed by **peers**.
- ➢ **Movement poetry** emphasized **realism** and **humanism**.
- ➢ Hughes used **mystical language** and **expansive ideas**.

➤ Hughes said, **"I hadn't had enough"** post-war rhetoric.
➤ Referenced **death camps** and **atomic bombs**.
➤ Hughes wanted to **"open negotiations" with the unknown**.
➤ **'The Thought-Fox'** symbolizes the **elusive poetic muse**.
➤ Fox disturbs the **poet's quiet night**, inspiring creation.

The Thought-Fox

I imagine this midnight moment's forest:
Something else is alive
Beside the clock's loneliness
And this blank page where my fingers move.

Through the window I see no star:
Something more near
Though deeper within darkness
Is entering the loneliness:

Cold, delicately as the dark snow
A fox's nose touches twig, leaf;
Two eyes serve a movement, that now
And again now, and now, and now

Sets neat prints into the snow
Between trees, and warily a lame
Shadow lags by stump and in hollow
Of a body that is bold to come

Across clearings, an eye,

A widening deepening greenness,
Brilliantly, concentratedly,
Coming about its own business

Till, with a sudden sharp hot stink of fox
It enters the dark hole of the head.
The window is starless still; the clock ticks,
The page is printed.

Question 116

Which two are the works of Ted Hughes?

- A. Wildtrack
- B. Wodwo
- C. Lupercal
- D. Jack Straw's Castle

Choose the correct answer from the options given below:

1. A and B only
2. A and C only
3. **B and C only**
4. B and D only

Correct Explanations:

Wodwo (1967) is named after a medieval mythical creature that is half-man, half-beast, and the collection includes poems that are infused with a sense of primal energy and wildness. The poems explore themes of identity, transformation, and the search for meaning in a rapidly changing world.

Lupercal (1960) is one of Hughes' earliest collections of poetry, and includes a number of his most well-known and frequently anthologized poems, such as "The Thought-Fox" and "Pike." The collection is notable for its vivid imagery and exploration of the darker, more primitive aspects of human experience.

Thom Gunn's "Jack Straw's Castle" (1976) is named after a pub in London that was a popular meeting place for writers and intellectuals in the 1960s and 1970s.

Question 117

Ted Hughes "Wodwo" is

1. a volume named after the wild men of the woods of Sir Gawain and the Green Knight.
2. a volume named after the elves of the masque of The Tempest.
3. a volume named after the central character of Pearl.
4. a volume named after the name of the monster of Beowulf.

Explanations

Answer: 1. a volume named from the wild men of the woods of Sir Gawain and the Green Knight.

Seamus Heaney (1939-2013)

Life and Career

- **Seamus Heaney**, Irish poet, evoked **rural life** and **history**.
- Awarded the **Nobel Prize for Literature in 1995**.
- First poetry collection: **Death of a Naturalist (1966)**.
- Early works explored **rural life** in **Northern Ireland**.
- **Wintering Out** (1972) and **North** (1975) addressed **violence**.
- Subjects viewed through **mythic and mystical** filters.
- Later volumes include **Field Work, Station Island**.
- **The Spirit Level** (1996) explored **balance and centredness**.
- **Opened Ground** (1998): Selected Poems, **1966–1996**.
- **Electric Light** (2001) revisited **youthful Irish experiences**.
- **Human Chain** (2010) reflected on **death and memory**.
- Essays appeared in **Preoccupations** and **Finders Keepers**.
- Translations include **The Cure at Troy (1991)**.
- Translated **Beowulf (1999)**; became an **international best seller**.
- **The Burial at Thebes (2004)** modernized **Sophocles' Antigone**.

Notable works:

- *Death of a Naturalist (1966)*
- *Digging*
- *Death of a Naturalist*
- *Mid-Term Break*
- *North (1975)*
- *Field Work (1979)*
- *The Spirit Level (1996)*
- *Beowulf: A New Verse Translation (translation, 1999)*
- *District and Circle (2006)*
- *Human Chain (2010)*

Death of a Naturalist (1966)

- **Death of a Naturalist (1966)** by **Seamus Heaney**.

- ➤ **Heaney won** the **1995 Nobel Prize in Literature**.
- ➤ Collection includes ideas presented at **The Belfast Group**.
- ➤ Won **Cholmondeley**, **Gregory**, **Somerset Maugham**, and **Faber Prize**.
- ➤ Contains **34 poems** exploring **childhood**, **identity**, and **rural life**.
- ➤ Begins with **"Digging"**, includes **"Death of a Naturalist"**.
- ➤ **"Death of a Naturalist"** recalls boy collecting **frogspawn**.
- ➤ Teacher explains **frogs**, symbolizing **childhood innocence**.
- ➤ Boy feels **threatened by frogs**, flees the **flax-dam**.
- ➤ **Loss of interest** in nature reflects **"naturalist's death"**.
- ➤ Extensive use of **onomatopoeia** and **war-like similes**.
- ➤ Frogs compared to **warfare**: "Some sat poised like grenades".

Death of a Naturalist

All year the flax-dam festered in the heart
Of the townland; green and heavy headed
Flax had rotted there, weighted down by huge sods.
Daily it sweltered in the punishing sun.
Bubbles gargled delicately, bluebottles
Wove a strong gauze of sound around the smell.
There were dragonflies, spotted butterflies,
But best of all was the warm thick slobber
Of frogspawn that grew like clotted water
In the shade of the banks. Here, every spring
I would fill jampotfuls of the jellied
Specks to range on window sills at home,
On shelves at school, and wait and watch until
The fattening dots burst, into nimble
Swimming tadpoles. Miss Walls would tell us how
The daddy frog was called a bullfrog
And how he croaked and how the mammy frog
Laid hundreds of little eggs and this was
Frogspawn. You could tell the weather by frogs too
For they were yellow in the sun and brown

In rain.
*   Then one hot day when fields were rank*
With cowdung in the grass the angry frogs
Invaded the flax-dam; I ducked through hedges

To a coarse croaking that I had not heard
Before. The air was thick with a bass chorus.
Right down the dam gross bellied frogs were cocked
On sods; their loose necks pulsed like sails. Some hopped:
The slap and plop were obscene threats. Some sat
Poised like mud grenades, their blunt heads farting.
I sickened, turned, and ran. The great slime kings
Were gathered there for vengeance and I knew
That if I dipped my hand the spawn would clutch it.

Digging

- ➢ **"Digging"** explores themes of **time** and **history**.
- ➢ Narrator admires father's **skill digging** on family farm.
- ➢ Declares he will **"dig with his pen"** instead.
- ➢ Pen symbolizes **Heaney's occupation** and **powerful tool**.
- ➢ Writing helps **excavate history** and **self-understanding**.
- ➢ Poem is **autobiographical**, narrator likely **Heaney himself**.
- ➢ Speaker recalls **father working** outside while writing.
- ➢ Memories of **father digging** potatoes resurface.
- ➢ Older memory of **grandfather digging** peat moss emerges.
- ➢ Speaker vividly **smells potatoes** and **peat moss**.
- ➢ Lacks **spade**, but vows to **"dig"** with pen.
- ➢ Poem highlights **generational connections** through **digging**.

Between my finger and my thumb
The squat pen rests; snug as a gun.

Under my window, a clean rasping sound
When the spade sinks into gravelly ground:
My father, digging. I look down

Till his straining rump among the flowerbeds
Bends low, comes up twenty years away
Stooping in rhythm through potato drills
Where he was digging.

The coarse boot nestled on the lug, the shaft
Against the inside knee was levered firmly.
He rooted out tall tops, buried the bright edge deep

To scatter new potatoes that we picked,
Loving their cool hardness in our hands.

By God, the old man could handle a spade.
Just like his old man.

My grandfather cut more turf in a day
Than any other man on Toner's bog.
Once I carried him milk in a bottle
Corked sloppily with paper. He straightened up
To drink it, then fell to right away
Nicking and slicing neatly, heaving sods
Over his shoulder, going down and down
For the good turf. Digging.

The cold smell of potato mould, the squelch and slap
Of soggy peat, the curt cuts of an edge
Through living roots awaken in my head.
But I've no spade to follow men like them.

Between my finger and my thumb
The squat pen rests.
I'll dig with it.

Mid-Term Break

- ➤ **"Mid-Term Break"** reflects on **Heaney's brother Christopher's death**.
- ➤ Heaney describes his **parents' contrasting displays of grief**.
- ➤ **Visitors** came to **pay their respects** to family.
- ➤ Encountered **brother's corpse in coffin** the next morning.
- ➤ Poem **"captures a boy's unfolding consciousness of death."**
- ➤ Final line emphasizes **death's finality: "A four foot box, a foot for every year."**

Mid-Term Break

I sat all morning in the college sick bay
Counting bells knelling classes to a close.
At two o'clock our neighbours drove me home.

In the porch I met my father crying—
He had always taken funerals in his stride—
And Big Jim Evans saying it was a hard blow.

The baby cooed and laughed and rocked the pram
When I came in, and I was embarrassed
By old men standing up to shake my hand

And tell me they were 'sorry for my trouble'.
Whispers informed strangers I was the eldest,
Away at school, as my mother held my hand

In hers and coughed out angry tearless sighs.
At ten o'clock the ambulance arrived
With the corpse, stanched and bandaged by the nurses.

Next morning I went up into the room. Snowdrops
And candles soothed the bedside; I saw him
For the first time in six weeks. Paler now,

Wearing a poppy bruise on his left temple,
He lay in the four-foot box as in his cot.
No gaudy scars, the bumper knocked him clear.

A four-foot box, a foot for every year.

North (1975)

- **North (1975)** is by **Seamus Heaney, Nobel Prize 1995**.
- First work directly addressing **The Troubles** in **Ireland**.
- Looks to **past symbols** for **violence context**.
- Heaney's reading recorded in **Collected Poems album**.
- First part includes **myths**, **bog bodies**, and **Vikings**.
- Second part focuses on **Northern Ireland's Troubles, dedications**.
- **Volume title "North" possibly inspired by poem.**
- **Manuscript drafts** reveal other poem **titles considered**.
- **No evidence Heaney considered another volume title.**
- **Rand Brandes writes**, "North was always North."
- Poem **"North" symbolizes Viking raiders invading Ireland.**

- ➢ Title suggests **raiders, bog bodies, and Northern Ireland**.

Bog Poems

- ➢ **Bog bodies inspire four poems**: "Bog Queen", "Punishment".
- ➢ **Wintering Out** featured **first bog-body poem**, "Tollund Man".
- ➢ Heaney inspired by **PV Glob's The Bog People**.
- ➢ Book studies **Iron-Age bodies** found in **Northern Europe**.
- ➢ In **"Feeling Into Words"**, Heaney explains poetry shift.
- ➢ Writing became about **"images and symbols adequate to our predicament"**.
- ➢ **Bog bodies** became **symbols** for Irish struggles.
- ➢ **Heaney**: Photographs "blended with atrocities, past and present".
- ➢ **Political and religious struggles** reflected in these poems.
- ➢ **Connections drawn** between the **past and present**.

Field Work (1979)

- ➢ **Field Work** followed Heaney's **North (1975)** collection.
- ➢ Reflects **four years (1972-1976)** in **rural Wicklow**.
- ➢ Heaney left **The Troubles** and moved to **Ireland**.
- ➢ Previously lived in **Belfast**, taught at **Queen's University**.
- ➢ Denis O'Donoghue called it **"years of retreat."**
- ➢ Period for **thinking**, renewal of **deep affiliations**.
- ➢ Joshua Weiner noted **"withdrawal" seemed politically deliberate**.
- ➢ **Field Work** showed **commitment** to the **long view**.
- ➢ Focused on **questions**, not fixed **political positions**.
- ➢ Themes reflect Heaney's **renewal and intellectual engagement**.

Question 118

In which of the Bog poems does Seamus Heaney speak about the "perishable treasure" of a body 'Murdered, forgotten, nameless, terrible?

1. "Bog Queen"
2. "Grauballe Man"
3. "Punishment
4. "Strange Fruit"

Explanations:

Answer: 4. "Strange Fruit

"Strange Fruit" is, importantly, linked to the terrible execution of two American Southern States Black men during the Jim Crow era. The bodies hanging from a tree in a ritualistic killing are the "strange fruit". Heaney used the title of the Billie Holiday song about the American executions for his poem.

In "Strange Fruit," Heaney describes the discovery of an Iron Age body found in a bog in Denmark. He writes:

> *"Here is the girl's head like an exhumed gourd.*
> *Oval-faced, prune-skinned, prune-stones for teeth.*
> *They unswaddled the wet fern of her hair*
> *And made an exhibition of its coil,*
> ***Let the air at her leathery beauty.***
> ***Pash of tallow, perishable treasure:***
> *Her broken nose is dark as a turf clod,*
> *Her eyeholes blank as pools in the old workings."*

Heaney uses vivid imagery to describe the body, emphasizing its fragility and perishability. The "pash of tallow" suggests the softness and melting of the flesh, while the "perishable treasure" highlights the fleeting nature of life and the inevitability of death. The broken nose and blank eyeholes serve to further emphasize the brutality and violence of the past, and the haunting legacy of those who have been forgotten or erased by history.

Question 119

Which two of the following poems by Seamus Heaney come under his Bog Poems?

    A.   "Personal Helicon"
    B.   "Punishment"
    C.   "The Early Purges"
    D.   "Tollund Man"

Choose the correct answer from the options given below:

    1.   (A) and (B) Only
    2.   (B) and (C) Only
    3.   (A) and (C) Only
    4.   (B) and (D) Only

Explanations:
Answer: 4. (B) and (D) Only

The two poems by Seamus Heaney that come under his Bog Poems are:

"Bogland": This poem explores the significance of bogs in Irish history and culture. Heaney delves into the layers of history and symbolism found within the bog landscape, reflecting on themes of preservation, identity, and the connection between the past and present.

"The Tollund Man": This poem is inspired by the discovery of a well-preserved Iron Age bog body in Denmark. Heaney uses the Tollund Man as a focal point to reflect on themes of sacrifice, violence, and the timeless nature of human suffering, drawing parallels to contemporary conflicts and societal issues.

Both poems exemplify Heaney's fascination with bogs as rich metaphorical landscapes that carry historical, cultural, and personal significance.

Question 120

Some of the following poets adorned the Oxford Professor of Poetry Chair:

A. James Fenton
B. Margaret Atwood
C. Seamus Heaney
D. Anne Sexton
E. Paul Muldoon

Choose the correct answer from the options given below:

1. B, C and D
2. A, B and C
3. A, C and E
4. C, D and E

Explanations
Answer: 3. A, C and E

The University of Oxford holds an esteemed academic position known as the Professor of Poetry, which was established in 1708 through a generous endowment from Henry Birkhead's estate. Those appointed to this prestigious chair have certain responsibilities, including delivering an inaugural lecture, giving public lectures each term on relevant literary topics, organising additional events like poetry readings or workshops, and delivering the Creweian Oration at Encaenia every other year. They also participate as judges for various literary prizes, such as the Newdigate Prize, the Jon Stallworthy Prize, the Lord Alfred Douglas Prize, and the Chancellor's English Essay Prize. Furthermore, they help judge the English poem on a sacred subject prize every third year and actively promote the art of poetry within the University.

Notable figures who have held the Oxford Professor of Poetry Chair include Seamus Heaney from 1989 to 1994, James Fenton from 1994 to 1999, Paul Muldoon from 1999 to 2004, and Christopher Ricks from 2004 to 2009. On 19th June 2015, Simon Armitage was elected as Geoffrey Hill's successor to this esteemed position.

Carol Ann Duffy (1955*)

- ➤ **Dame Carol Ann Duffy**, British poet and playwright.
- ➤ **Professor of contemporary poetry** at **Manchester Metropolitan University**.
- ➤ Appointed **Poet Laureate** in **May 2009**, resigned **2019**.
- ➤ **First woman, Scottish-born**, and **lesbian Poet Laureate**.
- ➤ Held **historic position** with profound **literary influence**.
- ➤ Her poems address issues such as oppression, gender, and violence in accessible language.
- ➤ **Her collections include:**
  - ○ *Standing Female Nude (1985)*, winner of a Scottish Arts Council Award.
  - ○ *Selling Manhattan (1987)*, which won a Somerset Maugham Award.
  - ○ *Mean Time (1993)*, which won the Whitbread Poetry Award.
  - ○ *Rapture (2005)*, which won the T. S. Eliot Prize.

Question 121

Which two poems in the following list are examples of dramatic monologue?

    A. Alfred Tennyson, "Ulysses"
    B. Philip Larkin, "Church Going"
    C. Carol Ann Duffy, "Medusa"
    D. Katherine Philips, "A Married State"

Choose the correct answer from the options given below:

1. A and D only
2. B and C only
3. C and D only
4. A and C only

Explanations:

Answer: 4. A and C only

- ➤ Alfred Tennyson's poem "***Ulysses***" is a **dramatic monologue**
- ➤ Carol Ann Duffy's poem "*Medusa*" is a **dramatic monologue**
- ➤ Katherine Philips' poem "*A Married State*" is a satirical poem that critiques the institution of marriage.
- ➤ Philip Larkin's poem "*Church Going*" is a meditation on the decline of religious belief and the loss of faith in modern society.

Other Poets

- ➤ **Michael Hofmann (1957)**
- ➤ **Lavinia Greenlaw (1962*)**
- ➤ **Glyn Maxwell (1962*)**
- ➤ **Simon Armitage (1963*)**

DRAMA AFTER WW II

- ➤ **Kitchen sink realism** developed in **1950s-60s** British theatre.
- ➤ Depicts **working-class domestic lives**, exploring **social issues**.
- ➤ **Angry Young Men** challenged **drawing room plays**.
- ➤ **John Osborne's Look Back in Anger** (1956) pivotal work.
- ➤ **Samuel Beckett's Waiting for Godot** (1955) influenced drama.
- ➤ **Theatre of the Absurd** shaped **Harold Pinter's works**.
- ➤ **Harold Pinter's The Birthday Party** (1958) themes of **menace**.
- ➤ **Tom Stoppard** influenced by Beckett, works include **wit**.
- ➤ **Rosencrantz and Guildenstern Are Dead** (1966), Stoppard's notable play.
- ➤ **BBC Radio** commissioned and adapted plays since **1920s**.
- ➤ **BBC radio launched careers** of major **playwrights**.
- ➤ **Caryl Churchill's first play** aired on BBC **radio**.
- ➤ **Dylan Thomas's Under Milk Wood** (1954) iconic radio play.
- ➤ **Harold Pinter's A Slight Ache** (1959) BBC production.
- ➤ **Robert Bolt's A Man for All Seasons** (1954), famed **radio play**.

Noel Coward (1899-1973)

- **Noël Coward**: English playwright, composer, director, actor, singer.
- Known for **wit**, flamboyance, and "personal style."
- *Blithe Spirit (1941):* Coward's **best farce**.
- Plot: **Jealous ghost** disturbs man's **domestic life**.
- Combines **drawing-room comedy** with **ghost story**.

Terence Rattigan (1911-1977)

- English playwright, a master of the well-made play.
- His plays are typically set in an upper-middle-class background.
- **Notable Work:**
  - *The Winslow Boy (1946),*
  - *The Browning Version (1948),*
  - *The Deep Blue Sea (1952)*
  - *Separate Tables (1954)*
- **The Winslow Boy (1946)**
  - Based on an incident involving George Archer-Shee in the Edwardian era.
  - The incident took place at the Royal Naval College, Osborne.

Christopher Fry (1907-2005)

- An English poet and playwright.
- He is best known for his verse dramas.
- *The Lady's Not for Burning* made him a major force in theatre.
- **Notable Works:**
  - *A Phoenix Too Frequent (1946)*
  - *The Firstborn (1946)*
  - ***The Lady's Not for Burning (1948)***
  - *Thor, With Angels (1948)*
  - *Venus Observed (1950)*
  - *Ring Round the Moon (1950),*
  - *A Winter's Tale (1951) music by Fry*
  - *A Sleep of Prisoners (1951)*
  - *The Dark is Light Enough (1954)*
  - *The Lark (1955),*
  - *Tiger At The Gates (1956),*
  - *Crown of the Year (1958),*
  - *Duel of Angels (1958),*
  - *Judith (1962),*

- o *The Boy and the Magic (1964),*
- o *Peer Gynt (1970),*
- o *A Yard of Sun (1970)*
- o *Cyrano de Bergerac (1975)*
- ➢ ***The Lady's Not for Burning (1948)***
  - o **Plot begins** with **disappearance of town's rag-and-bone man**.
  - o After **plot twists**, the **missing man turns up**.
  - o **Murder suspects released** after man's **reappearance**.

Angry Young Men

- ➢ **Angry Young Men** emerged in the **1950s Britain**.
- ➢ **Scorned sociopolitical order**, upper, and **middle classes**.
- ➢ Mostly from **working-class or lower middle-class origins**.
- ➢ Educated at **red-brick universities** or **Oxford**.
- ➢ Disliked **British class system** and **elitist universities**.
- ➢ Criticized **postwar welfare state's unmet aspirations**.
- ➢ Trend began with **Hurry on Down** and **Lucky Jim**.
- ➢ **Look Back in Anger** became **movement's hallmark**.
- ➢ John Osborne called an **"angry young man."**
- ➢ Writers expressed **rage at class distinctions**.
- ➢ Key novelists: **John Braine** and **Alan Sillitoe**.
- ➢ Key playwrights: **Bernard Kops** and **Arnold Wesker**.
- ➢ Movement ended in **early 1960s**, like **Beat movement**.
- ➢ **Associated writers:**
  - o Kingsley Amis
  - o John Arden
  - o Stan Barstow
  - o Edward Bond
  - o John Braine
  - o Michael Hastings
  - o Thomas Hinde
  - o Stuart Holroyd
  - o Bill Hopkins
  - o Bernard Kops
  - o John Osborne
  - o Harold Pinter
  - o Alan Sillitoe
  - o David Storey

- o   Kenneth Tynan
- o   John Wain
- o   Keith Waterhouse
- o   Arnold Wesker
- o   Colin Wilson

Kingsley Amis (1922-1995)

- ➤ English novelist, poet, critic, and teacher.
- ➤ He wrote more than 20 novels, six volumes of poetry.
- ➤ He is the father of the novelist Martin Amis.
- ➤ Amis was a representative of called "The Movement,"
- ➤ He is best known for satirical comedies such as:
  - o   *Lucky Jim (1954),*
  - o   *One Fat Englishman (1963),*
  - o   *Ending Up (1974),*
  - o   *Jake's Thing (1978),*
  - o   *The Old Devils (1986).*
  - o   *The Green Man (1969),*
  - o   *Jake's Thing (1978),*
  - o   *The Old Devils (1986).*
- ➤ *Lucky Jim (1954)*
  - o   Features **antihero Jim Dixon,** junior faculty member.
  - o   **Dixon despises pretensions** of provincial academic life.
  - o   Represents **lower-middle-class,** rising against **wellborn elite.**
  - o   Struggles with **academic hierarchy and social limitations.**
  - o   **Novel explores class dynamics** and societal tensions.

John Osborne (1929-1994)

- ➤ British playwright and film producer whose *Look Back in Anger.*
- ➤ Known as the first of the Angry Young Men.
- ➤ **First play**, *The Devil Inside Him* (1950), co-written with **Stella Linden.**
- ➤ Made **London acting debut** in **1956**, same year as *Look Back in Anger.*
- ➤ *The Entertainer* (1957) shows **Britain's diminished self-confidence.**
- ➤ *Luther* (1961) depicts **Reformation leader's rebellious nature.**
- ➤ *Plays for England* (1962) include satire, **The Blood of the Bambergs.**

- *Under Plain Cover* explores **incestuous dominance-submission games**.
- *Inadmissible Evidence* (1964): **tirade of Jimmy Porter reimagined**.
- *A Patriot for Me* (1965) features **homosexual Austrian officer**.
- *West of Suez* (1971) sympathizes with **British colonizer's struggles**.
- Osborne's **last play**, *Déjàvu* (1992), revisits **Jimmy Porter**.
- *Look Back in Anger* reflects **Osborne's own experiences**, per autobiography.
- Autobiography, *A Better Class of Person* (1981), **reveals Osborne's inspirations**.

Look Back in Anger (1956)

- **"Look Back in Anger"** (1956) by **John Osborne**.
- **Realist play** focusing on marital **struggles**.
- **Jimmy Porter**, working-class, angry, intelligent **protagonist**.
- **Alison**, his **upper-middle-class**, impassive **wife**.
- **Cliff Lewis**, Welsh lodger, tries to keep **peace**.
- **Helena Charles**, Alison's **snobbish** and urging **friend**.
- **Jimmy owns** a small **candy shop**, feels stuck.
- **Jimmy lashes out** and **insults Alison** often.
- **Helena urges Alison** to **leave Jimmy**.
- **Jimmy confronts Helena**, then they **become a couple**.
- Alison returns after **miscarriage**, feeling **grief-stricken**.
- **Helena reconciles** with Alison, **feeling guilty**.
- Alison and Jimmy **repair their marriage** eventually.
- Themes include **class conflict**, **anger**, and **reconciliation**.

The Entertainer (1957)

- **The Entertainer**, a play by **John Osborne**, debuted **1957**.
- **Published in 1959**, it has **13 parts**.
- Metaphor for **Great Britain's decline as power**.
- Uses **seedy comedian** and **Empire Music Hall**.
- **Decries pop culture** and radical political views.
- **Archie Rice**, a **troubled music-hall performer**, struggles.
- Relies on **nude tableaus** to attract **audience**.
- Set during the **Suez Crisis**, symbolizing **Britain's decline**.
- Alternates **family drama** with Archie's **stage acts**.
- **Archie** emotionally disconnected, **self-centered father**.
- Ridicules **father Billy**, insults **wife Phoebe**.

> **Jean**, his daughter, returns after **broken engagement**.
> Family **bickers, squabbles**, yet lacks **real communication**.
> **Archie's final performance** follows **family losses**.

Déjàvu (1992)

> **Déjàvu (1992)** is John Osborne's **final stage play**.
> **Failure on stage** led Osborne to **quit playwriting**.
> **Sequel to Look Back in Anger (1956)**.
> Portrays **Jimmy Porter (J.P.) in middle age**.
> **J.P. lives with daughter Alison**, who **irons**.
> **Relentless arguments** between **J.P. and Alison**.
> **Cliff smooths things; Helena supports Alison**.
> **J.P. consoles himself** with his **teddy bear**.
> Objects to **vulgarisation** of language, **social agencies**.
> **Alison leaves her father**, ending the play.

Arnold Wesker (1932-2016)

> **Sir Arnold Wesker** was an **English dramatist**.
> Wrote **50 plays, short stories, essays**, and journalism.
> **Plays translated into 20 languages**, performed worldwide.
> **Inspiration for The Kitchen** came from hotel work.
> Met his **future wife, Dusty**, at Bell Hotel.
> Themes include **self-discovery, love**, and **political disillusion**.
> **Chicken Soup with Barley (1958)** premiered in **Coventry Theatre**.
> Premiere **reflected Wesker's political views** as 'angry young man.'
> **Roots (1959)** explored **Beatie Bryant's struggles in Norfolk**.
> Critics praised **Roots** for "emotional authenticity."
> Plays staged at **Royal Court Theatre**, managed by **George Devine**.
> Later management by **William Gaskill** continued Wesker's success.

Kitchen sink realism

> **Kitchen sink realism** developed in **1950s-1960s** Britain.
> Focused on **working-class domestic situations** and struggles.
> Protagonists are **"angry young men," disillusioned** with society.
> Explores **controversial issues** like **abortion, homelessness**.
> **Style:** Harsh, realistic, unlike **"well-made plays"** escapism.
> Set in **industrial North England**, using local **slang, accents**.
> **Film precursor:** *It Always Rains on Sunday* (**1947**).

- ➤ **First play:** John Osborne's *Look Back in Anger* (**1956**).
- ➤ *Look Back in Anger* portrays **gritty love triangle**.
- ➤ Setting: **One-room flat** in English **Midlands**.
- ➤ Movement addressed **social, political issues realistically**.

Chicken Soup with Barley (1958)

- ➤ **Chicken Soup with Barley** written by **Arnold Wesker**, 1956.
- ➤ Part of the **'Wesker Trilogy'**, followed by **Roots**.
- ➤ First staged in **1958** at **Belgrade Theatre, Coventry**.
- ➤ Later transferred to **Royal Court Theatre**, London.
- ➤ **Key post-war British play**, showing **communist family**.
- ➤ Play spans **20 years** of the **Kahn family**.
- ➤ Set in **1936 London**, showing ideals' **downfall**.
- ➤ Explores struggles during **WWII**, **Stalinism**, **Hungarian Revolution**.
- ➤ **Sarah Kahn**: strong, socialist, family-minded, and bossy.
- ➤ **Harry Kahn**: weak, dishonest, lacking in **conviction**.
- ➤ **Ada**: passionate, romantic, **Marxist**, personal and political.
- ➤ **Ronnie**: youthful idealist with **romantic aspirations**.

Roots (1959)

- ➤ **Roots (1958)** is the second play by **Arnold Wesker**.
- ➤ Part of **The Wesker Trilogy**, preceded by **Chicken Soup with Barley**.
- ➤ Final play in the trilogy: **I'm Talking about Jerusalem**.
- ➤ Focuses on **Beatie Bryant**, transitioning to self-expression.
- ➤ Written in **Norfolk dialect**, a **kitchen sink drama**.
- ➤ First performed at **Belgrade Theatre**, Coventry, **May 1959**.
- ➤ Transferred to **Royal Court Theatre**, London, starring **Joan Plowright**.

- ➤ **Edward Bond (1934)**

- ➤ English playwright, theatre director, poet, theorist, and screenwriter.
- ➤ Other well-received works include:
  - ○ *Saved (1965)*
  - ○ *Narrow Road to the Deep North (1968),*
  - ○ *Lear (1971),*
  - ○ *The Sea (1973),*
  - ○ *The Fool (1975),*
  - ○ *Restoration (1981),*

- *War trilogy (1985).*

- **Lear (1971)** is a three-act play by **Edward Bond**.
- A **rewrite** of Shakespeare's **King Lear**.
- Bond, a **socialist**, critiques society through **politics**.
- Focuses on **social critique**, not just **artistic experience**.
- Plays aim to **"bring about change in society"**.
- Hilde Klein: Shakespeare's answers not valid **today**.
- **Lear** depicted as a **paranoid autocrat**.
- Builds a **wall** to keep out "enemies."
- Daughters **Bodice and Fontanelle** rebel, causing **war**.
- **Lear imprisoned**, starts a journey of **self-revelation**.
- **Blinded**, haunted by **Gravedigger's Boy's ghost**.
- **Gravedigger's Boy murdered** for showing Lear **kindness**.
- Lear attempts to **dismantle the wall**, leading to **death**.
- Lear's death symbolizes **hope** and **practical activism**.
- **Cordelia** becomes a **Stalinist-type dictator**.

John Arden (1930-2012)

- **John Arden** emerged as an **important mid-20th century playwright**.
- His plays combined **poetry, songs**, and **colloquial speech**.
- **Conflicts** in his works were **purposely left unresolved**.
- Associated with **English Stage Company** at **Royal Court Theatre**.
- **Serjeant Musgrave's Dance** (1959) is considered his **best play**.
- Influenced by **Bertolt Brecht** and **Epic Theatre techniques**.
- Other plays: **Live Like Pigs, Workhouse Donkey, Armstrong's Last Goodnight**.
- **Notable Works:**
  - *"All Fall Down"*
  - *"Left-Handed Liberty"*
  - *"Live Like Pigs"*
  - *"Serjeant Musgrave's Dance"*
  - *"The Happy Haven"*
  - *"The Island of the Mighty"*
  - *"The Life of Man"*
  - *"The Non-Stop Connolly Cycle"*

- o   *"The Workhouse Donkey"*
- o   *"Waters of Babylon"*

Alan Sillitoe (1928-2010)

- ➤ English writer and one of the so-called "angry young men" of the 1950s.
- ➤ He disliked the label, as did most of the other writers to whom it was applied.
- ➤ He is best known for his debut novel *Saturday Night and Sunday Morning*
- ➤ His early short story "*The Loneliness of the Long Distance Runner,* "adapted into films.
- ➤ Later novels, such as
  - o   *The Death of William Posters (1965)*
  - o   *The Widower's Son (1977),*
  - o   *Birthday (2001),*
  - o   *Saturday Night and Sunday Morning (1958)*
- ➤ Notable short-story collections are:
  - o   *The Ragman's Daughter* (1963; filmed 1974),
  - o   *Men, Women, and Children* (1974),
  - o   *The Second Chance* (1980).

Peter Shaffer (1926-2016)

- ➤ **Peter Levin Shaffer born** in **1926**, Liverpool, **a twin.**
- ➤ Brother **Anthony Shaffer** also became a **playwright.**
- ➤ Family **moved to London** in **1936.**
- ➤ Worked as a **'Bevin Boy'** in **coal mines.**
- ➤ Studied **History at Cambridge**, edited **Granta magazine.**
- ➤ **"The Woman in the Wardrobe" (1951)**, a **detective story.**
- ➤ Written under **Peter Antony**, co-authored with **brother.**
- ➤ First play, **The Salt Land** (1954), broadcast on **BBC.**
- ➤ **Five Finger Exercise** (1958) won **Evening Standard Award.**
- ➤ **Royal Hunt of the Sun** (1964) depicts **Peru's conquest.**
- ➤ **Black Comedy** (1967) uses a **pitch-black room** concept.
- ➤ **Equus** (1973), story of **troubled stable boy.**
- ➤ **Amadeus** (1980) explores **Mozart and Salieri's rivalry.**
- ➤ Films: **Royal Hunt** (1969), **Equus** (1977), **Amadeus** (1984).
- ➤ **Amadeus film** won **8 Oscars**, including **Best Screenplay.**

➢ **Yonadab** (1985), **Lettice and Lovage** (1987), **radio play** (1990).
➢ Final play: **Gift of the Gorgon** (1993).

Amadeus (1979)

➢ **Amadeus** by **Peter Shaffer**, premiered in **1979**.
➢ Inspired by **Pushkin's 1830 play Mozart and Salieri**.
➢ **Rimsky-Korsakov** adapted it into an **1897 opera**.
➢ Features **music of Mozart, Salieri**, and contemporaries.
➢ Settings include premieres of **Mozart's operas**.
➢ Premiered at **Royal National Theatre, London** in 1979.
➢ Won **1981 Tony Award**; adapted into **1984 film**.

Tom Stoppard (1937*)

➢ **Sir Tom Stoppard**: Czech-born British **playwright and screenwriter**.
➢ Known for **themes of human rights, censorship, freedom**.
➢ A **National Theatre playwright**, globally **performed dramatist**.
➢ **Knighted** in **1997** by **Queen Elizabeth II**.
➢ Born in **Czechoslovakia**, fled Nazi occupation as **refugee**.
➢ Lived in **Darjeeling (1943–1946)** before settling in **Britain**.
➢ Career began as **journalist, drama critic, then playwright**.
➢ Stoppard's most prominent plays include:
   o *Rosencrantz and Guildenstern Are Dead,*
   o *Jumpers,*
   o *Travesties,*
   o *Night and Day,*
   o *The Real Thing,*
   o *Arcadia,*
   o *The Invention of Love,*
   o *The Coast of Utopia,*
   o *Rock 'n' Roll*
   o *Leopoldstadt.*
➢ Stoppard is also known for his screenplays, including
   o *Brazil (1985),*
   o *Empire of the Sun (1987),*
   o *The Russia House (1990),*
   o *Billy Bathgate (1991),*
   o *Shakespeare in Love (1998),*

- ○ *Enigma (2001), and*
- ○ *Anna Karenina (2012).*

Rosencrantz and Guildenstern Are Dead (1966)

- ➤ **Rosencrantz and Guildenstern Are Dead**, absurdist tragicomedy, **Tom Stoppard**, 1966.
- ➤ Explores **two minor characters** from Shakespeare's **Hamlet**.
- ➤ **Primary setting** of the play is **Denmark**.
- ➤ Structured as **inverse of Hamlet**, focuses on **duo**.
- ➤ **Hamlet plays minor role**, actions occur **offstage**.
- ➤ Duo operates under **King's command** in Hamlet.
- ➤ **Hamlet mocks and outwits** them, leading to **death**.
- ➤ Events seen from **Rosencrantz and Guildenstern's perspective**.
- ➤ Actions seem **nonsensical, determined by Hamlet's plot**.
- ➤ Witness **The Murder of Gonzago** performance aboard ship.
- ➤ Ship transports **Hamlet to England**, troupe as **stowaways**.
- ➤ Hamlet replaces **execution letter**, duo becomes **targets**.
- ➤ Ship hijacked by **pirates**, Hamlet **disappears**.
- ➤ Duo accepts **quo fata ferunt**: "whither the fates carry us."
- ➤ Ends with **Hamlet's final scene**, "Rosencrantz and Guildenstern are dead."

Travesties (1974)

- ➤ **Travesties** is a **1974 play** by **Tom Stoppard**.
- ➤ Centres on **Henry Carr**, reminiscing about **Zürich 1917**.
- ➤ **Interacts** with **James Joyce, Lenin, and Tristan Tzara**.
- ➤ Set in **Zürich, Switzerland** during **First World War**.
- ➤ **James Joyce** writing **Ulysses, Lenin** planning revolution.
- ➤ **Tristan Tzara** involved in **Dada movement** origins.
- ➤ **Henry Carr**, British official, remembers these **figures**.
- ➤ Carr's **memory** is **distracted, creating unpredictable interpretations**.
- ➤ **Carr starred** in Wilde's **The Importance of Being Earnest**.
- ➤ Wilde's play frames themes of **art, war, revolution**.
- ➤ **Situations from Earnest** appear prominently in **Travesties**.
- ➤ Includes versions of **Gwendolen and Cecily** from Earnest.
- ➤ **Comedic elements** shared across Travesties' **characters**.
- ➤ **Linguistic devices** include **puns, limericks, parody songs**.
- ➤ Extended parody of **"Mister Gallagher and Mister Shean"**.

Which writer does not belong to the Angry Young Men Movement?

1. John Osborne
2. Kingsley Amis
3. Seamus Heaney
4. **Philip Larkin**

Correct Explanation:

The "angry young men" were mostly working- and middle-class British playwrights and novelists who became prominent in the 1950s. The group's leading figures included John **Osborne and Kingsley Amis; other popular figures included John Braine, Alan Sillitoe, and John Wain.**

Question 123

Match List I with List II:

List I	List II
(A) Malcolm Bradbury	(I) Masters
(B) David Lodge	(I) Lucky Jim
(C) Kingsley Amis	(II) The History Man
(D) CP Snow	(IV) Changing places

Choose the correct answer from the options given below:

1. (A)-(IV), (B)-(III), (C)-(I), (D)-(II)
2. (A)-(II), (B)-(III), (C)-(IV), (D)-(I)
3. (A)-(I), (B)-(II), (C)-(III). (D)-(IV)
4. **(A)-(III), (B)-(IV), (C)-(II), (D)-(I)**

Correct Explanations:

➢ *The Masters* is the fifth novel in **C. P. Snow**'s series *Strangers and Brothers*.
➢ *Lucky Jim* is a novel by **Kingsley Amis**, first published in 1954 by Victor Gollancz.
➢ **Bradbury**'s best-known novel, *The History Man*, a campus novel published in 1975.

➤ *Changing Places (1975)* is the first **"campus novel"** by British novelist **David Lodge.**

Question 124

Should poets bicycle-pump the human heart or squash it flat? Man's love is of man's life a thing apart:

Girls aren't like that.

The above lines are written by :

1. John Wain
2. Kingsley Amis
3. Donald Davie
4. Philip Larkin

Correct Explanations:

Bookdust in Camilla's shop must date to
when my mother was a girl, as masked up

like a surgeon, I step down the book encrusted
stair to the subterranean stacks, where shelves

of orphaned poetry is arranged
from Amis to Zephaniah, though

I've never yet made it past poor Sylvia Plath
without the need to surface for a breath of air.

Camilla keeps a raucous parrot in a cage and
a picture from when punk rock was all the rage.

I slide my bank card and the Life of Crow throug
the gap in her perspex shield then stand and wait

while she reads the message on the title page:
'I won't be gone forever, think of me, as I do you'.

She tells me poems are popular of late,

at least with those who live next door to fate.

Kingsley Amis
'A Bookshop Idyll' (1956)

Question 125

Which two of the following plays were written by John Osborne?

- A. Look Back in Anger
- B. Loot
- C. Funeral Games
- D. Dejavu

Choose the correct answer from the options given below.:

1. (A) and (B) Only
2. (A) and (C) Only
3. (A) and (D) Only
4. (B) and (C) Only

Explanations:

Answer: 3. (A) and (D) Only

The two plays written by John Osborne are:

- ➢ Look Back in Anger
- ➢ Dejavu

Question 126

Arrange the following plays in their chronological sequence:

- A. Sergeant Musgrave's Dance
- B. The Playboy of the Western World
- C. Look Back in Anger
- D. Man and Superman

Choose the correct answer from the options given below
1. D, B, A, C
2. B, D, A, C
3. **D, B, C, A**
4. B, D, C, A

Correct Explanations:

- ➤ *Man and Superman (1905)* is a four-act play by **George Bernard Shaw**.
- ➤ **The Playboy of the Western World** (1907) is a three-act play by **J M Synge**.
- ➤ *Look Back in Anger (1956)* is a three-act play by **John Osborne**.
- ➤ *Sergeant Musgrave's Dance (1959)* is a play by John **Arden**.

Choose from the following options the correct combination of playwrights who contributed to the movement called "Kitchen Sink Drama".

1. John Osborne, Arnold Wesker, Shelagh Delaney and John Arden
2. John Osborne, Arnold Wesker, Harold Pinter and Shelagh Delaney
3. John Osborne, Arnold Wesker, Antonin Artaud and John Arden
4. John Osborne, Harold Pinter, Shelagh Delaney and John Arden

Explanations:
Answer: 1) John Osborne, Arnold Wesker, Shelagh Delaney and John Arden

The "Kitchen Sink Drama" movement was a style of realistic theatre that emerged in the 1950s and 1960s in Britain, which aimed to present the lives of ordinary people in a gritty and truthful manner. The movement was characterized by its focus on **social issues, working-class life, and domestic realism.** Some of the major playwrights associated with the Kitchen Sink Drama movement include:

John Osborne: His play "Look Back in Anger" (1956) is considered a landmark of the movement.

Shelagh Delaney: Her play "A Taste of Honey" (1958) deals with issues of race, class, and gender.

Arnold Wesker: His play "Chicken Soup with Barley" (1958) is a drama about a Jewish family living in the East End of London.

Alan Sillitoe: His play "The Loneliness of the Long Distance Runner" (1960) deals with issues of class and social injustice.

John Arden: He is another playwright who is associated with the Kitchen Sink Drama movement. His plays, such as "Serjeant Musgrave's Dance" (1959) and "Live Like Pigs" (1961), deal with issues of class, war, and social injustice.

Name the celebrated actor who played the leading role in the first production of John Osborne's The Entertainer (1957).

1. Peter Brook
2. **Laurence Olivier**
3. Al Pacino
4. Robert De Niro

Explanations:

The celebrated actor who played the leading role in the first production **of John Osborne's The Entertainer (1957) was Laurence Olivier.** Olivier played the role of Archie Rice, a failing music hall performer who struggles to come to terms with his declining career and the changes in British society. Olivier's performance in the play is considered one of his greatest achievements and helped to establish him as one of the most talented actors of his generation.

Theatre of the Absurd

- **Theatre of the Absurd** emerged post-**World War II**.
- Refers to **absurdist fiction** by **European playwrights**.
- Plays explore **existentialism** and **meaningless human existence**.
- **Communication breakdown** is central to the plays' themes.
- Structures often have a **circular plot shape**.
- **Logical arguments** give way to **irrational speech**.
- Plays often conclude with **silence** as resolution.
- **Martin Esslin** coined the term in **1960 essay**.
- Defined the "absurd" as **"no purpose, goal, objective"**.
- Esslin identified **Beckett, Adamov, Ionesco, Genet.**
- Later added **Harold Pinter** to the group.
- **Albert Camus** described life as **meaningless, absurd.**
- Beckett's **Waiting for Godot** eliminates **traditional plot.**
- **Timeless, circular** structure emerges in **Waiting for Godot.**

- ➢ Characters in **The Bald Soprano** reveal **verbal inadequacies**.
- ➢ **Purposeless talk** highlights metaphysical distress in plays.
- ➢ Plays mix **comic surface** with **serious messages**.
- ➢ **Absurdist theatre** reflects existential **human condition**.
  - ○ Samuel Beckett,
  - ○ Arthur Adamov,
  - ○ Eugène Ionesco,
  - ○ Jean Genet,
  - ○ In subsequent editions, he added a fifth playwright, Harold Pinter.

Samuel Beckett (1906-1989)

- ➢ **Samuel Beckett**, an **Irish playwright**, settled in **Paris**.
- ➢ Supported himself as **farmworker** during **World War II**.
- ➢ Joined the **underground resistance** against the **Nazis**.
- ➢ Wrote **French trilogy: Molloy, Malone Dies, The Unnamable**.
- ➢ **Waiting for Godot** (1952) gained **immediate success**.
- ➢ Translated **Waiting for Godot** into **English**.
- ➢ Known for **minimal plot, existentialist ideas**, and **humor**.
- ➢ Works typify **Theatre of the Absurd**, as defined.
- ➢ Later plays include **Endgame, Krapp's Last Tape, Happy Days**.
- ➢ Awarded the **Nobel Prize** in **1969**.
- ➢ Explored **bleak, tragicomic experiences** of human **existence**.
- ➢ Increasingly **minimalist**, with **linguistic experimentation**.
- ➢ Recognized as a **modernist** and key **absurdist figure**.
- ➢ Coined by **Martin Esslin** as **Theatre of the Absurd**.

Selected works by Beckett

Dramatic works:

- ➢ *Human Wishes* (c. 1936; published 1984)
- ➢ *En attendant Godot* (published 1952, performed 1953) (*Waiting for Godot,* pub. 1954, perf. 1955)
- ➢ *Fin de partie* (published 1957); *Endgame* (published 1957)
- ➢ *Krapp's Last Tape* (first performed 1958)
- ➢ *Happy Days* (first performed 1961); Oh les beaux jours (published 1963)
- ➢ *Play* (performed in German, as Spiel, 1963; English version 1964)
- ➢ *Come and Go* (first performed in German, then English, 1966)

> *Breath* (first performed 1969)
> *Not I* (first performed 1972)
> *That Time* (first performed 1976)
> *Footfalls* (first performed 1976)
> *Neither* (1977) (An "opera", music by Morton Feldman)
> *A Piece of Monologue* (first performed 1979)
> ***Rockaby*** (first performed 1981)
> *Ohio Impromptu* (first performed 1981)
> *Catastrophe* (Catastrophe et autres dramatiques, first performed 1982)
> *What Where* (first performed 1983)

Prose
The Trilogy

> *Molloy (1951); English version (1955)*
> *Malone meurt (1951); Malone Dies (1956)*
> *L'innommable (1953); The Unnamable (1958)*

Novels

> *Dream of Fair to Middling Women* (written 1932; published 1992)
> ***Murphy*** (1938); 1947 Beckett's French version
> ***Watt*** (1943); 1968, Beckett's French version
> *Comment c'est* (1961); How It Is (1964)
> *Mercier and Camier* (written 1946, published 1970); English translation (1974)

Short prose

> ***More Pricks Than Kicks*** *(1934)*
> *"Echo's Bones"* (written 1933, published 2014)

Waiting For Godot (1953)

> **Samuel Beckett's tragicomedy** written in **two acts.**
> **Waiting for Godot** published in **1952 in French.**
> First staged in **1953,** Beckett's **theatrical success.**
> A **landmark in modern drama,** true **innovation.**
> Premiered in **Paris,** stunned the **audience initially.**
> Became a **new dramatic experience** for audiences.

- ➢ Translated and performed in **major cities worldwide**.
- ➢ Ran for **300 performances** in **Paris**.
- ➢ Critics praised; others found it **baffling**.
- ➢ **Reactions stemmed from misunderstanding** the play.
- ➢ **World War II chaos** inspired **Theatre of the Absurd**.
- ➢ **"Absurd" described "out of harmony" situations**.
- ➢ Theater broke from **traditional stage techniques**.
- ➢ **Raises questions**, no answers about **human life**.
- ➢ Godot's **absence symbolizes unresolved absurdity**.
- ➢ Lacks traditional **plot with beginning, middle, end**.
- ➢ **Act II repeats Act I's pattern**, emphasizing absurdity.

Act I:

- ➢ **Characters Introduced**: Vladimir (Didi) and Estragon (Gogo), waiting endlessly.
- ➢ **Setting**: A barren landscape, single tree, timelessness implied.
- ➢ **Dialogue**: Discuss futile attempts to hang themselves, indecision dominates.
- ➢ **Pozzo and Lucky Enter**: Pozzo arrogant; Lucky, his burdened servant.
- ➢ **Pozzo's Monologue**: On power, dominance, and Lucky's degrading state.
- ➢ **Lucky's Speech**: A nonsensical, chaotic monologue on God, knowledge.
- ➢ **Godot Mentioned**: Messenger tells them Godot will arrive tomorrow.
- ➢ **Key Line**: "Nothing to be done," highlighting existential futility.
- ➢ **Estragon's Pain**: His boots and recurring memory issues symbolize suffering.
- ➢ **End of Act**: Darkness falls; they consider leaving but don't.

Act II:

- ➢ **Same Setting**: Tree now has a few leaves, change hinted.
- ➢ **Vladimir's Reflection**: Highlights human misery, endless cycles.
- ➢ **Estragon's Struggles**: Physical pain, memory loss deepen existential angst.
- ➢ **Pozzo and Lucky Return**: Pozzo blind, Lucky mute, roles reversed.

- ➤ **Pozzo's Despair**: Claims time doesn't exist; no meaning in suffering.
- ➤ **Vladimir's Anguish**: Questions their purpose, awaiting Godot in vain.
- ➤ **Messenger Returns**: Again says Godot will come tomorrow.
- ➤ **Estragon's Attempt**: Removes boots, representing hopeless action cycles.
- ➤ **Key Line**: "They give birth astride a grave," on mortality.
- 11. **Final Scene**: They plan to leave but stay, echoing absurdity.

Endgame (1957)

- ➤ **Endgame**, written in **French** as **Fin de partie**.
- ➤ Produced and published in **1957, translated by Beckett**.
- ➤ Features **four characters** in a single **room**.
- ➤ **Hamm**, blind, wheelchair-bound, and **demanding master**.
- ➤ **Clov**, resentful servant, **cannot sit down**.
- ➤ **Nagg and Nell**, Hamm's **crippled parents**, live in cans.
- ➤ **Two windows** are the only **room features**.
- ➤ **Hamm and Clov's relationship** is the main focus.
- ➤ **Spare setting, copious stage directions** are characteristic.
- ➤ **Characters**: Hamm (blind), Clov (lame), Nagg, and Nell.
- ➤ **Setting**: Bare room, grey light, atmosphere of desolation.
- ➤ **Opening**: Clov looks outside; world appears lifeless.
- ➤ **Hamm's Control**: Orders Clov; themes of power and dependence.
- ➤ **Nagg and Nell**: Parents in bins; recall past happiness.
- ➤ **Existence's Futility**: Hamm says, "Can there be misery loftier?"
- ➤ **Clov's Desire**: Wants to leave but feels stuck.
- ➤ **Nell's Death**: Dies in her bin; unnoticed by Nagg.
- ➤ **Hamm's Soliloquy**: Reflects on life, loss, and looming death.
- ➤ **Ending**: Clov prepares to leave; Hamm remains seated.

Krapp's Last Tape (1958)

- ➤ **Krapp's Last Tape**, a **one-act monodrama** by **Samuel Beckett**.
- ➤ Written in **1958**, produced and published by **1959**.
- ➤ **Krapp listens** to **old tape recordings** at his desk.
- ➤ Considers younger self's voice naive and **foolish**.
- ➤ **Drawn** to recorded **hopeful self** despite critique.
- ➤ **Krapp**, aged **69**, sits with reel-to-reel tapes.
- ➤ **White light** illuminates desk; surroundings in **darkness**.
- ➤ Krapp **eats a banana** and consults his **ledger**.

- ➤ Finds tape recorded on **his 39th birthday.**
- ➤ **Records tape** each year for **most of life.**
- ➤ Younger Krapp describes **happy birthday spent alone.**
- ➤ Mentions **bananas cause bowel trouble** humorously.
- ➤ **Young Krapp recalls** earlier tape, mocks idealistic youth.
- ➤ Mentions **mother's death**; older Krapp focuses on **language.**
- ➤ Younger Krapp inspired by **incident at pier**; skipped.
- ➤ Romantic memory with **young woman listened to twice.**
- ➤ Krapp fetches **blank tape**, discards **notes** irritably.
- ➤ Describes **failure of book**, drunk in **church.**
- ➤ Romantic life reduced to **prostitute's pitiable visit.**
- ➤ Krapp **replays romantic memory**, sits silently afterward.

Trilogy: Molloy (1951-55), Malone Dies (1951-56) & The
Unnamable (1953-58)

Molloy (1951-55)

- ➤ **Molloy**, first of **Beckett's French prose trilogy.**
- ➤ Features **two monologues**: Molloy and **pursuer Moran.**
- ➤ Molloy narrates his **losses and search for mother.**
- ➤ Moran's **hunt for Molloy leaves him crippled.**
- ➤ Displays **black humor, despair**, linked to **Homer's Odyssey.**

Malone Dies (1951-56)

- ➤ **Second novel** in Beckett's **French prose trilogy.**
- ➤ Malone narrates his **dying condition and possessions.**
- ➤ Writes about a **character reflecting himself.**
- ➤ Satirizes the **creative process, exploring selfhood.**
- ➤ Translated into **English by Beckett himself.**

The Unnamable (1953-58)

- ➤ **Third novel** of Beckett's **trilogy on selfhood.**
- ➤ **No conventional plot**, focuses on **human suffering.**
- ➤ Narrator is **disembodied**, living in a **jar.**
- ➤ Explores **identity through shifting names**: Mahood, Worm.
- ➤ Famous line: **"I can't go on, I'll go on."**

Eugène Ionesco (1909-1994)

- **Eugène Ionesco**, Romanian-French **playwright**, wrote mainly in **French**.
- A **leading figure** of 20th-century **French avant-garde theatre**.
- Revolutionized **drama ideas** with his **anti-play** techniques.
- **The Bald Soprano** marked beginnings of **Theatre of the Absurd**.
- **Absurdist plays** reflect **Albert Camus' philosophical ideas**.
- Explored **absurdism**, emphasizing meaningless **human existence**.
- **Member of Académie française** from **1970**.
- Won **1970 Austrian State Prize for Literature**.
- Received **1973 Jerusalem Prize** for his contributions.
- Notable Works:
  - *Amédée, or How to Get Rid of It (1954)*
  - *The Killer (1958)*
  - ***Rhinoceros (1959)***
  - *Exit the King (1962)*
  - *Stroll in the Air (1962)*
  - *Hunger and Thirst (1964)*
  - *The Killing Game aka Here Comes a Chopper (1970)*
  - *Macbett (1972)*
  - ***The Bald Soprano (1950)***
  - *Salutations (1950)*
  - *The Lesson (1951)*
  - *The Motor Show (1951)*
  - *The Chairs (1952)*
  - *The Leader (1953)*
  - *Victims of Duty (1953)*
  - *Maid to Marry (1953)*
  - *Jack, or The Submission (1955)*
  - *The New Tenant (1955)*
  - *The Picture (1955)*
  - *Improvisation or the Shepherd's Chameleon (1956)*

The Bald Soprano (1950)

- Written by **Eugène Ionesco**, an **"antiplay"** in 11 scenes.
- First produced in **1950**, published as **La Cantatrice chauve**.
- Represents **Theatre of the Absurd** and meaningless conversations.
- Focuses on **two couples**: Smiths and Martins.

- ➤ Characters engage in **nonsensical banter** and stories.
- ➤ Joined by **Mary (maid)** and her lover, **fire chief**.
- ➤ Fire chief disappointed by **absence of fire**.
- ➤ Arguments escalate with **no resolution or sense**.
- ➤ Ends with **repetition of opening dialogue**.
- ➤ A modern classic, staged continuously for **longest time**.

Rhinoceros (1959)

- ➤ Written by **Eugène Ionesco**, explores **absurdist themes**.
- ➤ Inhabitants of a town **turn into rhinoceroses**.
- ➤ Central character **Bérenger resists mass metamorphosis**.
- ➤ **Bérenger**, an everyman, struggles with **drinking, tardiness**.
- ➤ Critiques **Fascism and Nazism** before **World War II**.
- ➤ Themes include **conformity, mob mentality, and responsibility**.
- ➤ Begins with **a rhinoceros running through town**.
- ➤ Transformation spreads, including **Bérenger's friend, Jean**.
- ➤ **Bérenger warns others** but remains the only human.
- ➤ Explores **philosophy, morality**, and resistance against **mass movements**.

Jean Genet (1910-1986)

- ➤ **Jean Genet**: French **criminal** turned **writer** and **dramatist**.
- ➤ Transformed **erotic, obscene themes** into **poetic vision**.
- ➤ Leading figure in **avant-garde theatre, Theatre of Absurd**.
- ➤ **Caught stealing** at **age 10**, sent to Mettray.
- ➤ **Mettray reform school** inspired **Miracle of the Rose**.
- ➤ **The Thief's Journal** recounts **tramp, pickpocket life**.
- ➤ Life in **Barcelona, Antwerp**, other cities shaped works.
- ➤ Wrote **Funeral Rites** and **Querelle of Brest** in 1947.
- ➤ Early plays reveal **Sartre's influence** in **structure**.
- ➤ **Deathwatch** explores **prison-world themes**, identity struggles.
- ➤ **The Maids** tackles complex **identity problems**.
- ➤ Genet excels in **Theatre of the Absurd** dramatists.
- ➤ Plays like **The Balcony** and **The Blacks** shock audiences.
- ➤ **Expressionist style** exposes **hypocrisy** and **complicity**.

> Genet's **Theatre of Hatred** critiques **social, political issues**.

Our Lady of the Flowers (1943)

> **Our Lady of the Flowers**, novel by **Jean Genet**.
> First published **anonymously** in **1943** in French.
> Published under **Genet's name** in **1944**.
> **Definitive French edition** appeared in **1951**.
> Written in **prison** while jailed for **burglary**.
> Championed by **Sartre** and **Cocteau**, securing **pardon**.
> Story of **Divine**, a drag queen **canonized**.
> Narrator tells stories for **amusement in prison**.
> **Sartre** called it "**the epic of masturbation.**"
> Divine lives with **lovers**, including **Darling Daintyfoot**.
> **Our Lady of the Flowers**, a **murderer**, appears.
> Genet redefines **betrayal**, **murder**, and **sexuality**.

Comedy of menace

> **Comedy of Menace** includes plays by **Pinter, Campton**, and others.
> **Irving Wardle** coined the term in **Encore (1958)**.
> Derived from **Campton's play** subtitle, **Comedy of Menace**.
> Term is a play on **Comedy of Manners**.
> **Merritt** highlights Wardle's insights on **The Birthday Party**.
> **Wardle**: Comedy shows **agents/victims of destruction** at work.
> Characters **joke while oiling revolvers**, showing **absurd features**.
> **"Menace" symbolizes destiny** in **Pinter's plays**.
> Destiny is like an **incurable disease** with jokes.
> Reflects an **age of conditioned behavior** and destruction.
> **Orthodox man** collaborates in his own **destruction**.
> Wardle retracted **"Comedy of Menace"** in **1960** review.
> Stated: "I rashly applied the phrase **to Pinter.**"
> **The Caretaker** led Wardle to retract his earlier **claim**.
> **Wardle's retraction** marked **shifting views** on Pinter's work.

Harold Pinter (1930-2008)

> **Harold Pinter**, British playwright, screenwriter, and director.
> Won **Nobel Prize**, influential **modern British dramatist**.
> Career spanned over **50 years** with notable plays.
> Famous plays: **The Birthday Party, The Homecoming**.

- ➢ Adapted **Betrayal (1978)** for screen.
- ➢ Wrote screenplays: **The Servant, The Trial, Sleuth.**
- ➢ Directed and acted in **radio, stage, film productions.**
- ➢ Born and raised in **Hackney, east London.**
- ➢ Educated at **Hackney Downs School**, excelled in **sports.**
- ➢ Studied at **Royal Academy of Dramatic Art**, didn't finish.
- ➢ Fined for refusing **national service**, conscientious objector.
- ➢ Trained at **Central School of Speech and Drama.**
- ➢ Married actress **Vivien Merchant**; son **Daniel** (1958).
- ➢ Left Merchant, married **Lady Antonia Fraser** (1980).
- ➢ Began career with **The Room** (1957) production.
- ➢ **The Birthday Party** initially closed after **eight performances.**
- ➢ Critics called early works **"comedy of menace".**
- ➢ Later plays, like **Betrayal**, known as **"memory plays".**
- ➢ Directed nearly **50 productions** for **stage and screen.**
- ➢ Awards include **Nobel Prize (2005), Légion d'honneur (2007).**
- ➢ **Notable Works:**
  - ○ ***The Room (1957)***
  - ○ ***The Birthday Party (1957)***
  - ○ ***The Dumb Waiter (1957)***
  - ○ *A Slight Ache (1958)*
  - ○ *The Hothouse (1958)*
  - ○ ***The Caretaker (1959)***
  - ○ *A Night Out (1959)*
  - ○ *Night School (1960)*
  - ○ *The Dwarfs (1960)*
  - ○ *The Collection (1961)*
  - ○ *The Lover (1962)*
  - ○ *Tea Party (1964)*
  - ○ ***The Homecoming (1964)***
  - ○ *The Basement (1966)*
  - ○ *Landscape (1967)*
  - ○ *Silence (1968)*
  - ○ *Old Times (1970)*
  - ○ *Monologue (1972)*
  - ○ *No Man's Land (1974)*
  - ○ *Betrayal (1978)*
  - ○ *Family Voices (1980)*
  - ○ *A Kind of Alaska (1982)*
  - ○ *Victoria Station (1982)*

- o *One for the Road (1984)*
- o *Mountain Language (1988)*
- o *The New World Order (1991)*
- o *Party Time (1991)*
- o *Moonlight (1993)*
- o *Ashes to Ashes (1996)*
- o *Celebration (1999)*
- o ***Remembrance of Things Past (2000)***

The Room (1957)

- ➢ **The Room** is **Harold Pinter's first play** (1957).
- ➢ Critics call it **earliest "comedy of menace"**.
- ➢ **Similar to The Birthday Party**, Pinter's second play.
- ➢ **"Pinteresque" dialogue**: familiar yet disturbingly unfamiliar.
- ➢ **Characters subtly contradictory**, ambiguous, and complex.
- ➢ Comic yet **menacing mood** reflects **tragicomedy**.
- ➢ **Plot includes reversals**, surprises, and emotional moments.
- ➢ **Unconventional ending** leaves **some questions unresolved**.

Act I:

- ➢ **Characters**: Rose, Bert in a dingy, claustrophobic room.
- ➢ **Setting**: A bleak room representing isolation and control.
- ➢ **Event**: Rose fears the outside, discussing dangers.
- ➢ **Dialogue**: Rose: "It's dark out there, always."
- ➢ **Conflict**: Landlord arrives, unsettling Rose's fragile security.

Act II:

- ➢ **Visitor**: Blind man (Riley) disrupts Rose's tranquility.
- ➢ **Event**: Riley claims to know Rose's past life.
- ➢ **Tension**: Rose struggles with Riley's haunting revelations.
- ➢ **Climax**: Bert returns, kills Riley violently, leaving silence.
- ➢ **Theme**: The play explores existential fear, isolation.

The Birthday Party (1957)

- ➢ **The Birthday Party** is a **drama in three acts**.
- ➢ **Written by Harold Pinter**, produced in **1958**.
- ➢ Pinter's first full-length play introduced **"comedy of menace"**.

➤ **"Vague horrors suddenly threaten a character"** outside.
➤ Set in a **shabby rooming house**, featuring **Stanley**.
➤ **Two mysterious men "punish" Stanley** for unknown crimes.
➤ **Birthday party turns into violence** and **terror**.
➤ Dialogue features **pauses, disjointed conversations, nonsequiturs**.

Act I

➤ **Characters**: Meg and Petey run a seaside boarding house.
➤ **Stanley**: Reclusive tenant, annoyed by Meg's overbearing care.
➤ **Meg**: Brags about two new guests arriving soon.
➤ **Goldberg and McCann**: Their arrival unnerves Stanley deeply.
➤ **Key Line**: "You'll be all right now, sonny."

Act II

➤ **Stanley**: Confronted by Goldberg and McCann's relentless questioning.
➤ **Interrogation**: Stanley accused of unknown, mysterious crimes.
➤ **Tension rises**: Stanley's mental state starts deteriorating rapidly.
➤ **Party**: Meg throws a surprise birthday party for Stanley.
➤ **Violence erupts**: Stanley attacks Lulu in chaotic confusion.

Act III

➤ **Morning**: Boarding house eerily quiet after the party.
➤ **Petey**: Attempts to protect Stanley from Goldberg and McCann.
➤ **Goldberg**: Manipulates Petey, asserting control over Stanley's fate.
➤ **Stanley silenced**: He is now catatonic and unresponsive.
➤ **Stanley taken**: Goldberg and McCann escort him away ominously.
➤ **Key Line**: Petey pleads, "Stan, don't let them tell you what to do!"
➤ **Meg returns**: Oblivious to the events that unfolded.
➤ **Meg's denial**: Cheerfully recalls the birthday party's "success."
➤ **Symbolism**: The play highlights isolation and existential dread.
➤ **End**: The audience left with more questions than answers.

The Dumb Waiter (1957)

- **The Dumb Waiter**: One-act play by **Harold Pinter**, 1957.
- **"Small but perfectly formed"**, best of **early plays**.
- Combines **paucity of information, atmosphere of menace**.
- Features **working-class talk** in **claustrophobic setting**.
- Contains **political edge, germ of Pinter's oeuvre**.
- **Act I - Characters**: Ben and Gus, two hitmen, await orders.
- **Setting**: Basement room with a mysterious dumb waiter system.
- **Gus' Questions**: Gus repeatedly asks Ben questions about work.
- **Ben's Silence**: Ben avoids answers, creating tension between them.
- **Dumb Waiter Messages**: Notes demand food, though kitchen lacks supplies.
- **Confusion**: Gus wonders who's sending the orders upstairs.
- **Tension Builds**: Discussion about loyalty and past killings arises.
- **Final Order**: Ben receives instructions for their next assignment.
- **Plot Twist**: Gus realizes he is the target victim.
- **Cliffhanger**: Ben points gun at Gus; lights fade.

The Caretaker (1959)

- **The Caretaker** is a play by **Harold Pinter**.
- A **psychological study** exploring **power and corruption**.
- Became **Pinter's first significant commercial success**.
- Premiered at **Arts Theatre Club** on **27 April 1960**.
- Ran **444 performances**, moved to **Broadway** after London.
- **Action occurs** in flat of **Aston and Mick**.
- **Aston**, slow-witted, befriends **garrulous tramp Davies**.
- **Mick**, smarter but unstable, vies for **Davies's friendship**.
- Both brothers **offer Davies** role as **caretaker**.
- **Brothers realize equilibrium** is in **jeopardy**.
- They **ultimately reject Davies** to maintain balance.

The Homecoming (1964)

- **The Homecoming**, a two-act play by **Harold Pinter**.
- Written in **1964**, published in **1965**.
- Premiered in **London (1965)** and **New York (1967)**.
- Directed by **Sir Peter Hall, Tony Award 1967**.
- Set in **North London**, features **six characters**.

- ➢ Five men: **Max, Sam, Teddy, Lenny, Joey**.
- ➢ **Max**, retired butcher; **Sam**, chauffeur; **Teddy**, professor.
- ➢ **Lenny**, discreet **pimp**; **Joey**, aspiring **boxer**.
- ➢ One woman, **Ruth**, wife of **Teddy**.
- ➢ **Vivien Merchant** played Ruth in early productions.

Betrayal (1978)

- ➢ **Harold Pinter's Betrayal** (1978) uses **reverse chronology**.
- ➢ Inspired by Pinter's **seven-year affair** with Joan Bakewell.
- ➢ Bakewell wrote **Keeping in Touch** to share **her side**.
- ➢ **Betrayal explores multiple betrayals** in personal relationships.
- ➢ **Emma** has an affair with **Jerry**, Robert's **close friend**.
- ➢ **Jerry** is also **married to Judith**, adding complexity.
- ➢ Emma's affair remains **secret for five years**.
- ➢ Emma **confesses infidelity** to Robert, another **betrayal**.
- ➢ The play starts in **1977** and ends in **1968**.
- ➢ First scene shows Jerry, Emma meet after **affair ends**.
- ➢ **Final scene shows** Jerry declares love at **party**.
- ➢ **Nine scenes** explore shifting dynamics among characters.
- ➢ **Emma, Jerry use London flat** for clandestine meetings.
- ➢ Pivotal **Venice hotel scene** reveals Jerry's **letter**.
- ➢ **Emma admits** her affair to Robert in **Venice**.
- ➢ Affair continues, but **relationships are permanently altered**.
- ➢ Reverse chronology adds **emotional weight** to the narrative.
- ➢ **Audience knows future outcomes**, intensifying dramatic tension.
- ➢ Dialogue is **economical, meaningful, and power-laden**.

Question 129

Arrange the following literary movements in chronological order of their emergence:

    A. Imagism
    B. Impressionism
    C. Absurdism
    D. Futurism
    E. Pre-Raphaelitism

Choose the correct answer from the options given below :

(1) A, C, D, E, B
(2) B, D,C, E, A
(3) D, A, B, C, E
(4) E, B, D, A, C

Explanations:
Answer: **(4) E, B, D, A, C**

The Pre-Raphaelite Brotherhood (1848)

The **Pre-Raphaelite Brotherhood** was formed in **1848** by three young Royal Academy students: **Dante Gabriel Rossetti**, a gifted poet and painter, **William Holman Hunt**, and **John Everett Millais**, all under 25 years of age. This movement sought to return to the detailed and vibrant styles that existed before Raphael's influence on art, emphasizing sincerity and realism in their work.

Literary Impressionism (Late 19th to Early 20th Century)

Literary Impressionism drew inspiration from the European **Impressionist art movement** of the late 19th century. It focused on subjective perceptions, blurring the edges of reality by adopting unconventional points of view. Prominent influences include the **Dutch Tachtigers** and **Symbolist poets** such as **Baudelaire, Mallarmé, Rimbaud, Verlaine,** and **Laforgue**. The movement aimed to capture fleeting moments and individual perceptions, often using fragmented and associative language.

Futurism (Early 20th Century)

Futurism emerged in the early 20th century as a **modernist avant-garde movement**. It officially debuted in literature with the publication of **Filippo Tommaso Marinetti's Manifesto of Futurism (1909)**. This movement celebrated speed, technology, youth, and industrial progress, rejecting traditional forms and themes. It was particularly influential in Italy, becoming a major force in modernist art and literature.

Imagism (1914–1917)

Imagism was an early 20th-century poetry movement that emphasized precise imagery and clear, sharp language. It is considered the first organized

modernist literary movement in English. Between **1914 and 1917**, Imagist publications featured works by prominent modernists, including **Ezra Pound, H.D. (Hilda Doolittle), Amy Lowell, Ford Madox Ford, William Carlos Williams, F. S. Flint**, and **T. E. Hulme**. Imagism influenced modern poetry by advocating for simplicity and directness.

Theatre of the Absurd (1950s)

The **Theatre of the Absurd**, named after **post–World War II** absurdist fiction, became prominent in the **late 1950s**. It is associated with the works of European playwrights who explored existential themes and the absurdity of human existence. Prominent figures include **Samuel Beckett, Arthur Adamov, Eugène Ionesco, Jean Genet**, and later **Harold Pinter**. These plays often defied traditional plot structures, using nonsensical dialogue and surreal scenarios to reflect the fragmented and meaningless nature of modern life.

Question 130

Which of the following are features of the 'Theatre of the Absurd'?

    A.   Emphasis on the central role of God in the universe
    B.   **presentation of futile actions devoid of any goal**
    C.   portrayal of situations that point to the meaningfulness of life
    D.   **lacking in conflicts and dramatic tensions**
    E.   **presenting players in stasis or drift without definite roles**

Choose the correct answer from the options given below:
1. A, C and E only
2. **B, D and E only**
3. A, B and D only
4. B, C and D only

Correct Explanations:

The features of the 'Theatre of the Absurd' are:

➢ Questions of Existence.
➢ Distrust in Language.
➢ **Illogical Speeches and Meaningless Plots.**
➢ Re-establishment of man's communion with the Universe.

- ➤ Emphasize Abstract Values of Life.
- ➤ Vagueness about Time, Place, and Character.
- ➤ Lack of communication amid characters.
- ➤ **Presentation of futile actions devoid of any goal**
- ➤ **Lacking in conflicts and dramatic tensions**
- ➤ **Presenting players in stasis or drift without definite roles**

Question 131

Name the dramas which fall within the category of the Theatre of the Absurd.

- A. The Birthday Party
- B. Endgame
- C. Mrs. Warren's Profession
- D. The Rhinoceros
- E. Riders to the Sea

Choose the correct answer from the options given below:

1. A, B and E
2. B, C and D
3. A, B and D
4. C, D and E

Explanations:

Ans: A, B and D

Among the given options, the dramas which fall within the category of the Theatre of the **Absurd are "Endgame" and "The Rhinoceros." "The Birthday Party"** can also be considered a precursor to the Theatre of the Absurd, but it is not a typical example of the genre. "Mrs. Warren's Profession" and "Riders to the Sea" do not fall within this category.

Question 132

Arrange the works in chronological sequence:

- A. The Theatre of Revolt by Robert Brustein
- B. The Theater of the Absurd by Martin Esslin
- C. The Playwright as Thinker by Eric Bentley

D.   Modern American Drama by C)W.E Bigsby
E.   Modern Drama in Theory and Practice by L. N. Styan

Choose the correct answers from the options given below:

1.   A, D, C, D and E
2.   E, C, D, A and B
3.   B, D, A, E and C
4.   C, B, A, E and D

Explanations:
Ans: C, B, A, E and D

> ➢   *The Playwright as Thinker by Eric Bentley (1946)*
> ➢   *The Theater of the Absurd by Martin Esslin (1961)*
> ➢   *The Theatre of Revolt by Robert Brustein (1964)*
> ➢   *Modern Drama in Theory and Practice by L. N. Styan (1981)*
> ➢   *Modern American Drama by C. W. E. Bigsby (1992)*

Question 133

In Absurd Theatre, the characters often use disjointed, repetitive and clichéd speech to

A. Suggest that meaninglessness is also about a meaning.
B. Suggest the working of the subconscious.
C. Bring about the comic action and relief.
D. Illustrate the illogical and purposelessness of human condition.
E. Defy the self-professed 'modern' notion of dignity and wisdom.

Choose the correct answer from the options given below:

1. (A) and (B) Only
2. (B) and (C) Only
3. (D) and (E) Only
4. (A) and (D) Only

Explanations:
Answer: 4. (A) and (D) Only

Who makes the following speech in Samuel Beckett's Waiting for Godot?
"Astride of a grave and a dificult birth. Down in the hole, lingeringly, the grave-digger puts on the forceps."

1. Estragon
2. Lucky
3. Vladimir
4. Pozzo

Explanations:

Answer: 3. Vladimir

Vladimir's speech in Waiting for Godot is a part of the play's larger theme of existential crisis and waiting for something that may never come. The metaphor of "astride of a grave and a difficult birth" suggests the precariousness of human existence, as we are born into a world that is already heading towards our inevitable end. The image of the grave-digger putting on the forceps suggests that this existence is not only precarious but also painful and difficult, as we struggle to find meaning and purpose in a world that seems indifferent to our struggles.

Question 135

Which of these characters figure in Samuel Beckett's Waiting for Godot?

A. Estragon
B. Pozzo
C. Bassanio
D. Murphy

Choose the correct answer from the options given below:

1. **A and B only**
2. B and C only
3. C and D only
4. A and D only

Correct Explanation:

Estragon and Pozzo are two of the main characters in Samuel Beckett's play, Waiting for Godot. Estragon is one of the two tramps who are waiting for the arrival of Godot, while Pozzo is a wealthy landowner who passes through the area with his slave, Lucky.

Question 136

Which of the following is true about Samuel Beckett's Waiting for Godot?

(A) It illustrates vanity of human kind.
(B) It has uncompromising views on humanitarian communism.
(C) It projects self-deception, striving to disguise failure.
(D) It is a static representation without structure or development.
(E) It's incoherent dialogue suggests despair of a society.

Choose the correct answer from the options given below:

1. (A) and (C) Only
2. (C) and (D) Only
3. (A) and (B) Only
4. (D) and (E) Only

Explanations:

Answer: 4. (D) and (E) Only

The correct answer is (D) and (E) Only, which are "It is a static representation without structure or development" and "Its incoherent dialogue suggests despair of a society." Samuel Beckett's "Waiting for Godot" epitomizes the Theatre of the Absurd, characterized by its lack of conventional plot, structure, or character development. The play **focuses on the existential condition, highlighting human life's static and repetitive nature through its characters' endless wait for the never-appearing Godot**. This static quality underscores the absence of meaningful action or progress, reflecting a profound societal despair and the futile search for purpose. The dialogue, often seen as incoherent, mirrors the breakdown of communication in society and the individuals' isolation, contributing to the overall theme of existential despair.

Why Other Statements are Wrong:

(A) "It illustrates vanity of human kind." While "Waiting for Godot" does explore existential themes, including the potential futility of life, saying it merely illustrates vanity oversimplifies its depth and philosophical undertones.

(B) "It has uncompromising views on humanitarian communism." The play does not explicitly deal with political ideologies such as communism; instead, it focuses on existential and philosophical themes.

(C) "It projects self-deception, striving to disguise failure." Although the play touches on self-deception, it is not the primary focus; the core lies in existential waiting and the human condition.

Question 137

Which one of the following statements is appropriately true of Harold Pinter's plays?

1. Menace is in the air, and it leads to bloody violence.
2. Menace is in the air, and it is realised through the female characters.
3. Menace is in the air, but it is not pinned down or explained.
4. Menace is in the air, and anarchy follows in a systematic manner.

Explanations:

Answer: 3. Menace is in the air, but it is not pinned down or explained.

The statement that appropriately characterises Harold Pinter's plays is **"Menace is in the air, but it is not pinned down or explained." Pinter's plays are known for their use of language, often involving pauses, silences, and non-sequiturs, which create a sense of tension and unease.** This tension is often never fully resolved, and the source of the menace is often left unexplained, creating a sense of ambiguity and mystery.

The term **"Comedy of Menace" is often used to describe Pinter's plays.** It refers to the way in which Pinter **combines elements of comedy and humour with moments of extreme violence and aggression.** In Pinter's plays, characters often engage in seemingly innocent conversations, only to have the conversation take a darker turn, with threats, intimidation, and violence lurking just beneath the surface. This creates a sense of unease and tension for the audience, who are never quite sure what will happen next.

Question 138

What game do the characters play in Act II of Harold Pinter's The Birthday Party?

1. A game of chess
2. A game of cards
3. Blind Man's Buff
4. Musical chairs

Explanations:

Answer: 3. Blind man's buff

In Act II of Harold Pinter's play The Birthday Party, the characters play a game of blind man's buff. This is a game where one person is blindfolded and tries to catch and identify the other players without being able to see them. In the play, the game becomes increasingly chaotic and violent as the characters become more aggressive and disoriented. The game is used as a metaphor for the confusion and power struggles that are happening between the characters throughout the play. It also serves to highlight the idea that the characters are playing a dangerous game of deception and manipulation, where no one is quite sure who is in control or what is really going on.

Question 139

In Harold Pinter's play The Birthday Party, who suggests the idea of having a birthday party?

1. Meg
2. Lulu
3. Goldberg
4. McCann

Explanations:

Answer: 3. Goldberg

Goldberg suggests that they throw a party for Stanley as it's his birthday. They corner and interrogate Stanley, their questions become ever more aggressive and absurd. They talk about a mysterious 'organisation' and are generally threatening in their demeanour.

Question 140

Which two of the following stage directions are from Harold Pinter's The Birthday Party?

A. The living room of a house on a seaside town.

B.   A garbage pail on the ground next to the porch steps.
C.   A light shows from the upstairs bedroom, with dark lower-floor windows.
D.   He hangs the drum around his neck, taps it gently with the sticks, then marches round the table, beating it regularly.

Choose the correct answer from the options given below:

1.   **A and D only**
2.   C and D only
3.   B and C only

Correct Explanations:

The Birthday Party opens in the living-dining area of a seedy rooming **house at an unnamed seaside resort in England**. Stanley returns just before Meg comes back. He grills her about the men, trying to find out if she knows who they are. **He also denies that it is his birthday, but he accepts her present, left by Lulu on the sideboard. It is a toy drum. He straps it on his neck, then marches around banging on it.** Just before the curtain, his beating becomes erratic and finally "savage and possessed."

Question 141

Which among the following are true about Harold Pinter?

A.   Harold Pinter was born in the year 1925.
B.   He was influenced by Samuel Beckett and the Theatre of the Absurd,
C.   The Caretaker and The Alchemist are his famous plays.
D.   Stanley is a character in The Birthday Party.
E.   Betrayal is a story of a married couple.

Choose the correct answer from the options given below :

1.   A, D and E only
2.   A, C and D only
3.   **B, D and E only**
4.   B, C and D only

Correct Explanations:

➢   **Harold Pinter** was born **October 10, 1930, London.**

- Died **December 24, 2008**, and was an **English playwright**.
- Renowned post-WWII dramatist, challenging and complex works.
- His plays use silence and understatement for depth.
- Characters' thoughts often contradict their spoken words.
- **Pinter won the Nobel Prize for Literature (2005).**
- **Theatre of the Absurd** reflects existential absurdity and purposelessness.
- Influenced by Camus's essay **"The Myth of Sisyphus" (1942).**
- Absurdist dramatists include **Beckett, Ionesco, Genet, Pinter,** and others.
- **The Caretaker (1960)** explores familial trust and betrayal.
- **The Birthday Party (1958)** established **"comedy of menace."**
- Action happens in a rooming house with Stanley.
- Two mysterious men punish Stanley for unknown crimes.

Question 142

Which of the following are plays written by Harold Pinter?

A. Family Voices
B. A Moon for the Misbegotten
C. The Room
D. No Man's Land
E. Krapp's Last Tape

Choose the correct answer from the options given below:

1. A, B and E
2. B, C and D
3. A, C and D
4. C, D and E

Explanations:

Ans: A, C and D

- *Family Voices* was first produced in 1981.
- *The Room* is an early play first performed in 1957.
- *No Man's Land* is a play first produced in 1975.

BRITISH POSTMODERN FICTION: 1950 TILL THE PRESENT

George Orwell (1903-1950)

- **Eric Arthur Blair**, pen name **George Orwell**.
- Known for **lucid prose** and **social criticism**.
- Opposed **totalitarianism** and supported **democratic socialism**.
- Born in **India**, raised and educated in **England**.
- Worked as an **Imperial policeman** in **Burma**.
- Adopted pen name inspired by **River Orwell**.
- Lived as **journalist**, teacher, bookseller in **London**.
- Attended **Wellington** and **Eton**, taught by **Aldous Huxley**.
- Published **first writings** in **college periodicals**.
- Wounded in the **Spanish Civil War**, health worsened.
- Worked as **BBC journalist** during **World War II**.
- **Animal Farm** brought fame during his **lifetime**.
- **Nineteen Eighty-Four** written in **final years**.
- Nonfiction works: **The Road to Wigan Pier** (1937).
- **Homage to Catalonia** (1938) on **Spanish Civil War**.
- Novels: **Burmese Days, A Clergyman's Daughter**.
- **Keep the Aspidistra Flying** critiques middle-class **materialism**.
- Coined neologisms like **Big Brother, doublethink, Newspeak**.
- Influential, adjective **"Orwellian"** describes **authoritarian practices**.
- Ranked **second** by **The Times** in **2008**.
- Themes include **politics, language**, and **culture critique**.
- Works remain influential in **popular and political culture**.

Novels

- *1934 – Burmese Days*
- *1935 – A Clergyman's Daughter*
- *1936 – Keep the Aspidistra Flying*
- *1939 – Coming Up for Air*
- *1945 – Animal Farm*
- *1949 – Nineteen Eighty-Four*

Nonfiction

- *1933 – Down and Out in Paris and London*
- *1937 – The Road to Wigan Pier*
- *1938 – Homage to Catalonia*

- **Animal Farm** published in **1945** by **George Orwell**.
- Allegory of the **Russian Revolution of 1917**.
- **Tsarist autocracy** overthrown; **Bolsheviks** seize power.
- **Joseph Stalin** betrayed revolution's **supporters**.
- Uses **fable conventions** with animals as characters.
- **Pigs represent Lenin, Trotsky, Stalin** in story.
- **Animals rebel** against Mr. Jones, symbolizing **tsar**.
- Set on a **small English farmyard**.
- **Pigs manipulate**, animals believe in a **republic**.
- Written at **WWII's end**, praising **USSR victories**.
- Orwell struggled to **find willing publishers**.
- Rejected by **Gollancz, Faber and Faber**.
- Jonathan Cape **abandoned publishing**, influenced by **spy**.
- **Runaway success** in England (1945) and US (1946).
- Marked the **Cold War's beginning**, dissolving alliances.
- Among **Orwell's finest works**, critically acclaimed.
- **Animals overthrow humans**, creating egalitarian society.
- **Pigs subvert rebellion**, become oppressive rulers.
- Famous quote: **"All animals are equal..."**
- Ranked second in **The Times'** 2008 list.
- **Rebellion Begins**: Animals overthrow humans, inspired by Old Major.
- **Key Characters**: Napoleon, Snowball, Boxer, and Squealer emerge.
- **Seven Commandments**: "All animals are equal" introduced as law.
- **Windmill Debate**: Snowball advocates progress; Napoleon opposes violently.
- **Power Grab**: Napoleon expels Snowball, consolidates leadership alone.
- **Corruption Grows**: Pigs enjoy luxuries, animals face growing hardships.
- **Propaganda**: Squealer manipulates, changing commandments to justify tyranny.
- **Boxer Betrayed**: Loyal horse sent to slaughter, breaking spirits.
- **Final Betrayal**: Pigs resemble humans, breaking equality promise.
- **Important Line**: "All animals are equal, but some..."
- Initially, there were seven commandments:
    - *Whatever goes upon two legs is an enemy.*
    - *Whatever goes upon four legs, or has wings, is a friend.*

- o *No animal shall wear clothes.*
  - o *No animal shall sleep in a bed.*
  - o *No animal shall drink alcohol.*
  - o *No animal shall kill any other animal.*
  - o *All animals are equal.*
- ➢ These commandments are also refined into the maxim *"Four legs good, two legs bad!"*

Nineteen Eighty-Four (1949)

- ➢ **Nineteen Eighty-Four is a dystopian social science fiction novel.**
- ➢ Written by **George Orwell**, published **8 June 1949**.
- ➢ **Themes**: Totalitarianism, **mass surveillance**, repressive regimentation.
- ➢ Modeled after **Stalinist Russia** and **Nazi Germany**.
- ➢ Explores **truth, facts in politics**, and manipulation.
- ➢ Set in **1984**, in totalitarian state **Oceania**.
- ➢ **Oceania ruled** by Party, led by **Big Brother**.
- ➢ Party enforces obedience through **Newspeak** and **doublethink**.
- ➢ **Slogans** include: "War is peace," "**Freedom is slavery**."
- ➢ **Thought Police** ensure control with **constant surveillance**.
- ➢ **Hero Winston Smith**, Outer Party member, rewrites **history**.
- ➢ Works at **Ministry of Truth**, alters political records.
- ➢ **Winston rebels**, longs for **truth and decency**.
- ➢ Begins forbidden affair with **Julia**, like-minded rebel.
- ➢ Rents room in neighborhood of **Proles (proletariats)**.
- ➢ Grows interested in **Brotherhood**, opposing **Party doctrines**.
- ➢ Posters warn: **"Big Brother is watching you."**
- ➢ **O'Brien**, Inner Party member, sets a **trap**.
- ➢ O'Brien is a **Party spy**, hunting **thought-criminals**.
- ➢ **Winston and Julia** caught, sent to **Ministry of Love**.
- ➢ **Torture destroys Winston's independence**, dignity, and **humanity**.
- ➢ In **Room 101**, Winston faces **his worst nightmare**.
- ➢ Betrays Julia, screams: **"Do it to Julia!"**
- ➢ **Winston released**, loves **Big Brother**, and abandons **Julia**.

Why I Write (1946)

- ➢ **"Why I Write"** (1946) by **George Orwell**.
- ➢ Published in **Summer 1946 edition** of **Gangrel**.
- ➢ Editors **J.B. Pick** and **Charles Neil** requested essays.

- Orwell recounts his journey to becoming a **writer**.
- Describes early works: **poems, short stories, self-stories**.
- Sets out **four motives** driving all **writers**.
- **Motive proportions** vary between **writers and times**.
- **Sheer egoism**: Desire to seem **clever and remembered**.
- Writers want to **"get back"** at childhood snubs.
- Serious writers are **vainer**, less money-focused than **journalists**.
- **Aesthetic enthusiasm**: Love for **good prose, rhythm, impact**.
- Writing's **beauty and sound** bring **pleasure** to authors.
- Some writers have **weak aesthetic enthusiasm** but **present**.
- **Historical impulse**: Desire to see **facts as they are**.
- Writers aim to **store true facts** for **posterity**.
    1. Sheer egoism
    2. Aesthetic enthusiasm
    3. Historical impulse
    4. Political purpose
- **Political purpose**: No book is free from **political bias**.
- Desire to **"push the world"** in specific directions.
- Belief that art should avoid politics is **political**.
- Orwell connects writing to **human motives** universally.
- Writing mixes **egoism, aesthetics, history, and politics**.

Question 143

Match List - I with List - II.

List - I (Original name)	List - II (Penname / Pseudonym)
A. Charles Lutwidge Dodgson	I. George Eliot
B. Mary Ann Evans	II. Mark Twain
C. Eric Arthur Blair	III. George Orwell
D. Samuel Langhorne Clemens	IV. Lewis Carroll

Choose the correct answer from the options given below :

(1) A-IV, B-I, C-III, D-II.

(2) A-III, B-IV, C-II, D-I

(3) A-I, B-II, C-III, D-IV

(4) A-II, B-I, C-III, D-IV

Explanations:
Answer: (1) A-IV, B-I, C-III, D-II.

A. Charles Lutwidge Dodgson → IV. Lewis Carroll
(Lewis Carroll is the pseudonym of Charles Lutwidge Dodgson, famous for *Alice's Adventures in Wonderland*.)
B. Mary Ann Evans → I. George Eliot
(George Eliot is the pen name of Mary Ann Evans, known for *Middlemarch* and *Silas Marner*.)
C. Eric Arthur Blair → III. George Orwell
(George Orwell is the pen name of Eric Arthur Blair, known for *1984* and *Animal Farm*.)
D. Samuel Langhorne Clemens → II. Mark Twain
(Mark Twain is the pen name of Samuel Langhorne Clemens, known for *The Adventures of Tom Sawyer* and *The Adventures of Huckleberry Finn*.)

Question 144

Match List I and List II List I

List I Essayist	List II Essay
A. George Orwell	I. "On the Artificial Comedy of the Last Century"
B. Michel de Montaigne	II. 'Why I Write"
C. Charles Lamb	**III.** "A Modest Proposal"
E. Jonathan Swift	**IV.** "On the Cannibals"

Choose the correct answer from the options given below:

1. A – III, B – IV, C – III, D – I
2. A – II, B – IV, C – I, D – III
3. A – IV, B – III, C – II, D – I
4. A – II, B – III, C I, D – IV

Explanations:
Answer: 2. A–II, B – IV, C – I, D – III

The correct sequence of the publication dates for these essays is:

1. **Michel de Montaigne - "On the Cannibals" (1580)**
2. **Charles Lamb - "On the Artificial Comedy of the Last Century" (1822)**

3. Jonathan Swift - "A Modest Proposal" (1729)
4. George Orwell - 'Why I Write" (1946)

Who is the author of the essay "Lear, Tolstoy and the Fool"?

1. Aldous Huxley
2. **George Orwell**
3. Virginia Woolf
4. Somerset Maugham

Correct Explanations:

"Lear, Tolstoy and the Fool" is an essay by George Orwell. It was inspired by a critical essay on Shakespeare by Leo Tolstoy and was first published in Polemic No. 7 (March 1947).

Match List I with List II

List I (Character)	List II (Novel)
A. Winston Smith	I. Sons and Lovers
B. Paul Morel	II. Ulysses
C. 'whiskey priest'	III. Nineteen Eighty-four
D. Leopold Bloom	IV. Decline and Fall
E. Paul Pennyfeather	V. The Power and the Glory

Choose the correct answer from the options given below:

1. **A-III, B-I, C-V, D-II, E-IV**
2. A-I, B-V, C-II, D-III, E-IV
3. A-IV, B-III, C-V, D-II, E-I
4. A-V, B-I, C-IV, D-II, E-III

Correct Explanations:

A. Winston Smith is a character in the novel "Nineteen Eighty-Four" by George Orwell.
B. Paul Morel is a character in the novel "Sons and Lovers" by D.H. Lawrence.

C. The "whiskey priest" is a character in the novel "The Power and the Glory"
D. Leopold Bloom is a character in the novel "Ulysses" by James Joyce.
E. Paul Pennyfeather is a character in the novel "Decline and Fall" by Evelyn Waugh.

In "Politics and the English Language" which two of the following 'tricks' are mentioned by George Orwell as 'bad habits' of English use?

   A. obsolete words
   B. pretentious diction
   C. dying metaphors
   D. false modifiers

Choose the correct answer from the options given below:

   1. A and B only
   2. **B and C only**
   3. B and D only
   4. C and D only

Correct Explanations:

In "Politics and the English Language," George Orwell argues that bad writing is often a symptom of lazy or unclear thinking and that it can have insidious political consequences. He identifies several "tricks" of bad writing that are often used to mask a lack of content or to manipulate the reader. **Two of these tricks are "dying metaphors,"** which are metaphors that have been overused to the point of losing their meaning, and "pretentious diction," which involves using unnecessarily complex or abstract language in an attempt to sound intelligent or sophisticated.

Match List - I with List - II.

List - I (Character)	List - II (Novel)
A. Sethe	**I.** The Handmaid's Tale
B. Okonkwo	**II.** Beloved

| C. Offred | **III.** Things Fall Apart |
| D. Winston Smith | **IV.** Nineteen Eighty Four |

Choose the correct answer from the options given below :

    1. (A)-(II), (B)-(III), (C)-(I), (D)-(IV)
    2. (A)-(III), (B)-(II), (C)-(IV), (D)-(I)
    3. (A)-(I), (B)-(III), (C)-(II), (D)-(IV)
    4. (A)-(IV), (B)-(I), (C)-(III), (D)-(II)

Explanations:

Answer: 1. (A)-(II), (B)-(III), (C)-(I), (D)-(IV)

Toni Morrison's 1987 novel, Beloved, unfolds in the aftermath of the American Civil War and centers on the haunting of a Cincinnati home by a vengeful ghost. This home belongs to **Sethe, a woman who once endured the horrors of enslavemen**t, and her daughter Denver. Drawing inspiration from the true story of Margaret Garner, an enslaved woman who escaped to Ohio from Kentucky in 1856, Morrison weaves a narrative set in 1873 that explores the enduring scars of slavery and the search for identity and home.

Chinua Achebe's Things Fall Apart, published in 1958, marks a seminal moment in English African literature, offering a nuanced portrayal of life in pre-colonial Igboland and the disruptive advent of European colonialism and Christianity. Through the experiences of **Okonkwo, a respected leader in the Umuofia clan,** Achebe delves into Igbo society, its values, and the clash between traditional ways and the new order brought by colonial influence, narrating a tale of cultural upheaval and personal tragedy.

Margaret Atwood's The Handmaid's Tale, a novel released in 1985, presents a grim vision of the future where the Republic of Gilead, a theocratic state, replaces the United States. **The story, narrated by Offred**, revolves around the lives of Handmaids, women forced into childbirth roles by the state's elite. Atwood crafts a dystopian world that examines themes of power, gender, and resistance within the confines of a totalitarian society.

Nineteen Eighty-Four, penned by George Orwell in 1949, introduces readers to **Winston Smith,** an ordinary man navigating life under the oppressive regime of Big Brother in a dystopian future.

Match List I with List II

List I (Author)	List II (Work)
A. Nigel Dennis	I. "Technique as Discovery"
B. George Orwell	II. The Gay Science
C. Mark Schorer	III. Cards of Identity
D. Nietzsche	IV. Down and Out in Paris and London

Choose the correct answer from the options given below

1. (A) - (III), (B) - (IV), (C) - (I), (D) - (II)
2. (A) - (III), (B) - (IV), (C) - (II), (D) - (I)
3. (A) - (IV), (B) - (III), (C) - (II), (D) - (I)
4. (A) - (IV), (B) - (III), (C) - (I), (D) - (II)

Explanations:
Answer: 1. (A) - (III), (B) - (IV), (C) - (I), (D) - (II)

Nigel Forbes Dennis (January 16, 1912 – July 19, 1989) was a British author known for his versatility across novels, criticism, drama, and editorial work. His writing journey began notably in 1949 with "Boys and Girls Come out to Play" (released as "A Sea Change" in the USA), leading to his acclaimed **1955 novel, "Cards of Identity."** This work, celebrated for its sharp satirical edge on psychological themes, won him a cult following. "A House in Order," his subsequent novel, explored personal dimensions of identity through the lens of a prisoner's mental resilience. Dennis's literary contributions, though sparse, were significant and included "Two Plays and a Preface" (1958), "Dramatic Essays" (1962), and a praised study on Jonathan Swift that received the Royal Society of Literature Award in 1966. His later years saw the publication of "Exotics: Poems of the Mediterranean and Middle East" (1970) and "An Essay on Malta" (1972), enriched with Osbert Lancaster's illustrations.

Eric Arthur Blair, known by his pen name George Orwell (June 25, 1903 – January 21, 1950), was an influential English writer celebrated for his clear prose, insightful social commentary, and firm stance against totalitarianism. **Novels**

➢ *1934 – Burmese Days*
➢ *1935 – A Clergyman's Daughter*
➢ *1936 – Keep the Aspidistra Flying*
➢ *1939 – Coming Up for Air*
➢ *1945 – Animal Farm*
➢ *1949 – Nineteen Eighty-Four*

Nonfiction
➢ ***1933 – Down and Out in Paris and London***
➢ *1937 – The Road to Wigan Pier*
➢ *1938 – Homage to Catalonia*

Mark Schorer (May 17, 1908 – August 11, 1977) was an American writer, critic, and scholar born in Sauk City, Wisconsin. A leading critic of his time, he was best known for his work, Sinclair Lewis: An American Life.

Literary works
➢ *A House Too Old (1935)*
➢ *William Blake: The Politics of Vision (1946)*
➢ *"The State of Mind" (1947)*
➢ ***Technique as Discovery (1948)***
➢ *Wars of Love (1954)*
➢ *Sinclair Lewis: An American Life (1961)*
➢ *Colonel Markesan and Less Pleasant People (1966) with August Derleth*
➢ *The World We Imagine (1968)*
➢ *Pieces of Life (1977)*

Friedrich Nietzsche (October 15, 1844 – August 25, 1900) was a German philosopher, cultural critic, composer, poet, and philologist..

List of Works:
➢ ***The Birth of Tragedy (1872)***
➢ *On Truth and Lies in a Nonmoral Sense (1873)*
➢ *Philosophy in the Tragic Age of the Greeks (1873; first published in 1923)*
➢ *Untimely Meditations (1876)*
➢ *Human, All Too Human (1878)*
➢ *The Dawn (1881)*
➢ ***The Gay Science (1882)***
➢ *Thus Spoke Zarathustra (1883)*
➢ *Beyond Good and Evil (1886)*
➢ *On the Genealogy of Morality (1887)*
➢ *The Case of Wagner (1888)*

> *Twilight of the Idols (1888)*
> *The Antichrist (1888)*
> *Ecce Homo (1888; first published in 1908)*
> *Nietzsche contra Wagner (1888)*
> *The Will to Power*

William Golding (1911-1993)

> **Sir William Golding**: British novelist, playwright, **poet**.
> Best known for **Lord of the Flies (1954)**.
> Published **12 volumes of fiction** in lifetime.
> Won **Booker Prize** in 1980 for **Rites of Passage**.
> Awarded **Nobel Prize in Literature** in **1983**.
> Educated at **Marlborough Grammar School** and **Oxford**.
> Worked in **settlement house** and **small theatres**.
> Became a **schoolmaster** at Bishop Wordsworth's School.
> Joined **Royal Navy (1940)**, helped sink **Bismarck**.
> Commanded **rocket-launcher** in France's **1944 invasion**.
> Resumed teaching after **WWII** until **1961**.
> **Lord of the Flies** explores **savagery among boys**.
> **The Inheritors** depicts Neanderthal man's **final days**.
> **Pincher Martin** reflects on **guilt and survival**.
> **Free Fall** and **The Spire** explore **man's evil**.
> **Darkness Visible** tells of boy burned in **WWII blitz**.
> Sea trilogy: **Rites of Passage, Close Quarters, Fire Down Below**.
> Knighted in **1988** for **literary achievements**.
> **Novels:**
>> *Lord of the Flies (1954)*
>> *The Inheritors (1955)*
>> *Pincher Martin (1956)*
>> *Free Fall (1959)*
>> *The Spire (1964)*
>> *The Pyramid (1967)*
>> *Darkness Visible (1979)*
>> *To the Ends of the Earth (trilogy)*
>>> 1. *Rites of Passage (1980)*
>>> 2. *Close Quarters (1987)*
>>> 3. *Fire Down Below (1989)*
>> *The Paper Men (1984)*

Lord of the Flies (1954)

- **Lord of the Flies** published in **1954** by **William Golding**.
- Explores **dark human nature** and **reason's importance**.
- Children evacuated from **Britain** during a **nuclear war**.
- **Plane crashes** on uninhabited island, **adults killed**.
- Boys attempt to form **social order**, devolve into **savagery**.
- Boys abandon **moral constraints**, commit **murder**.
- Plane crashes near **Pacific island** during **evacuation**.
- Only survivors are **middle childhood** or **preadolescent boys**.
- **Ralph** and **Piggy** find **conch**, summon survivors.
- **Conch symbolizes authority**, and Ralph becomes **chief**.
- Policies: **fun**, **survival**, maintain **smoke signal fire**.
- **Piggy's glasses** used to light the **signal fire**.
- Boys develop **paranoia** over an imaginary **beast**.
- Ralph argues no **beast**, Jack vows to **hunt it**.
- Jack's **hunting party** neglects fire; **ship passes unseen**.
- Ralph confronts Jack, considers quitting, Piggy **persuades him**.
- **Aerial battle** leads to **pilot's corpse** landing.
- **Sam and Eric** mistake parachutist for the **beast**.
- Ralph, Jack, Roger find corpse, **flee terrified**.
- Jack forms his **own tribe**, boys **join gradually**.
- **Simon** often isolates in forest for **solitude**.
- Jack offers **pig's head** to the **beast**.
- **Lord of the Flies** warns Simon of **boys' violence**.
- Simon realizes **beast is parachutist**, rushes to tell.
- **Frenzied boys mistake Simon**, beat him to **death**.
- **Ralph and Piggy** deeply disturbed by Simon's **murder**.
- Jack steals **Piggy's glasses** to light **fire**.
- Ralph's group confronts Jack at **Castle Rock**.
- **Roger kills Piggy**, shatters the **conch shell**.
- Roger tortures **Sam and Eric**, forcing allegiance.
- Sam and Eric warn Ralph of **Jack's hunt**.
- Jack sets **forest on fire**, Ralph narrowly **escapes**.
- Fire consumes **island**, Ralph chased by **hunters**.
- Ralph trips, encounters **British naval officer**.
- Ralph weeps for **Simon and Piggy's deaths**.
- Jack and boys revert to **childlike sobbing**.

➢ Officer **disappointed** by boys' **feral behavior**.
➢ Themes of **civilization vs. savagery** dominate story.
➢ Symbols include **conch**, **fire**, and **Lord of the Flies**.
➢ **Profound allegory** of human nature and societal **collapse**.

Question 150

Which of the following authors have been correctly matched with their works?

    A. Malcolm Bradbury - The History of Man
    B. William Golding - Rites of Passage
    C. Seamus Heaney - Darkness visible
    D. Brian Friel - Dancing at Lughnasa
    E. Molly Keane - The Norman Conquests

Choose the correct answer from the options given below;

    1. **A, B and E only**
    2. B, C and E only
    3. C, D and E only
    4. A, B and D only

Correct Explanations:

Malcolm Bradbury - The History Man: This novel is a satire of academic life in 1970s England, focusing on the character of Howard Kirk, a charismatic but morally dubious history professor.

William Golding - Rites of Passage: This novel is the first in Golding's "Sea Trilogy," and it follows the journey of Edmund Talbot, a young aristocrat, on a ship bound for Australia in the early 19th century. The book explores themes of class, power, and morality in a microcosm of society aboard the ship.

"Darkness Visible" is a novel by William Golding, and it was indeed awarded the James Tait Black Memorial Prize in 1979. The novel tells the story of a young Englishman named Matty, who struggles to come to terms with his own mortality and the meaning of life. The title of the novel comes from a line in John Milton's epic poem "Paradise Lost," and refers to the idea of a spiritual or existential darkness that can be more palpable than physical darkness.

Seamus Heaney - Station Island: This collection of poems by Seamus Heaney is divided into several sections, including "Sweeney Redivivus" and "Glanmore Sonnets." The poems address a range of themes, including personal identity, Irish history and mythology, and the role of poetry itself.

Brian Friel - Dancing at Lughnasa: This play is set in rural Ireland in 1936 and follows the lives of the five Mundy sisters, who live together in a modest cottage. The play explores themes of family, memory, and cultural change in Ireland.

Molly Keane - Good Behaviour: This novel is a darkly comic portrayal of an Anglo-Irish family in the 1920s and 30s, focusing on the character of Aroon St. Charles, who is desperate for the approval of her socially ambitious mother. The book explores themes of family dysfunction, class, and gender.

"The Norman Conquest," there are multiple books with that title by different authors. The book you may be referring to by Marc Morris is a non-fiction history book that describes the events leading up to and following the Norman Conquest of England in 1066. It explores the political and social changes that occurred in England during this period and the impact that the Norman Conquest had on English society.

Anthony Burgess (1917-1993)

- **Anthony Burgess**, original name **John Anthony Burgess Wilson**.
- **English novelist**, critic, and man of **letters**.
- Known for **wit**, moral **earnestness**, and the **bizarre**.
- Best known for dystopian satire **A Clockwork Orange**.
- **1971 adaptation** by **Stanley Kubrick** boosted novel's popularity.
- Other works include **Enderby quartet, Earthly Powers**.
- Wrote **librettos**, screenplays, and **TV mini-series Jesus of Nazareth**.
- Worked as **literary critic** for **The Observer, The Guardian**.
- Studied **James Joyce** and classic literary **figures**.
- Translated **Cyrano de Bergerac, Oedipus Rex**, and **Carmen**.

A Clockwork Orange (1962)

- **A Clockwork Orange** is a **1962 dystopian novel**.
- Set in **near-future society** with **extreme youth violence**.

- ➤ **Teen protagonist Alex** narrates his **violent exploits**.
- ➤ **"Nadsat" argot** influenced by **Russian suffix '-teen'**.
- ➤ Written by **Anthony Burgess** in **three weeks**.
- ➤ A **satirical black comedy** exploring **state reform**.
- ➤ **Characters**: Alex, leader of Droogs, loves violence, Beethoven.
- ➤ **Plot**: Alex narrates dystopian life of crime, betrayal.
- ➤ **Event**: Droogs turn on Alex during a robbery.
- ➤ **Line**: "What's it going to be then, eh?"
- ➤ **Event**: Alex undergoes Ludovico Technique, brainwashing aversion therapy.
- ➤ **Line**: "Goodness is something to be chosen."
- ➤ **Plot Twist**: Alex becomes a victim of societal violence.
- ➤ **Resolution**: Alex regains free will, reflects on future.
- ➤ **Line**: "I was cured all right."
- ➤ **Themes**: Free will, violence, morality, societal control.

Question 151

The lives of which of the following writers have been the subject matter of novels by Anthony Burgess?

    A. Milton
    B. Marlowe
    C. Shelley
    D. Keats

Choose the correct answer from the options given below:

    1. A and B only
    2. A and D only
    3. B and C only
    4. B and D only

Explanations:

Answer: 4. B and D only

Anthony Burgess, in addition to being a novelist and critic, was also a scholar of English literature. He was particularly interested in the lives and works of Romantic poets, **including Christopher Marlowe, Percy Bysshe Shelley, and John Keats**. Burgess wrote several novels that revolve around these poets, often exploring their lives, works, and the historical contexts in which they lived.

For example, his novel **"A Dead Man in Deptford" explores the life and death of Marlowe,** while "Byrne" is a fictionalized account of Shelley's life. Burgess's novel **"Nothing Like the Sun" is a fictionalized biography of William Shakespeare** that also features Marlowe as a character. Finally, **his novel "Abba Abba" is a fictionalized account of the final days of Keats's life.** In each of these novels, Burgess uses his extensive knowledge of literature and history to create rich and complex portraits of these writers and the worlds in which they lived.

Match List I and List II

List I (Author)	List II (Text)
A. Thomas Pynchon	I. G.
B. Howard Jacobson	II. V
C. Anthony Burgess	III. J
D. John Berger	IV. M/F

Choose the correct answer from the options given below:

1. A – II, B – IV, C – I, D – III
2. A – II, B – III, C – IV, D – I
3. A – II, B – III, C – I, D – IV
4. A – IV, B – III, C – I, D – II

Explanations:

Answer: 2. A–II, B – III, C – IV, D – I

V. is the debut novel of Thomas Pynchon, published in 1963. It describes the exploits of a discharged U.S. Navy sailor named Benny Profane, his reconnection in New York with a group of pseudo-bohemian artists and hangers-on known as the Whole Sick Crew, and the quest of an aging traveler named Herbert Stencil to identify and locate the mysterious entity he knows only as "V." It was nominated for a National Book Award.

J is a 2014 novel by Howard Jacobson. It was shortlisted for the 2014 Man Booker Prize. Howard Eric Jacobson (born 25 August 1942) is a British novelist and journalist. He is known for writing comic novels that often revolve around the dilemmas of British Jewish characters. He is a Man Booker Prize winner.

M/F is a 1971 novel by the English author Anthony Burgess. It was first published as MF by Jonathan Cape and Alfred A. Knopf; though M/F first appeared on the spine of Knopf's dust jacket. Burgess has called the novel a personal favorite of all his writings.

G. is a 1972 novel by John Berger, set in pre-First World War Europe, and its protagonist, named "G.", is a Don Juan or Casanova-like lover of women who gradually comes to political consciousness after misadventures across the continent. Berger's experimental, non-linear narrative novel won both the James Tait Black Memorial Prize for Fiction and the Booker Prize. At the Booker Prize ceremony, Berger criticized the sponsor Booker-McConnell for exploiting trade in the Caribbean for the past 130 years. Berger also gave half of the prize money to the British Black Panther movement.

S/Z, published in 1970, is Roland Barthes' structural analysis of "Sarrasine", the short story by Honoré de Balzac. Barthes methodically moves through the text of the story, denoting where and how different codes of meaning function. Barthes' study made a major impact on literary criticism and is historically located at the crossroads of structuralism and post-structuralism.

Muriel Spark (1918-2006)

- ➢ **Muriel Spark**, British writer, known for **satirical wit**.
- ➢ Began writing **post-World War II** under **married name**.
- ➢ Started with **poetry and literary criticism**.
- ➢ Became **editor of Poetry Review** in **1947**.
- ➢ One of the **few female editors** of her time.
- ➢ Left **Poetry Review** in **1948**.
- ➢ Baptized into **Church of England** in **1953**.
- ➢ Converted to **Roman Catholic Church** in **1954**.
- ➢ Spark: Conversion key to **"seeing existence as whole."**
- ➢ Gained **confidence** in writing after **conversion**.
- ➢ Supported by **Graham Greene, Fielding**, and **Waugh**.
- ➢ Published **The Comforters** in **1957**, praised highly.
- ➢ **Catholicism and conversion** referenced in the novel.
- ➢ **Prime of Miss Jean Brodie (1961)** achieved **greater success**.
- ➢ Known for **flashforwards** and **imagined conversations**.
- ➢ **James Gillespie's High School** inspired **Marcia Blaine School**.
- ➢ **Helena Club** inspired May of Teck Club in **The Girls of Slender Means**.
- ➢ Published **The Girls of Slender Means** in **1963**.
- ➢ **Notable Works:**
    - ○ *"The Go-Away Bird and Other Stories"*

- o   *"Memento Mori"*
- o   *"The Comforters"*
- o   *"The Girls of Slender Means"*
- o   *"The Prime of Miss Jean Brodie"*

The Prime of Miss Jean Brodie (1961)

- ➤ **The Prime of Miss Jean Brodie** published in **1961**.
- ➤ Adapted for the **stage in 1966**.
- ➤ Story of **eccentric Edinburgh teacher** inspiring **cultlike reverence**.
- ➤ Themes of **innocence, betrayal, rationality**, and **Miss Brodie's downfall**.
- ➤ **Characters**: Miss Jean Brodie, Sandy, and "Brodie set" girls.
- ➤ **Plot**: Miss Brodie influences students in 1930s Edinburgh.
- ➤ **Miss Brodie**: "Give me a girl at impressionable age."
- ➤ **Themes**: Loyalty, betrayal, control, and personal growth.
- ➤ **Key Event**: Brodie idolizes fascist leaders like Mussolini.
- ➤ **Sandy's Betrayal**: Reports Brodie's actions to school authorities.
- ➤ **Climax**: Brodie loses her job after Sandy's betrayal.
- ➤ **Brodie's Line**: "I am in my prime!" defines story.
- ➤ **Sandy's Growth**: Becomes a nun, reflecting on Brodie's influence.
- ➤ **Ending**: Explores morality, leadership, and misguided devotion.

Iris Murdoch (1919-1999)

- ➤ **Dame Jean Iris Murdoch**: Irish and British **novelist, philosopher**.
- ➤ Known for exploring **good, evil, and morality**.
- ➤ **Under the Net** (1954): **Modern Library's Top 100 novels**.
- ➤ **The Sea, the Sea** (1978): Won **Booker Prize**.
- ➤ First work: **Sartre, Romantic Rationalist** (1953).
- ➤ Novels include **Under the Net** and **The Flight from the Enchanter**.
- ➤ Admired for **intelligence, wit, and high seriousness**.
- ➤ Work explores **tensions in sexual relationships**.
- ➤ Rich **comic sense** distinguished Murdoch's literary **style**.
- ➤ **Notable Work:**
    - o   *The Bell (1958),*
    - o   *A Severed Head (1961),*
    - o   *The Red and the Green (1965),*
    - o   *The Nice and the Good (1968),*
    - o   *The Black Prince (1973),*

- o *Henry and Cato (1976),*
- o *The Philosopher's Pupil (1983),*
- o *The Good Apprentice (1985),*
- o *The Book and the Brotherhood (1987),*
- o *The Message to the Planet (1989),*
- o *The Green Knight (1993).*

Under the Net (1954)

- ➢ **Under the Net** is a **1954 novel** by **Iris Murdoch.**
- ➢ It was Murdoch's **first published novel.**
- ➢ Set in **London**, follows writer **Jake Donaghue.**
- ➢ Mixes **philosophical** and **picaresque**, gaining **fame.**
- ➢ **Dedicated** to **Raymond Queneau.**
- ➢ Jake takes **Murphy by Beckett** and **Queneau's Pierrot mon ami.**
- ➢ Both books **echo themes** in **this story.**
- ➢ Epigraph is from **Dryden's Secular Masque.**
- ➢ Refers to **misunderstandings** driving **main character**'s actions.
- ➢ Jake's eviction starts his journey to stability and truth.
- ➢ He reconnects with Hugo, questioning past ideas and philosophies.
- ➢ Jake chases Sadie, leading to comedic and reflective misadventures.
- ➢ A heist of Hugo's manuscript uncovers deeper misunderstandings.
- ➢ Jake confronts his selfishness, seeking personal and moral growth.
- ➢ Jake realizes the value of human connection over intellectual theories.

Question 153

Under the Net (1954) is written by

1. **Iris Murdoch**
2. Edmund Goose
3. William Cooper
4. John Fowles

Correct Explanation:

Under the Net is a 1954 novel by Iris Murdoch. It was Murdoch's first published novel.

Doris Lessing (1919-2013)

- ➢ **Doris May Lessing** was a **British-Zimbabwean novelist.**

- ➤ Born in **Iran** to **British parents**, lived until 1925.
- ➤ Family moved to **Southern Rhodesia (now Zimbabwe)**.
- ➤ Moved to **London, England**, in **1949**.
- ➤ Novels include **The Grass Is Singing (1950)**.
- ➤ Wrote **Children of Violence** (1952–1969) series.
- ➤ Published **The Golden Notebook (1962)**, a milestone.
- ➤ Wrote **The Good Terrorist (1985)**.
- ➤ Authored **Canopus in Argos: Archives** series (1979–1983).
- ➤ Won **2007 Nobel Prize in Literature**, oldest recipient.
- ➤ Described as **"that epicist of the female experience."**
- ➤ **Notable Work:**
  - o *The Grass Is Singing (1950)*
  - o *The Golden Notebook (1962)*
  - o *The Memoirs of a Survivor (1974)*
  - o *The Good Terrorist (1985)*
  - o *The Fifth Child (1988)*
  - o *Ben, in the World (2000) – the sequel to The Fifth Child*
  - o *The Sweetest Dream (2001)*
  - o *The Cleft (2007)*
- ➤ **Children of Violence series (1952–1969)**
  - o *Martha Quest (1952)*
  - o *A Proper Marriage (1954)*
  - o *A Ripple from the Storm (1958)*
  - o *Landlocked (1965)*
  - o *The Four-Gated City (1969)*

The Grass Is Singing (1950)

- ➤ **The Grass Is Singing**, Doris Lessing's **first novel** (1950).
- ➤ Set in **Southern Rhodesia** (now **Zimbabwe**) during 1940s.
- ➤ Explores **racial politics** in British **colonial society**.
- ➤ Centers on **Mary Turner**, her **mental decline**, and **murder**.
- ➤ Novel caused a **sensation** and was an **instant success**.
- ➤ Adapted into **Gräset Sjunger**, filmed in **1981**.
- ➤ Title derived from T.S. Eliot's **The Waste Land**.
- ➤ Quoted from **Part V: 'What the Thunder Said.'**
- ➤ Theme contrasts **destruction's power** with **growth**.
- ➤ Quotes anonymous: **"Failures and misfits judge weaknesses."**
- ➤ Begins with **newspaper clipping** about Mary's **murder**.
- ➤ Mary had a **loveless childhood** but a content **city life**.

- ➢ **Friends mocked** her as **sexless, immature**; resolves to marry.
- ➢ Marries **Dick Turner**, a struggling, **lonely farmer**.
- ➢ **Marriage cold**, bound by **fear, poverty**, and loneliness.
- ➢ Mary discovers Dick's **incompetence**, increasing her **resentment**.
- ➢ Rejects neighbors' **friendship**, ashamed of **poverty**.
- ➢ Mary treats **black workers** with **frigid contempt**.
- ➢ **Moses**, the servant, forms a **tense connection** with her.
- ➢ Story unfolds in **intimacy, despair**, ending in **death**.

The Golden Notebook (1962)

- ➢ **The Golden Notebook**, a 1962 novel by **Doris Lessing**.
- ➢ Explores **"inner space fiction"**, societal and mental breakdowns.
- ➢ Contains **anti-war** and **anti-Stalinist messages**.
- ➢ Analyzes **communism** in England (1930s to 1950s).
- ➢ Examines **sexual revolution** and **women's liberation movements**.
- ➢ Story of **Anna Wulf** and her **notebooks**.
- ➢ Anna ties four notebooks into a **golden notebook**.
- ➢ Includes **realistic narratives** about Anna and **Molly Jacobs**.
- ➢ Depicts lives of **children, ex-husbands, and lovers**.
- ➢ Intersperses **Free Women** narrative with Anna's **colored notebooks**.
- ➢ **Black**: Anna's experience in Southern Rhodesia inspired best-selling novel.
- ➢ **Red**: Anna's Communist Party membership shaped her experiences.
- ➢ **Yellow**: Ongoing novel reflects painful love affair ending.
- ➢ **Blue**: Anna's journal captures memories, dreams, emotional life.

Children of Violence series (1952–1969)

- ➢ *The Children of Violence*
  - o Five semi-autobiographical novels by Doris Lessing.
  - o Protagonist Martha Quest's life spans adolescence to 1997.
  - o Set in Southern Rhodesia and dystopian future London.
- ➢ *Martha Quest (1952)*
  - o Fifteen-year-old Martha grows up in Southern Rhodesia.
  - o Struggles with narrow family life and societal conventions.
  - o Becomes a typist, eager for real-life experiences.
- ➢ *A Proper Marriage (1954)*
  - o Martha's rebellious nature reacts to marriage constraints.
  - o Feels trapped by domesticity and societal expectations.

- o World War II impacts her husband's departure.
- ➤ ***A Ripple from the Storm (1958)***
  - o Explores Communist group growth in Central Africa.
  - o Martha divorces and marries a Communist leader.
  - o Set during Soviet admiration in wartime years.
- ➤ ***The Four-Gated City (1969)***
  - o Post-WWII Britain marked by Cold War tensions.
  - o Chronicles poverty, social anarchy, and societal changes.
  - o Ends in 1997 with Martha's death post-WWIII.

Question 154

Match List I with List II

List I (Author)	List II (Autobiography/Memoir)
A. Pablo Neruda	(i) Under My Skin
B. Graham Greene	(ii) Speak, Memory
C. Doris Lessing	(iii) Memoirs
D. Vladimir Nabakov	(iv) A Sort of Life

Choose the correct answer from the options given below :

1. (a)-(iv), (b)-(iii), (c)-(i), (d)-(ii)
2. (a)-(iii), (b)-(iv) (c)-(ii), (d)-(i)
3. (a)-(ii), (b)- iv), (c)-(iii) (d)-(i)
4. (a)-(iii), (b)-(iv), (c)-(i), (d)-(ii)

Explanations:

Answer: 4. (a)-(iii), (b)-(iv), (c)-(i), (d)-(ii)

The correct matching of authors with their respective autobiographies/memoirs is:

A. Pablo Neruda - (iii) Memoirs
B. Graham Greene - (iv) A Sort of Life
C. Doris Lessing - (i) Under My Skin
D. Vladimir Nabokov - (ii) Speak, Memory

A. Pablo Neruda - "Memoirs": In this autobiography, Pablo Neruda recounts his personal and political experiences, capturing the essence of his life as a poet and political activist.

B. Graham Greene - "A Sort of Life": Graham Greene's memoir takes readers on a journey through his early years, exploring his upbringing, education, and the formative experiences that shaped his literary career.

C. Doris Lessing - "Under My Skin": Doris Lessing's memoir delves into her early life in Southern Rhodesia (now Zimbabwe), highlighting her struggles, relationships, and her emergence as a prominent writer.

D. Vladimir Nabokov - "Speak, Memory": Nabokov's memoir offers a richly detailed account of his life, from his aristocratic upbringing in Russia to his exile and literary success, filled with vivid recollections and reflections on art, love, and identity.

Question 155

Choose the right chronological sequence of the publication of the following books:

- A. Margaret Atwood, The Handmaid's Tale
- B. Alice Walker, The Color Purple
- C. Doris Lessing, The Golden Notebook
- D. Toni Morrison, The Bluest Eye

Choose the correct answer from the options given below:

1. A, B, D, C
2. B, A, D, C
3. **C, D, B, A**
4. D, C, B, A

Correct Explanations:
- ➢ Doris Lessing, The Golden Notebook (1962)
- ➢ Toni Morrison, The Bluest Eye (1970)
- ➢ Alice Walker, The Color Purple (1982)
- ➢ Margaret Atwood, *The Handmaid's Tale (1985)*

Question 156

Which of these is a correct combination of the works by Doris Lessing and their respective themes?

- A. The Golden Notebook deals with Johor travelling to Rhonda
- B. The Good Terrorist is about a doomed love affair.

C.   Shikasta is about a planet cut off due to the advanced influence of civilisation.
D.   Alfred and Emily explore the life of her parents
E.   The Grass is Singing draws from her experiences in Africa.

Choose the correct answer from the options given below:

1. B, A and D only
2. A, B and E only
3. C, D and E only
4. E, B and A only
5. **DROP**

CORRECT EXPLANATIONS:

The Golden Notebook is the story of writer Anna Wulf, the four notebooks in which she records her life and attempts to tie them together in a fifth, gold-coloured notebook.

The Good Terrorist is a 1985 political novel by the British novelist Doris Lessing. **The book's protagonist is the naïve drifter Alice,** who squats with a group of radicals in London and is drawn into their terrorist activities. **Alice fell in love with him, only to become frustrated by his aloofness and burgeoning homosexuality.**

Re: Colonised Planet 5, Shikasta (often shortened to Shikasta) is a 1979 science fiction novel by Doris Lessing and is the first book in her five-book Canopus in Argos series. **Shikasta is the history of the planet Shikasta** (whose inhabitants call it Earth) under the influence of three galactic empires, Canopus, Sirius, and their mutual enemy, Puttiora.

Alfred and Emily is a book by Doris Lessing in a new hybrid form. Part fiction, part notebook, part memoir, it was first published in 2008. The book is based on the lives of Lessing's parents. **Part one is a novella, a fictional portrait of how her parents' lives might have been without the interruption of the First World War. Part two is a retelling of how her parents' lives developed.**

Published in 1950, **The Grass Is Singing** is the first novel by the British author Doris Lessing. It takes place in Southern Rhodesia (now Zimbabwe), in southern Africa, during the 1940s and deals with the racial politics between whites and blacks in that country (which was then a British Colony). It follows an emotionally immature woman's hasty marriage to an unsuccessful farmer, her ensuing mental deterioration, her murder, and the colonial British society's reactions to it.

Identify the correct pairs:

    A. Ewan McEwan — Amsterdam
    B. Italo Calvino — If on a Winters Night A Traveller
    C. Amitav Ghosh — The Circle of Reason
    D. D M Thomas - Everest Hotel
    E. Doris Lessing — The Testaments

Choose the correct answer from the options given below:

    1. **A, B and C only.**
    2. A, B and E only.
    3. B, C and D only.
    4. C, D and E only.

Explanations:

Ewan McEwan's *Amsterdam* is a novel that explores the moral dilemma of two lifelong friends and their involvement in a politician's scandalous death.

Italo Calvino's *If on a Winters Night A Traveller* is a postmodern novel that follows the reader's quest to find the ending of a novel, only to be interrupted by different books and characters along the way.

Amitav Ghosh's *The Circle of Reason* is a novel that tells the story of a young man named Alu who is accused of a crime he did not commit, and his journey to escape persecution and find a place in the world.

"The Testaments" is a novel by Margaret Atwood, published in 2019, and is a sequel to her 1985 novel "The Handmaid's Tale."

John Fowles (1926-2005)

- **John Robert Fowles**: Renowned **English novelist** between **modernism/postmodernism**.
- Influenced by **Jean-Paul Sartre** and **Albert Camus**.
- Taught **English in Spetses**, inspiring **The Magus** (1965).
- **The Magus** reflected **1960s hippy anarchism** and philosophy.
- Wrote **The French Lieutenant's Woman** (1969), a **postmodern romance**.
- Set in **Lyme Regis**, where Fowles later **lived**.
- Published **The Ebony Tower** in **1974**.
- Followed by **Daniel Martin** (1977) and **Mantissa** (1982).
- Concluded major works with **A Maggot** (1985).
- Fowles explored **experimental themes** in **all major novels**.
- **List of works:**
    - *(1963) The Collector*
    - *(1964) The Aristos, essays (ISBN 0-586-05377-8)*
    - *(1965) The Magus (revised 1977)*
    - *(1969) The French Lieutenant's Woman*
    - *(1973) Poems by John Fowles*
    - *(1974) The Ebony Tower*
    - *(1974) Shipwreck*
    - *(1977) Daniel Martin*
    - *(1978) Islands*
    - *(1979) The Tree*
    - *(1980) The Enigma of Stonehenge*
    - *(1982) A Short History of Lyme Regis*
    - *(1982) Mantissa*
    - *(1985) A Maggot*
    - *(1985) Land (with Fay Godwin)*
    - *(1990) Lyme Regis Camera*
    - *(1998) Wormholes - Essays and Occasional Writings*

The French Lieutenant's Woman (1969)

- **The French Lieutenant's Woman** by **John Fowles**, published **1969**.
- **Pastiche** of historical romance with **Victorian ethos**.
- **Plot** follows **Charles Smithson**, amateur Victorian **paleontologist**.
- Engaged to **Ernestina Freeman**, breaks it for **Sarah Woodruff**.
- **Sarah**, a social outcast, known as **French lieutenant's lover**.
- **Author intrudes**, offers **three different endings** for readers.

- ➢ **Set in mid-nineteenth century**, Sarah Woodruff is protagonist.
- ➢ Known as **"Tragedy"** and **"French Lieutenant's Whore"**.
- ➢ Lives in **Lyme Regis**, disgraced by **Varguennes**.
- ➢ **Varguennes abandoned her**, returned to France, and married.
- ➢ Employed by **Mrs. Poulteney**, a **pious household mistress**.
- ➢ Spends time on **The Cobb**, staring at sea.
- ➢ **Charles Smithson** and fiancée **Ernestina Freeman** spot Sarah.
- ➢ Ernestina tells Charles about **Sarah's story**.
- ➢ **Charles becomes curious** and meets Sarah **three times**.
- ➢ Sarah shares her **history**, seeks **emotional support**.
- ➢ Charles fears losing **inheritance** to uncle's possible child.
- ➢ Charles's servant **Sam** loves Mary, Ernestina's aunt's maid.
- ➢ **Charles loves Sarah**, advises her to leave **Lyme**.
- ➢ Stops in **Exeter**, seemingly to visit Sarah.
- ➢ Narrator offers **three different endings** for the novel.
- ➢ **Narrator becomes a character**, intervening throughout story.
- ➢ **First Ending**
  - o Charles marries Ernestina, joins trade under Mr. Freeman.
  - o Marriage unhappy, no clarity on Sarah's fate.
  - o Narrator dismisses as a daydream of Charles.
- ➢ **Second Ending**
  - o Charles and Sarah's rash encounter reveals her virginity.
  - o Sam fails to deliver proposal letter to Sarah.
  - o Sarah bears Charles' child, found living in London.
- ➢ **Third Ending**
  - o Narrator changes events by turning back time.
  - o Reunion with Sarah sour, unclear child's parentage.
  - o Charles leaves, questioning Sarah's motives and honesty.

JG Ballard (1930-2009)

- ➢ **J.G. Ballard**, English novelist, satirist, and essayist.
- ➢ Explored **human psychology**, **technology**, **sex**, and **mass media**.
- ➢ Associated with **New Wave** science fiction movement.
- ➢ Known for **post-apocalyptic novels** like **The Drowned World**.
- ➢ Courted controversy with **The Atrocity Exhibition (1970)**.
- ➢ **Crash (1973)** explored **car crash fetishists' lives**.
- ➢ **Empire of the Sun** brought **broader recognition** in 1984.
- ➢ Adapted into **Steven Spielberg's 1987 film** version.
- ➢ Chronicled life in **The Kindness of Women (1991)**.

- ➢ **Ballardian**: Defined as **dystopian modernity** and **psychological effects**.
- ➢ Films include **Crash (1996)** and **High-Rise (2015)**.
- ➢ Works reflect **bleak man-made landscapes** and **technology's impacts**.

Empire of the Sun (1984)

- ➢ **Empire of the Sun**: Novel by **J.G. Ballard**.
- ➢ **Published in 1984**, awarded **James Tait Black Prize**.
- ➢ **Shortlisted for Man Booker Prize**, notable achievement.
- ➢ Fiction inspired by Ballard's **WWII experiences**.
- ➢ Name derived from **Japan's etymological meaning**.
- ➢ Ballard's **autobiography** discusses novel and film adaptation.
- ➢ Story follows **Jamie "Jim" Graham**, young **British boy**.
- ➢ **Jim lives in Shanghai** with **his parents**.
- ➢ After **Pearl Harbor**, Japan occupies **Shanghai Settlement**.
- ➢ Jim becomes **separated from his parents** in chaos.
- ➢ Survives in **abandoned mansions**, eating **packaged food**.
- ➢ Surrenders to **Japanese Army**, interned at **Lunghua Camp**.
- ➢ **Admires Japanese pilots**, despite being **official enemies**.
- ➢ War causes **food shortages**, many prisoners **starve**.
- ➢ Saved from **starvation by American air drops**.
- ➢ Reunites with parents at **pre-war residence**.

Question 158

Which book by J.G. Ballard is about a virus that freezes anything it comes in contact with?

1. The Drowned World
2. Concrete Island
3. **The Crystal World**
4. Kingdom Come

Correct Explanations:

The Crystal World is a science fiction novel by English author J. G. Ballard, published in 1966. The novel tells the story of a physician trying to make his way deep into the jungle to a secluded leprosy treatment facility. **While trying to make it to his destination, his chaotic path leads him to try to** come to terms with an apocalyptic phenomenon in the jungle that crystallises everything it touches.

CAMPUS NOVEL

- **Campus novel** focuses on **university campus settings**.
- Genre dates back to the **early 1950s**.
- **Mary McCarthy's The Groves of Academe (1952)** is pivotal.
- **Elaine Showalter** mentions earlier works like **C. P. Snow's The Masters**.
- Examples include **Willa Cather's The Professor's House (1925)**.
- Other examples: **Régis Messac's Smith Conundrum (1928-1931)**.
- **Dorothy L. Sayers's Gaudy Night (1935)** also fits.
- **Kingsley Amis's Lucky Jim** uses comic or **satirical themes**.
- **David Lodge's works** highlight **intellectual pretensions, weaknesses**.
- Serious examples: **C. P. Snow's The Masters, Coetzee's Disgrace**.
- Others include **Philip Roth's The Human Stain**.
- **Faculty perspective** (e.g., **Lucky Jim**) often dominates narratives.
- **Student perspective** (e.g., **I Am Charlotte Simmons**) also features.
- **Varsity novels** focus more on **students than faculty**.
- Subgenre: **Campus murder mystery**, e.g., **Gaudy Night**.

David Lodge (1935)

- **David John Lodge** is an **English author and critic**.
- **Literature professor** at **University of Birmingham** until **1987**.
- Known for **"Campus Trilogy"**, **satirizing academic life**.
  - *Changing Places: A Tale of Two Campuses (1975)*,
    - The subtitle is *"A Tale of Two Campuses,"*
    - Thus, both the title and subtitle are literary allusions to **Charles Dickens' A Tale of Two Cities**.
  - *Small World: An Academic Romance (1984)*
  - *Nice Work (1988)*

Malcolm Bradbury (1932-2000)

- **Sir Malcolm Bradbury**, British novelist, critic, satirist.
- Best known for **The History Man (1975)**.
- Studied at **Leicester, Queen Mary, Manchester universities**.
- Earned a **doctorate from Manchester** in **1964**.

- ➢ **Taught in Hull, Birmingham**, later at **East Anglia**.
- ➢ Helped establish **East Anglia's first creative writing course**.
- ➢ Taught **Ian McEwan** and **Kazuo Ishiguro**.
- ➢ First novel, **Eating People Is Wrong (1959)**, acclaimed.
- ➢ **Stepping Westward (1965)** reflects American campus experience.
- ➢ **The History Man** introduced harsher tone, technical innovation.
- ➢ **Rates of Exchange (1983)** satirizes Eastern Europe.
- ➢ Created fictional country Slaka in **Why Come to Slaka? (1986)**.
- ➢ Final novel, **To the Hermitage (2000)**.
- ➢ Wrote critical essays, literary history, and **TV plays**.
- ➢ Honored as **CBE in 1991**, knighted in **2000**.
- ➢ **The History of Man (1975)**
    - ○ A dark satire of academic life in the "glass and steel" universities.
    - ○ British universities established in the 1960s which followed their "redbrick" predecessors.

AS Byatt (1936*)

- ➢ **A.S. Byatt**: English scholar, literary critic, and novelist.
- ➢ Known for **erudite works** featuring academics and artists.
- ➢ Published **The Shadow of a Sun** (1964) and **The Game** (1967).
- ➢ Gained recognition with **The Virgin in the Garden** (1978).
- ➢ Novel set during **Queen Elizabeth II's coronation**.
- ➢ First of a **tetralogy spanning 1953 to 1980**.
- ➢ Second volume, **Still Life** (1985), explores **painting**.
- ➢ Followed by **Babel Tower** (1995) and **A Whistling Woman** (2002).
- ➢ Wrote **Possession** (1990), part **mystery, part romance**.
- ➢ **Possession** awarded the **Booker Prize** in 1990.
- ➢ **The Children's Book** (2009) blends history with fiction.
- ➢ **Ragnarok** (2011) retells **Norse myth during WWII**.
- ➢ Byatt's work combines **history, myth, and postmodernism**.
- ➢ **Notable Works:**
    - ○ *"A Whistling Woman"*
    - ○ *"Babel Tower"*
    - ○ *"Elementals: Stories of Fire and Ice"*
    - ○ *"Passions of the Mind"*
    - ○ *"Peacock & Vine"*
    - ○ *"Possession"*
    - ○ *"Ragnarok: The End of the Gods"*

- o *"Still Life"*
- o *"Sugar and Other Stories"*
- o *"The Biographer's Tale"*
- o *"The Children's Book"*
- o *"The Matisse Stories"*
- o *"The Virgin in the Garden"*
- ➢ ***Possession: A Romance (1990)***
  - o **Possession: A Romance** is a **1990 Booker Prize** winner.
  - o Explores **postmodern concerns**, categorized as **historiographic metafiction**.
  - o Follows two **academics** researching fictional poets' **love lives**.
  - o Set in both the **present** and **Victorian era**.
  - o Contrasts time periods, satirizes **academia** and **mating rituals**.
  - o Incorporates **diary entries, letters, poetry**, and **narrative styles**.
  - o Explores **postmodern concerns** of textual **authority**.
  - o Title **Possession** highlights themes of **ownership** and **independence**.
  - o Examines **collecting cultural artifacts** of historical significance.
  - o Reflects biographers' **"possession" over their subjects**.
  - o Scholar Roland Michell discovers Ash's secret letter drafts.
  - o Suspects Ash had an affair with poet LaMotte.
  - o He enlists Maud Bailey, a LaMotte scholar.
  - o Letters reveal a romance between Ash and LaMotte.
  - o Modern scholars parallel Ash and LaMotte's relationship.
  - o Ash's unconsummated marriage contrasted with his affair.
  - o LaMotte's companion Blanche suicides; secrets unravel further.
  - o LaMotte secretly births Ash's illegitimate daughter, Maia.
  - o LaMotte's sister raises Maia as her own child.
  - o Great Storm of 1987: scholars exhume Ash's documents.
  - o Maud discovers she's descended from Ash and LaMotte.
  - o Ash's grave holds a lock of Maia's hair.
  - o Roland avoids consequences, sees career opportunities ahead.
  - o Maud opens up emotionally, envisions love with Roland.
  - o Epilogue: Ash unknowingly meets daughter Maia briefly.

Angela Carter (1940-1992)

- **Angela Carter** was an **English novelist, poet, journalist.**
- Known for **feminist, magical realism, picaresque works.**
- Famous for **The Bloody Chamber** (1979).
- **Nights at the Circus** won **James Tait Black** prize
- **Novels**
  - *Shadow Dance (1966; also published as Honeybuzzard)*
  - *The Magic Toyshop (1967; filmed in 1986)*
  - *Several Perceptions (1968)*
  - *The Infernal Desire Machines of Doctor Hoffman (1972)*
  - *The Passion of New Eve (1977)*
  - *Wise Children (1991)*
- **Short Story Collection**
  - *The Bloody Chamber (1979)*
- **Non-Fiction**
  - *The Sadeian Woman: An Exercise in Cultural History (1979)*
  - *Screenplay*
  - *The Company of Wolves (1984; based on a story from The Bloody Chamber)*
- ***Night at the Circus (1984)***
  - **Nights at the Circus** by **Angela Carter**, published **1984.**
  - Won the **1984 James Tait Black Memorial Prize.**
  - Focuses on **Sophie Fevvers**, a **Cockney virgin.**
  - **Fevvers claims** to have hatched from an **egg.**
  - Becomes a celebrated **aerialiste** with **fully-fledged wings.**
  - **Jack Walser**, journalist, joins circus, encounters **magic.**
  - Blends **postmodernism**, **magical realism**, and **postfeminism.**
  - Dissects **fairy tale structure** and **literary traditions.**
  - **London Section**
    - Journalist Walser interviews winged performer Sophie Fevvers.
    - Fevvers claims wings appeared during puberty.
    - Ma Nelson's brothel burns after her death.
    - Fevvers joins a freak show, escapes sacrifice.
    - Joins Colonel Kearney's circus, gains fame.
  - **Petersburg Section**
    - Walser joins circus as a clown.
    - Saves Mignon from tigress, gains trust.

- Fevvers introduces Mignon to Princess Abyssinia.
        - Buffo loses control, attacks Walser.
        - Fevvers narrowly escapes Grand Duke's advances.
    - **Siberia Section**
        - Circus train attacked by runaway outlaws.
        - Walser rescued by escaped murderesses' group.
        - Fevvers declares her legend a lie.
        - Blizzard scatters clowns and convicts.
        - Fevvers reunites with Walser at dawn.

Margaret Drabble (1939*)

- **Dame Margaret Drabble** is an **English novelist, biographer, critic**.
- Her **first novel appeared in 1963**.
- Won **John Llewellyn Rhys Prize** for **The Millstone** (1966).
- Won **James Tait Black Prize** for **Jerusalem the Golden** (1967).
- Edited two editions of **The Oxford Companion to English Literature**.
- Published **19 novels** as of **2016**.
- Her **first novel: A Summer Bird-Cage** (1963).
- Early novels published by **Weidenfeld & Nicolson**.
- Later works published by **Penguin** and **Viking**.
- **The Millstone** (1965) brought **her first major prize**.
- **The Needle's Eye** published in **1972**.
- Themes link **society** and **individuals** in contemporary **England**.
- **Characters reflect political, economic situations, conservative restrictions**.
- **Protagonists are mostly women**, facing societal conflicts.
- Realistic descriptions often based on **personal experiences**.
- Early novels explore **motherhood vs. intellectual challenges**.
- **The Witch of Exmoor** depicts withdrawn **old author**.
- Written **screenplays, plays, short stories, biographies**.
- Notable works: **A Writer's Britain**, biographies of **Bennett, Wilson**.
- **Short story collection: A Day in the Life of a Smiling Woman** (2011).
- **Novels:**
    - *A Summer Bird-Cage (1963)*
    - *The Garrick Year (1964)*
    - *The Millstone (1965)*
    - *Jerusalem the Golden (1967)*

- o *The Waterfall (1969)*
  - o *The Needle's Eye (1972)*
  - o *The Realms of Gold (1975)*
  - o *The Ice Age (1977)*
  - o *The Middle Ground (1980)*
  - o *The Radiant Way (1987)*
  - o *A Natural Curiosity (1989)*
  - o *The Gates of Ivory (1991)*
  - o *The Witch of Exmoor (1996)*
  - o *The Peppered Moth (2001)*
  - o *The Seven Sisters (2002)*
  - o *The Red Queen (2004)*
  - o *The Sea Lady (2006)*
  - o *The Pure Gold Baby (2013)*
  - o *The Dark Flood Rises (2016)*
- ➢ **A Summer Bird-Cage (1963)**
  - o **Sarah and Louise**, two **sisters**, are central characters.
  - o **Sarah returns** from **Paris** for Louise's wedding.
  - o **Sarah**, an **Oxford graduate**, feels **directionless** post-degree.
  - o **Sarah loves Francis**, a **historian at Harvard**.
  - o **Tensions arise** as Sarah views **Halifax arrogant**.
  - o Sarah discovers **Louise's affair** with **actor John Connell**.
  - o **Friction leads** to Sarah confronting **Louise's life choices**.
  - o Novel focuses on **sisters' personalities**, not **plot action**.

Julian Barnes (1946*)

- ➢ **Julian Patrick Barnes** is an **English writer**.
- ➢ **Won Man Booker Prize** in 2011 for **The Sense of an Ending**.
- ➢ Previously shortlisted for **Flaubert's Parrot, England, England**, and **Arthur & George**.
- ➢ Wrote **crime fiction** under pseudonym **Dan Kavanagh**.
- ➢ Published **essays** and **short stories** alongside novels.
- ➢ Known for **literary versatility** across multiple genres.
- ➢ **Novels**
  - o *Metroland (1980)*
  - o *Before She Met Me (1982)*
  - o *Flaubert's Parrot (1984) – shortlisted for the Booker Prize*
  - o *Staring at the Sun (1986)*
  - o *A History of the World in 10½ Chapters (1989)*

- *Talking It Over (1991)*
- *The Porcupine (1992)*
- *England, England (1998) – shortlisted for the Booker Prize*
- *Love, etc. (2000) – the sequel to Talking it Over*
- *Arthur & George (2005) – shortlisted for the Booker Prize*
- *The Sense of an Ending (2011) – winner of the Booker Prize*
- *The Noise of Time (2016)*
- *The Only Story (2018)*
- *Elizabeth Finch (2022)*

➢ *Flaubert's Parrot (1984)*
- **Flaubert's Parrot** by **Julian Barnes, Booker-shortlisted 1984**.
- Won the **Geoffrey Faber Memorial Prize** next year.
- Follows amateur **Flaubert expert Geoffrey Braithwaite's musings**.
- Braithwaite searches for the **stuffed parrot** inspiring Flaubert.

➢ **The Sense of an Ending (2011)**
- **The Sense of an Ending** is a **2011 novel** by **Julian Barnes**.
- **Barnes's eleventh novel** under his own name.
- Published on **4 August 2011** in the **UK**.
- Narrated by **Tony Webster**, a retired man.
- Tony recalls meeting **Adrian Finn** at **school**.
- Reflects on paths as **past catches up**.
- Won the **Man Booker Prize** in **October 2011**.
- Nominated for **Costa Book Awards** in **November**.

Ian McEwan (1948*)

➢ **Ian McEwan** is an **English novelist** and **screenwriter**.
➢ In **2008**, *The Times* listed him among **"50 greatest British writers since 1945"**.
➢ *The Daily Telegraph* ranked him **19th** in **"100 most powerful people in British culture"**.
➢ Renowned for his **influence** in **British literature**.
➢ **Novels:**
- *The Cement Garden (1978)*
- *The Comfort of Strangers (1981)*
- *The Child in Time (1987)*
- *The Innocent (1990)*

- o *Black Dogs (1992)*
  - o *Enduring Love (1997)*
  - o ***Amsterdam (1998)***
  - o ***Atonement (2001)***
  - o ***Saturday (2005)***
  - o *On Chesil Beach (2007)*
  - o *Solar (2010)*
  - o *Sweet Tooth (2012)*
  - o *The Children Act (2014)*
  - o *Nutshell (2016)*
  - o *Machines Like Me (2019)*
  - o *The Cockroach (2019) (novella)*
  - o *Lessons (2022)*
- ➢ **Amsterdam (1998)**
  - o **Amsterdam** is a **1998 novel** by **Ian McEwan.**
  - o Won the **1998 Booker Prize** for its brilliance.
  - o **Story of a euthanasia pact** between **two friends**.
  - o Focuses on a **composer** and **newspaper editor's relationship**.
- ➢ **Atonement (2001)**
  - o **Atonement**, a **2001 British metafiction novel** by Ian McEwan.
  - o Set in **1935 England, WWII France**, and **present-day England**.
  - o Explores a **girl's mistake** that **ruins lives**.
  - o Reflects on **adulthood**, **regret**, and **nature of writing**.
  - o Widely considered one of **McEwan's best works**.
  - o **Shortlisted** for the **2001 Booker Prize for Fiction**
- ➢ Saturday (2005)
  - o **Saturday (2005)** is a novel by **Ian McEwan.**
  - o Set in **Fitzrovia, London**, on **15 February 2003**.
  - o **Henry Perowne**, a **48-year-old neurosurgeon**, is protagonist.
  - o **Protest against Iraq invasion** forms the backdrop.
  - o Day disrupted by a **violent, troubled man**.
  - o McEwan researched by spending time with **neurosurgeons**.
  - o Novel explores **existence** in the **modern world**.
  - o **Perowne struggles** to understand his **life's meaning**.

Martin Amis (1949*)

- ➤ **Martin Amis** born in **Oxford in 1949.**
- ➤ Son of **writer Kingsley Amis.**
- ➤ Educated in **Britain, Spain, and the USA.**
- ➤ Graduated **First Class Honours** from **Exeter College, Oxford.**
- ➤ Wrote **The Rachel Papers** while at **Times Literary Supplement.**
- ➤ **The Rachel Papers** won **Somerset Maugham Award (1974).**
- ➤ Published **Dead Babies** (1975) and **Success** (1978).
- ➤ Served as **Literary Editor** at **New Statesman** (1977-1979).
- ➤ Influential voice in **contemporary British fiction.**
- ➤ Associated with **Rushdie, McEwan, and Julian Barnes.**
- ➤ Influenced by **Philip Roth, John Updike, Saul Bellow.**
- ➤ Trilogy: **Money (1984), London Fields (1989), The Information (1995).**
- ➤ **Time's Arrow (1991)** shortlisted for **Booker Prize.**
- ➤ Wrote **Experience (2000)**, won **James Tait Black Prize.**
- ➤ Published **Koba the Dread (2002)** on **communism.**
- ➤ **Novels:**
  - ○ *The Rachel Papers (1973)*
  - ○ *Dead Babies (1975)*
  - ○ *Success (1978)*
  - ○ *Other People (1981)*
  - ○ *Money (1984)*
  - ○ *London Fields (1989)*
  - ○ *Time's Arrow: Or the Nature of the Offence (1991)*
  - ○ *The Information (1995)*
  - ○ *Night Train (1997)*
  - ○ *Yellow Dog (2003)*
  - ○ *House of Meetings (2006)*
  - ○ *The Pregnant Widow (2010)*
  - ○ *Lionel Asbo: State of England (2012)*
  - ○ *The Zone of Interest (2014)*
  - ○ *Inside Story (2020)*
- ➤ **Short fiction:**
  - ○ *Einstein's Monsters (1987)*
  - ○ *Two Stories (1994)*
  - ○ *God's Dice (1995)*
  - ○ *Heavy Water and Other Stories (1998)*

Peter Ackroyd (1949*)

- ➢ **Peter Ackroyd**: English **biographer, novelist**, and **critic.**
- ➢ Known for focus on **history, culture of London.**
- ➢ Won **Somerset Maugham** and two **Whitbread Awards.**
- ➢ Biographies include **Blake, Dickens, Eliot, Chaplin, More.**
- ➢ Renowned for **volume, styles**, and **research depth.**
- ➢ Skilled at assuming **different voices** in works.
- ➢ Noted for novels about **English history, culture.**
- ➢ **Notable Works**
  - ○ *A Study of Transvestism*
  - ○ *Notes for a New Culture: An Essay on Modernism (1976)*
- ➢ **Biographies**
  - ○ *Ezra Pound and His World (1980, revised as Ezra Pound, 1987)*
  - ○ *T.S. Eliot (1984)*
  - ○ *Dickens (1990)*
  - ○ *Blake (1995)*
  - ○ *The Life of Thomas More (1998)*
  - ○ *Charlie Chaplin (2014)*
  - ○ *Alfred Hitchcock (2015)*
- ➢ **Novels**
  - ○ *The Great Fire of London (1982)*
  - ○ *The Last Testament of Oscar Wilde (1983)*
  - ○ *Hawksmoor (1985)*
  - ○ *Chatterton (1987)*
  - ○ *First Light (1989)*
  - ○ *English Music (1992)*
  - ○ *The House of Doctor Dee (1993)*
  - ○ *The Trial of Elizabeth Cree: A Novel of the Limehouse Murders (1995)*
  - ○ *The Fall of Troy (2006)*
  - ○ *Three Brothers (2013)*
  - ○ *Mr. Cadmus (2020)*
- ➢ **Historical Retellings**
  - ○ *A Retelling of The Canterbury Tales (2009)*
  - ○ *Historical Surveys*
  - ○ *Ancient Egypt (2004, part of Voyages Through Time series)*
  - ○ *Ancient Greece (2005, part of Voyages Through Time series)*
  - ○ *History of England (multivolume, first book published in 2011)*

Graham Swift (1949*)

- ➢ **Graham Swift** is an **English writer**.
- ➢ Born in **London**, educated at **Dulwich College**.
- ➢ Studied at **Queens College** and **University of York**.
- ➢ Swift's **books filmed** include **Waterland** and **Shuttlecock**.
- ➢ **Last Orders** won **1996 James Tait Black Prize**.
- ➢ **Booker Prize winner** despite **controversy over similarities**.
- ➢ Compared to Faulkner's **As I Lay Dying**.
- ➢ **Novels**
    - ○ *The Sweet-Shop Owner (1980)*
    - ○ *Shuttlecock (1981) – winner of the 1983 Geoffrey Faber Memorial Prize*
    - ○ *Waterland (1983) – shortlisted for Booker Prize*
    - ○ *Out of This World (1988)*
    - ○ *Ever After (1992)*
    - ○ *Last Orders (1996) – winner of the 1996 Booker Prize*
    - ○ *The Light of Day (2003) – long-listed for the Man Booker Prize.*
    - ○ *Tomorrow (2007)*
    - ○ *Wish You Were Here (2011)*
    - ○ *Mothering Sunday (2016)*
    - ○ *Here We Are (2020)*

Hilary Mantel (1952*)

- ➢ Hilary Mantel was born in Glossop, Derbyshire, England, on 6 July 1952.
- ➢ She is famous for *Wolf Hall (2009)* and *Bring Up the Bodies (2012)*.
- ➢ **Notable Works:**
    - ○ *Eight Months on Ghazzah Street (1988)*
    - ○ *Fludd (1989)*
    - ○ *A Place of Greater Safety (1992)*
    - ○ *A Change of Climate (1994)*
    - ○ *An Experiment in Love (1995)*
    - ○ *The Giant, O'Brien (1998)*
    - ○ *Giving Up the Ghost: A Memoir (2003)*
    - ○ *Learning to Talk: Short Stories (2003)*
    - ○ *Beyond Black (2005)*
    - ○ *Wolf Hall (2009)*
    - ○ *Bring Up the Bodies (2012)*

QUESTIONS

Question 159

Which of the following are novels by David Lodge?

    A.   The British Museum is Falling down
    B.   The Seven Sisters
    C.   Changing Places
    D.   Nice Work
    E.   Empire of the Sun

Choose the correct answer from the options given below:
1. A, B and C only
2. B, D and E only
3. **A, C and D only**
4. C, D and E only

Correct Explanatiions:
    A.   *The British Museum is Falling Down* (1965) is a comic novel by British author David Lodge.
    B.   The Seven Sisters is a 1992 novel by British novelist Margaret Drabble.
    C.   *Changing Places* (1975) is the first "campus novel" by British novelist David Lodge.
    D.   *Nice Work* is a 1988 novel by British author David Lodge.
    E.   *Empire of the Sun* is a 1984 novel by English writer J. G. Ballard.

Question 160

Match List I with List II:

List I	List II
(A) Malcolm Bradbury	(I) Masters
(B) David Lodge	(I) Lucky Jim
(C) Kingsley Amis	(II) The History Man
(D) CP Snow	(IV) Changing places

Choose the correct answer from the options given below:

1.   (A)-(IV), (B)-(III), (C)-(I), (D)-(II)
2.   (A)-(II), (B)-(III), (C)-(IV), (D)-(I)
3.   (A)-(I), (B)-(II), (C)-(III). (D)-(IV)
4.   **(A)-(III), (B)-(IV), (C)-(II), (D)-(I)**

Correct Explanations:

The Masters is the fifth novel in C. P. Snow's series Strangers and Brothers. It involves the election of a new Master at narrator Lewis Eliot's unnamed Cambridge College, which resembles Christ's College, where Snow was a fellow. The 1951 novel's dedication is "In memory of G. H. Hardy", the Cambridge mathematician.

Lucky Jim is a novel by Kingsley Amis, first published in 1954 by Victor Gollancz. It was Amis's first novel and won the 1955 Somerset Maugham Award for fiction. The novel follows the exploits of the eponymous James (Jim) Dixon, a reluctant lecturer at an unnamed provincial English university.

Bradbury's best-known novel, The History Man, a campus novel published in 1975, is a satire of academic life in the "glass and steel" universities, the ones established in the 1960s which followed the "redbricks". In 1981 the book was made into a successful BBC television serial.

Changing Places (1975) is the first "campus novel" by British novelist David Lodge. The subtitle is "A Tale of Two Campuses", and thus both the title and subtitle are literary allusions to Charles Dickens's A Tale of Two Cities. It is the first novel, followed by Small World (1984) and Nice Work (1988).

Question 161

Identify the correct pairs:

A.   Gabriel Garcia Marquez - The Feast of the Goat
B.   Jorge Luis Borges - The Autumn of the Patriarch
C.   Salman Rushdie - The Enchantress of Florence
D.   EL Doctorow - Ragtime
E.   AS. Byatt - Possession

Choose the correct answer from the options given below:

1.   A, B and C

2. A, B and E
3. B, C and D
4. C, D and E

Explanations:

Ans: C, D and E

"The Feast of the Goat" is a historical novel written by Mario Vargas Llosa. It deals with the last days of the dictatorship of Rafael Trujillo in the Dominican Republic and its aftermath. It is known for its complex narrative structure and its exploration of themes such as power, violence, and memory.

"The Autumn of the Patriarch" is another novel by Gabriel Garcia Marquez. It tells the story of a mythical dictator in an unnamed Latin American country and his slow descent into madness and isolation. The novel uses a nonlinear narrative structure and a highly poetic language to explore themes of power, loneliness, and the human condition.

"The Enchantress of Florence" is a novel by Salman Rushdie. It tells the story of a mysterious traveler who arrives in the court of the Mughal Emperor Akbar in the 16th century and claims to be the son of a lost princess. The novel blends historical fact and fiction, and uses magical realism to explore themes such as identity, power, and storytelling.

"Ragtime" is a novel by E.L. Doctorow. It is set in early 20th century America and explores the lives of various characters from different social backgrounds. The novel uses a nonlinear narrative structure and a collage-like approach to storytelling, blending historical fact and fiction to explore themes such as identity, race, and social change.

"Possession" is a novel by A.S. Byatt. It tells the story of two academics who uncover a secret love affair between two Victorian poets. The novel uses a complex narrative structure and multiple points of view to explore themes such as love, identity, and the relationship between the past and the present.

Question 162

Which of the following are novels by Ian McEwan?

A. Atonement

B. The Man with Two Left Feet
C. The Child in Time
D. The Rachel Papers

Choose the correct answer from the options given below:

1. **A and C only**
2. B and D only
3. C and D only
4. D and A only

Correct Explanations:

Atonement is a novel by Ian McEwan and published in 2001. It is a postmodern novel that explores the nature of memory, storytelling, and the relationship between fiction and reality. The novel has been adapted into a film and a play.

The Child in Time is a novel by Ian McEwan and published in 1987. It is a work of literary fiction that explores the themes of loss, grief, and the search for meaning in the aftermath of a tragic event. The novel has been adapted into a television film.

Other Explanations

The Man with Two Left Feet is a collection of short stories by P. G. Wodehouse, first published in 1917. The stories are humorous and lighthearted, and many feature Reggie Pepper, who would later evolve into Wodehouse's famous character Bertie Wooster.

The Rachel Papers is a novel by Martin Amis published in 1973. It is a coming-of-age novel that follows the romantic pursuits of the protagonist, Charles Highway, and his attempts to win the affection of a girl named Rachel. The novel is notable for its use of metafictional techniques, such as self-reflexivity and breaking the fourth wall.

Question 163

Which two of the following are non-fictional works by Peter Ackroyd?

(A) Escape from Earth

(B) The Great Fire of London
(C) The English Ghost
(D) English Music

Choose the correct answer from the options given below:

1. (A) and (B) Only
2. (B) and (C) Only
3. (A) and (C) Only
4. (B) and (D) Oniy

Explanations:

Answer: 2. (A) and (C) Only

Peter Ackroyd CBE, FRSL (born 5 October 1949) is an English biographer, novelist and critic with a specialist interest in the history and culture of London. For his novels about English history and culture and his biographies of, among others, William Blake, Charles Dickens, T. S. Eliot, Charlie Chaplin and Sir Thomas More, he won the Somerset Maugham Award and two Whitbread Awards. He is noted for the volume of work he has produced, the range of styles therein, his skill at assuming different voices, and the depth of his research.

Fiction
- **1982 The Great Fire of London**
- 1983 The Last Testament of Oscar Wilde
- 1985 Hawksmoor
- 1987 Chatterton
- 1989 First Light
- **1992 English Music**

Usage Policy for NerdSchool Notes

Created by: Instructors from NerdSchool
Owned by: NERDSTABLE PVT LTD

The following notes are the intellectual property of **NERDSTABLE PVT LTD** and are made available exclusively to students who have paid for access. By using these notes, you agree to the terms and conditions outlined below:

Policy of Usage:

Personal Use Only: These notes are intended for your **personal study and exam preparation**. You are permitted to **read** and **print** them for your own reference.

No Unauthorized Distribution or Sale: You **may not sell**, **distribute**, or **replicate** these notes in any form, whether digitally or physically. This includes sharing copies with others, regardless of the medium (online platforms, printed materials, etc.).

No Plagiarism: You **may not claim** the contents of these notes as your own. Any form of direct publication or submission under your name, without proper citation, is strictly prohibited.

Non-Transferable Access: Access to these notes is restricted to the individual purchaser. **Sharing your login credentials** or any other means of access to these materials with others is a violation of this policy.

Additional Guidelines:

For Educational Use Only: These notes are designed to help students succeed in their academic exams and should be used responsibly. They are meant to supplement your learning, not to replace the guidance of instructors or textbooks.

No Commercial Use: The content in these notes cannot be used for **commercial purposes**. This includes using the material in any form of paid tutoring or educational courses that you offer without the explicit permission of NERDSTABLE PVT LTD.

Proper Attribution: If you wish to reference any part of these notes in your own academic work, proper **citation** must be made to **NerdSchool and NERDSTABLE PVT LTD.**

Legal Action: Any violation of these terms, including unauthorized distribution or commercial use, may result in **legal action**.